SPIRITUAL INTERROGATIONS

SPIRITUAL INTERROGATIONS

CULTURE, GENDER, AND COMMUNITY
IN EARLY AFRICAN AMERICAN
WOMEN'S WRITING

Katherine Clay Bassard

PRINCETON UNIVERSITY PRESS
PRINCETON, NEW JERSEY

Library of Congress Cataloging-in-Publication Data

Bassard, Katherine Clay, 1959–
Spiritual interrogations : culture, gender and community in early
African American women's writing / Katherine Clay Bassard.
p.   cm. — (Princeton studies in culture/power/history)
Includes bibliographical references and index.

ISBN 0-691-01639-9 (hardcover : alk. paper)
ISBN 0-691-01647-X (pbk. : alk. paper)
1. American literature—Afro-American authors—History and criticism.
2. American literature—Women authors—History and criticism.
3. American literature—19th century—History and criticism. 4. Christianity
and literature—United States—History. 5. Women and literature—United
States—History. 6. Spirituals (Songs)—History and criticism. 7. Wheatley,
Phillis, 1753–1784—Religion. 8. Afro-American women—Religious life.
9. Afro-American women in literature. 10. Community life in literature.
11. Spiritual life in literature. 12. Religion and literature. I. Title.   II. Series.
PS153.N5B33   1999
810.9′382—dc21   98-23197   CIP

This book has been composed in Galliard

Princeton University Press books are printed
on acid-free paper and meet the guidelines
for permanence and durability of the Committee
on Production Guidelines for Book Longevity
of the Council on Library Resources

http://pup.princeton.edu

Printed in the United States of America

1   3   5   7   9   10   8   6   4   2

1   3   5   7   9   10   8   6   4   2
(pbk.)

For my husband, Mark, and my daughter, Angelique

Contents

Acknowledgments

THIS project began as a dissertation for my Ph.D. at Rutgers University and was funded generously by a Ford Foundation Disseration Fellowship from the National Research Council. As I revised it into its present form, financial support for research and leave time came from several sources at the University of California–Berkeley: the Doreen B. Townsend Center for the Humanities, the Center for the Study of American Cultures, a Junior Faculty Mentor Grant, a Junior Faculty Fellowship, and a Junior Faculty Summer Fellowship.

I wish to thank librarians and staff at the Schomburg Center for Black Culture, the Historical Society of Pennsylvania, and the church archivists at "Mother Bethel" African Methodist Episcopal Church in Philadelphia. Thanks also to Professor James Miller of Trinity College (Hartford) for sending me available information on Ann Plato.

I am blessed by wonderful mentors from Rutgers, Donald B. Gibson and Cheryl A. Wall, and colleagues at Berkeley, Barbara Christian, Waldo Martin, Mitchell Breitweiser, Elizabeth Abel, and Abdul JanMohammed, and I thank them for their encouragement and support.

I also want to thank my graduate student researchers, Donna Hunter, Diane Matlock, and Anthony Hale, who not only helped with archival research but offered computer assistance and advice.

I am grateful as well to editors and staff of Princeton University Press, especially Deborah Malmud and Lauren Lepow, for their patience and diligence in bringing this book to its present form, and to my friend and colleague John Lynch, who prepared the index.

Finally, but most important, I want to thank God for the gifts and the "great cloud of witnesses" He has placed in my path in the form of family and friends: my husband, Mark, and daughter, Angelique; my mother and father, Mary and Add Thomas; my brothers, David Clay and Dwayne Thomas; my sisters-in-law, Sharon Bassard, Oleta Clay, and Leila Khetib; my mother- and father-in-law, Bettye and Knowlton Bassard; a special aunt, Charlotte B. Wood; and dear friends, Angelique Martin, Judylyn S. Ryan, Caryl Loney, and Pastor and Mrs. Charles R. Mixson.

Excerpts from chapters 1 and 2 appeared as "The Daughters' Arrival: The Earliest Black Women's Writing Community" in *Callaloo* 19, no. 2 (1996): 508–18 © 1996 by the Johns Hopkins University Press.

SPIRITUAL INTERROGATIONS

Introduction

> Methinks I heard a spiritual interrogation—
> "Who shall go forward, and take off the reproach
> that is cast upon the people of color? Shall it be a
> woman?" And my heart made this reply—"If it is
> thy will, be it even so, Lord Jesus!"
> (*Maria W. Stewart, "Lecture Delivered at
> Franklin Hall"*)

IN HER "Lecture Delivered at Franklin Hall" in Boston on September 22, 1832, Maria W. Stewart includes this conversation with God.[1] Significantly, this dialogue harkens back to an earlier encounter with divinity in Stewart's life for which this dialogue serves as a response. The call to political and social action is preceded by Stewart's conversion experience in 1830, which commands her "to come out of the world and be separate; to go forward and be baptized":

> Methought I heard a spiritual interrogation, are you able to drink of that cup that I have drank of? And to be baptized with the baptism I have been baptized with? And my heart made this reply: Yea, Lord, I am able. (66)

In the public forum of oratorical performance, Stewart speaks of the most private of communications—between self and Spirit. And it is this public utterance of private communication that marks so much of early African American women's writings, as the experience of Christian conversion figures so prominently in their texts. As Stewart's theological formulation makes clear, communication with Spirit is dialogical, a give-and-take signified by its interrogative nature. Unlike the commands, demands, catechisms, and chastisements that often characterized black women's interactions with white male and female owners/employees, and black male fathers, spouses, and community leaders, dialogue with Spirit signifies neither conquest nor coercion.[2] Rather, God as spiritual interrogator asks questions that prompt a response from the "heart."

It is within these private encounters with Spirit that African American women often experienced a conferral of personhood denied by larger social constructions of African American and female subjectivity. For it is within this divine dialogue that black women's subjectivity is produced even as her agency is acknowledged and affirmed. The "I" that

hears the interrogative in the conversion account becomes the empowered "I" who is "able." As Stewart writes in *Religion and the Pure Principles of Morality*, "From the moment I experienced the change, I felt a
strong desire, with the help and assistance of God, to devote the remainder of my days to piety and virtue, and now possess that spirit of inde-
pendence that, were I called upon, I would willingly sacrifice my life for
the cause of God and my brethren" (Richardson 29). Stewart views her
conversion as nothing short of a mandate to free her "brethren" (and
presumably, sisters) from the material demands of nineteenth-century
African American life.

The sense of a dialogue between metadiscursive realms—between different "worlds," we might say—for the purpose of both self-empower-
ment and communal political engagement informs this book. *Spiritual
Interrogations* begins with two cases of revisionism in early African
American women's literature. The first instance connects two Congregationalist women—eighteenth-century enslaved poet Phillis Wheatley
(1753?–1784) and nineteenth-century free black poet and essayist Ann
Plato (1820?–?)—through Plato's inclusion of six lines of Wheatley's
"On Recollection" in one of her own poems. The second case involves
two nineteenth-century contemporaries with varying degrees of connection to African Methodism—itinerant preacher Jarena Lee (1783–?) and
Rebecca Cox Jackson (1795–1871), who later became a Shaker
eldress—through an entry in Jackson's journal that describes Lee unflat-
teringly as "one of my most bitter persecutors." Yet what seem to be two
literary historical footnotes open out onto a series of historical, literary,
and theoretical displacements that involve questions of subjectivity,
agency, and racial and gendered configurations of culture.

In the spring of 1994, I stood in front of a weathered wooden door
inside the stone slave holds of Cape Coast Castle, Ghana, on what was
called "The Point of No Return," the last African soil the captives
touched before embarking on the notorious Middle Passage. I was
struck by the irony of my own position as an African American woman
intellectual whose possible return to the African continent had already
been both foreseen and prohibited. Indeed, my return could scarcely be
called a return at all given at least ten generations of genealogy on
American soil, and the irretrievability of any certainty as to the spot on
the massive continent from which I might construct a history of origins.
And yet there had been something compelling about the view of the
Atlantic from "the other side" that challenged many of my assumptions
about the theorizing of African American subjectivity and discourse before Emancipation. While I had no inclination to return to a positivistic
search for "roots," I found that my scholarly positionality had shifted

somewhat off the mainland of North America, only to remain in a kind of suspension over the Atlantic.

The practice of reading black women's intertextuality that I call "spiritual interrogation" refers first of all to a scholarly positionality which does not assume that terms like "diaspora," "culture," and "community" necessarily conjure up essentializing categories of "ontological blackness."[3] Thus I view figurations of diaspora and Africanity not as empirically knowable and quantifiable categories but as *structures of vision* which open onto terrains of reading early African American writing that promise to challenge and to expand some of our most central understandings of African collective identity and literary tradition. In this vein I follow scholars like Barbara Christian, Hortense Spillers, Peter Paris, Kwame Anthony Appiah, and Paul Gilroy, all of whom have worked to bring an Africanist and diasporic vision to bear on African Americanist intellectual work.[4]

Spiritual interrogation proceeds, as well, from an understanding of the relationship between the archival and the theoretical as two necessary parts of a common project of restoration and revision in any study of what Abdul R. JanMohamed and David Lloyd have termed "minority discourse." Since minority discourses are subject to "institutional forgetting" and historical neglect, JanMohamed and Lloyd argue that archival work acts as "a form of counter-memory" and is thus essential to the overall project of ethnic and women's studies. "However," they continue, "if the previously marginalized production of minority cultures is not to be relegated to mere repetition of ethnic or feminine exotica, theoretical reflection cannot be omitted" (6). Moreover, given the violence enacted against black women's histories, bodies, and texts, the archives will remain incomplete and inadequate as sources for an empirically complete counternarrative of black women's literary production.[5] On the other hand, a purely theoretical approach that does not attend to the demands of history as, at least in part, determinative of the range of available signs and subject positions runs the risk of subsuming African American women's literary production into yet another anecdotal proof of a theory or validation of Theory per se.

By "theory" I mean a nexus of theoretical discourses—psychoanalytic, deconstructionist, dialogical, and so forth—that inhabit various historical, literary, and philosophical domains. As a matrix of critical discursive interventions rather than a "methodology," spiritual interrogation occurs within the shifts between and among these various discursive domains. In most cases, for example, I will begin a chapter or a discussion with the historical, proceed to the literary, and open out onto the theoretical. With each shift, the prior discourse is simultaneously reaffirmed and destabilized. For example, the juxtaposition of the historical and the literary brings the narrativity of history into relief even as it "grounds" the literary representation within a contextual field. Likewise, when discussions of genre and literary history and close readings of texts are laid alongside theoretical considerations of subjectivity, agency, utterance, and the like, the "literary" becomes accountable for the power relations inhering in representation even as the theoretical is made responsible for the tropological field that drives its metaphors.

The reader will notice in *Spiritual Interrogations* intermittent engagements with Lacan, Derrida, Foucault—often oblique, sometimes direct—and a more sustained dialogue with the late writings of M. M. Bakhtin. Bakhtin has long been important to the study of African American literature, as is evident in the work of scholars such as Henry Louis Gates, Jr. (*Signifying Monkey* and *Figures in Black*), and Mae Gwendolyn Henderson ("Speaking in Tongues"); however, Bakhtin's later work, collected in *Speech Genres and Other Late Essays*, has been ignored.[6] Yet it is in these essays that Bakhtin advances theories of discourse and utterance which are the most fruitful for African American literary study, especially as his theory of "speech genres" engages with social constructions of identity and discourse. The formulations I make the most extensive use of are:

1. Bakhtin's theory of "the change of speaking subjects" for discussions of literary tradition and revisionism in chapter 1 and the politicizing of black women's challenges to black male authority in chapter 5.

2. Genre as "form-shaping ideology" for considerations of black women writers' engagements with specific genres (Wheatley and the elegaic in chapter 3, Plato and autobiography in chapter 4, Lee and Jackson and spiritual autobiography in chapters 5 and 6).

3. The category of "speech genres" as a descriptor for Wheatley's appropriation of others' speech in chapter 2, the use of the "speech genres" of black religiosity—black sacred music, preaching, singing, tongues, and testifying, in chapter 5.

4. Finally, Bakhtin's understanding of "finalization" and the boundaries of the utterance for discussions of black women as a "writing community" in chapter 1 and for theorizing early black culture and community in chapter 7.

It is important to note, however, that while I use Bakhtinian dialogics in the analysis of early African American women's writings, I also, in turn, show how early black women's writing often anticipates, critiques, or challenges Bakhtin's theorizing.

As one of a growing number of scholars interested in what Theophus Smith has dubbed "the nascent field of African American spirituality" (ix), I have been greatly influenced by the work of several scholars in religious studies. First and foremost I have been impressed with the work of womanist ethicists, theologians, and biblical scholars, including Katie Cannon, Jacqueline Grant, Renita Weems, Delores Williams, and Cheryl Kirk-Duggan, for the centrality of African American women's literature in their theologizing.[7] I have also studied with great interest the work of other theologians and religion scholars, including cultural critics Theophus Smith and Victor Anderson, ethicist Peter Paris, theomusicologist Jon Michael Spencer, and theologian Dwight Hopkins.[8] In bringing this work to bear on African American literary study, I take my cue from the early writers themselves, for whom issues of spirituality and religiosity were central and not peripheral to their self- and communal inscriptions.

I have given *Spiritual Interrogations* a kind of "bookend" structure: the more literary considerations of revisionism are framed by the more theoretical meditations. Thus readers interested primarily in an overview of African American literary theory and discourse and early African American culture and subjectivity are directed to chapters 1 and 7.

In chapter 1, "The Daughters' Arrival: Histories, Theories, Vernaculars," I attend to the historical, literary, and theoretical displacements that occasion the arrival of African American women's bodies and texts to the auction block and to the literary critical marketplace, respectively. I then retrace the theorizing of literary tradition and vernacularity that were the principle preoccupations of African American literary theorists of the 1980s, the decade that saw the reprinting and publication of so much of early African American literature. Finally, I offer "writing community" and "spirituals matrix" as figures that both continue and challenge these earlier projects.

In chapter 2, "Diaspora Subjectivity and Transatlantic Crossings: Phillis Wheatley's Poetics of Recovery," I reread Phillis Wheatley's poetry in the context of the Middle Passage, the "metaoccasion" for a body of work often dismissed as merely "occasional" verse. Wheatley's own theorizing of a subjectivity of displacement in *Poems on Various Subjects Religious and Moral* (1773) recasts her survival of the Middle Passage as an "event" whose constituent parts (capture, enslavement, transport, sale) and results (catechism, conversion, poetic authorship) are explored and developed in her poetic utterance. Wheatley's careful explication of her positionality as, simultaneously, an African woman enslaved in the United States and a poet recovers the cultural specificity of her poetics, which is representative of her deepening awareness of the meaning of her own displacement.

Chapter 3, "'The Too Advent'rous Strain': Slavery, Conversion, and Poetic Empowerment in Phillis Wheatley's Elegies," takes up Wheatley's engagements with a specific genre in the Puritan funeral elegies that constitute over one-third of her surviving corpus. I argue for a reading of these poems, which have been almost universally denigrated by Wheatley scholars, that revisions them as a part of Wheatley's overall project of constructing an empowered poetic persona from which to launch a critique of existing social structures while simultaneously seeking to gain entry into eighteenth-century Boston community. Ultimately, I argue that in the elegies Wheatley comes closest to voicing her own deeply felt alienation and isolation as her mediations on grief and mourning enact a repetitious replay of the central drama of her own displaced family and kin networks.

Chapter 4, "'Social Piety' in Ann Plato's *Essays*," is the first extended critical treatment of Ann Plato's *Essays; Including Biographies and Miscellaneous Pieces in Prose and Poetry*, which was published in 1841. Tracing the literary lineage from Wheatley to Plato necessitates a shift from an interracial to an intracommunal frame of reference, which in turn demands a corresponding shift in the meanings assigned to analytical categories of race and gender as the formation of free black communities at the turn of the nineteenth century forced black women's renegotiations of the terms of self and community. Thus Plato's engagements with prevailing contestations over black women's voice and place within African American communities and institutions led to a subtle but distinct struggle with the pietistic expectations of her social positionality. Moreover, I read the four prose biographical sketches included in *Essays*, which depict the lives of four African American women who died very young, as continuing Wheatley's strategy in the elegies of speaking the "self" through the voice of the "other."

Chapter 5, "'I Took a Text': Itinerancy, Community, and Intertextuality in Jarena Lee's Spiritual Narratives," traces Lee's recounting of her call to preach the gospel in her 1836 *Life and Religious Experience* and 1849 *Religious Experience and Journal* as a simultaneous repetition of and subversion of Anglo-Protestant morphologies of conversion. Specifically, I argue that the narrative line which enacts a search for religious community becomes the point of entry for the cultural as Lee encodes black oral forms of preaching and spirituals as structuring devices for her texts. This reading restores cultural specificity to a text that has been described as concerned only with religious transcendence. The multiple strategies of voice within the narrative(s) underscore Lee's unique formulation of the place of community, culture, race, and gender in the conversion experience.

Chapter 6, "Rituals of Desire: Spirit, Culture, and Sexuality in the Writings of Rebecca Cox Jackson," explores Jackson's rewriting of the central narrative line of Lee's 1836 *Life and Religious Experience*—the search for religious community—in her own spiritual journals, which were written in the 1830s–1850s but first published in 1981 as *Gifts of Power*. I show that Jackson's recounting of her journey through the A.M.E. Church, itinerancy, and the Shaker community of Watervliet, New York, constitutes a direct revision of important scenes in Lee's text. Thus while Jackson "witnesses" to Lee's testimony of black women's challenges to black male religious authority, she offers a competing definition of community and an alternative paradigm for the place of race, gender, and sexuality in conversion experience. This instance of African American women's "competitive revisionism," I argue, is rooted in differences in Lee's and Jackson's religious visions and spiritual investments. The second movement of this chapter, therefore, presents a rereading of Jackson's enigmatic dream visions in light of striking similarities between the ritual mappings of Jackson's written visions and Central African Kongo cosmograms and religious art that appear, as well, in North American versions of "conjure" or "Hoodoo." Thus I posit a reading of Jackson's journals as a "ritual space" that occasions the meeting of biblical and African religiosity and calls for a redefinition of early African American women's spirituality and cultural performance.

Finally in chapter 7, "Performing Community: Culture, Community, and African American Subjectivity before Emancipation," I argue for a reformulation of the interrelationship of race, culture, and community as signifiers of African American collective subjectivity. Reading written texts of spirituals and "eyewitness" accounts of white observer-recorders from the pre-Emancipation period, I theorize an African American culture whose primary function was *performing community*, encoding in oral cultural forms the means by which boundaries of self/other, insider/outsider become negotiated, as a challenge to racial proscriptions and definitions that served the material and economic interests of the larger white society.

CHAPTER ONE

The Daughters' Arrival:
Histories, Theories, Vernaculars

RITUAL MISNAMINGS

TO BE SOLD. A parcel of likely NEGROES,
imported from Africa, cheap for Cash, or short
credit with Interest; enquire of John Avery, at his
House next Door to the White Horse, or at a
Store adjoining to said Avery's Distill-House, at
the South End, near the South Market: Also if
any Persons have any Negro Men, strong and
hearty, tho' not of the best moral character,
which are proper Subjects for Transportation,
may have an Exchange for Small Negroes.
(Boston Evening Post, *August 3, 1761*)

[S]hift does not produce a contending theory,
it announces an existence that has not yet been
named, or one that has been subsumed, erroneously,
under the rubric of an inappropriate title.
(*Karla F. C. Holloway,* Moorings and Metaphors)

I been 'buked and I been scorned,
I been talked about sho's you born.
(*African American spiritual*)

In the slave auction notice above, eighteenth-century slave poet Phillis
Wheatley's arrival to the Boston auction block as a captive African girl is
unceremoniously misnamed, a misnaming that functions to erase a gendered and cultural subjectivity.[1] Positioned at the end of the advertise-
ment, the details about this cargo of "likely Negroes" emerge through
the language of commodification; the slave seller offers the exchange of
"Small Negroes" for "Negro Men, strong and hearty, tho' not of the
best moral character." The black woman's misnaming occurs, then, via
a chiastic displacement that exchanges the gendered sign "Men,"

which holds, at least, the possibility of subjecthood, for the adjective "Small," which not only connotes an object status but carries with it the space-conscious priorities of a trade that described the transport of human beings in terms like "loose pack" and "tight pack." Sold in 1761 at the age of seven or eight, Phillis Wheatley might well have been the object of such an exchange, one that designates "Negro Men" as possible "proper Subjects for Transportation" while solidifying her own status as object. Yet the complexity of how gender also misnames black women is not so easily discerned. The geocultural displacements signified in the descriptor "NEGROES, imported from Africa" encode overlapping narratives of race and culture whose underlying tensions are neither immediately comprehended nor easily resolved. That is, an analysis based solely on "race" as it is currently used in literary study—defined, deconstructed, and de-essentialized as a dialectic of biology/trope, body/language, skin color/social positioning—often masks the ways in which black women and men are equally victims of *cultural* theft and misappropriation, a violation signaled by "NEGROES" as a misnaming of *African* peoples.

These ritual misnamings mark the various port-side auction blocks and slave pens of the North American continent, from the Caribbean to the southern and northern United States, as an archipelago of Ellis/Angel Islands for African entry into Euramerican/Western usurped spaces and discourses. We therefore come to understand the figure of the slave auction block not only as a point of departure for critical analyses of African American history, culture, and subjectivity but as a point of arrival as well. This relocation of the trajectories of departure and arrival performs a ritual renaming that shifts the terms of origin and destination, memory and desire, in the theorizing of black women's subjectivity and literary tradition.

Moreover, the arrival of African women—many, like Wheatley, as small children to the slave-trading ports of Boston; Narragansett and Newport, Rhode Island; Perth Amboy, New Jersey; New York; and Philadelphia in the late eighteenth century—points to the need for a new configuration of the history of black women under slavery and the writings occasioned by their northern exposures.[2] Although throughout the eighteenth century New England bore the distinction of being "the greatest slave-trading section of the country" (Greene, 24),[3] historians, concerned with "representativeness," have situated the majority of studies of American slavery in the nineteenth-century U.S. South. Thus the plantation system has been treated as "normative" of pre-Emancipation black experience, an assumption with serious consequences for theories of African American subjectivity and discourse.[4] While the number of slaves in the North never even approximated the number in the South owing to starkly different labor demands, and despite the consensus that northern slavery was "milder" and less "rooted" than its southern counterpart, the northern system bore all the legal, economic, social, and racial markings of a slave system. Understanding slavery in the North requires a shift not only in terms of region but often from rural to urban as well. It requires, moreover, a departure from the plantation model to the Yankee brand of paternalism or "family slavery," where slaves' residing in the slaveholding family's household was more the rule than the exception. It means relinquishing the notion of "house niggers" as pet slaves co-opted by the master and mistress in favor of a conceptualization of domestic slave labor (especially with regard to black women) that was primary rather than a system of "rewards" for white blood ties or Sambo-type behavior.[5] Indeed, the northern markets overwhelmingly preferred young black males, needing only one or two female slaves per household to perform domestic labor. Thus in 1773, black male slaves in a collective petition for their freedom to the Massachusetts legislature cried: "We have no Property! We have no Wives!"[6]

Not only do geographical markers open onto a need to refigure much of our ways of conceptualizing African American subjectivity and discourse, but temporal/historical designations come under critique as well. Thus I designate the literary/historical period from 1760 to 1865 as the pre-Emancipation period (rather than antebellum) because the status of free or unfree was a more important influence on African American subjectivity and literary production than was the fact of the Civil War, though, clearly, African Americans were beneficiaries of the war's outcome. Despite various gradual emancipation laws that began to appear in the northern states as early as 1780, the procedures for actually emancipating enslaved men and women were often clumsy, long and drawn-out, or full of legal pitfalls and loopholes. Moreover, the presence of legal slavery in the southern states shaped northern conceptions of African Americans, the legal status of "free" blacks, and, most important, African Americans' conceptions of themselves. Free black northerners understood their fate as irrevocably linked to their "brothers and sisters in bondage," not only in terms of ideologies of black inferiority used to justify enslavement and oppressive to enslaved and "free" African Americans alike, but materially as well. Before general Emancipation, all blacks in the United States faced the possibility of capture and enslavement.[7] Thus even though an individual African American might be legally free, the existence of chattel slavery within U.S. borders was constitutive, though to varying degrees, of African American subjectivity before 1863, the year the Emancipation Proclamation took effect. In addition, though the year 1863 theoretically ushered in legal emancipation for African Americans, there were cases, especially in the deep

South, in which masters chose to withhold the information about freedom from their slaves for up to two years after the Emancipation Proclamation became effective.[8]

African Americanists from a variety of disciplines have designated the historical period between 1760 and 1830 in America as the beginning of African American community building, black collective consciousness, and African American cultural production. This period saw the rise of the first black Masonic lodge and Freemasonry under Prentice Hall in 1787; the first African American churches and denominations, culminating in the incorporation of the African Methodist Episcopal denomination in 1816; the establishment of the black press with newspapers like *Freedom's Journal* and the *Colored American* in the first third of the nineteenth century; and the formation of African American holidays and celebrations like Negro Election Day, July 5th celebrations (as a protest against the exclusion of free African Americans from Anglo-Americans' Fourth of July celebrations), and January 1st observances of the abolition of the U.S. slave trade in 1808. Thus during this period, African Americans became an identifiable collective in terms of language, religious practice, and literary and cultural production.[9] African American women's early literature emerges, then, as a part of a larger project of African American cultural production[10] and community building in which black women played an active and vital role as cocreators in the community's artistic and intellectual life.

THEORIZING TRADITIONS

In addition to the historical displacements and arrivals I sketched in very broad strokes above, the arrival to literary study of volumes of texts written by black women in America before Emancipation points to the need to rethink current theories of black vernacular traditions, revisionism, and African American subjectivity. Following the work of African Americanist and black feminist scholars who posed important challenges to the white and male hegemonies of the literary canon, the decade of the 1980s saw the reprinting of volumes of literature written by African Americans during the pre-Emancipation period, moving a wealth of early African American writing from the historical archives to the literary critical marketplace. Noteworthy among these editions are Jean Humez's edition of the writings of Rebecca Cox Jackson, *Gifts of Power* (1981); Henry Louis Gates's edition of Harriet E. Wilson's novel *Our Nig; or Sketches from the Life of a Free Black*, in which Gates established Wilson's African American identity (1983); Gates's edition of *The Classic Slave Narratives* (1987), which includes the slave narratives of Olaudah Equiano, Mary Prince, Frederick Douglass, and Harriet Jacobs; Jean Fagan Yellin's annotated edition of Harriet Jacobs's *Incidents in the Life of a Slave Girl* (1987); and William L. Andrews's edited volume, *Sisters of the Spirit: Three Black Women's Autobiographies of the Nineteenth Century* (1987). However, the largest publishing endeavor of the decade, the Schomburg Library of Nineteenth-Century Black Women Writers (1988) under the series editorship of Henry Louis Gates, made available to literary scholars over thirty volumes of writing by African American women.

Although much of this writing had been known to historians, the "rediscovery" of these texts as objects of literary critical inquiry quickly changed the shape and contours of African American literary history. Thus scholars within the field suddenly had to deal with an enormous increase in available materials (both historical materials and, I might add, contemporary writing by African Americans) and with the new critical theories spawned by poststructuralist thought, which destabilized both the text as "object" of study and the subject as knowable and unitary. African Americanist literary scholars, then, were in the position of having to pursue two antithetical projects at once: construct a "canon" of literature and deconstruct that canon in the very process of its formation. Henry Louis Gates, one of the primary proponents both of the process of defining and shaping an African American literary canon and of the move to critical theory, recognized the dilemma: "You cannot . . . critique the notion of the subject until a tradition's subjectivity has been firmly established."[11] As Gates's remarks make clear as well, questions of textuality and subjectivity overlap so profoundly in African American literature that discussions around African American literary history remain tied to issues of black collective identity; theories of intertextuality presume some working concept of intersubjectivity as well.

The work of incorporating so much writing into taxonomies of African American and African American women's literary traditions has resulted in three primary metanarratives of African American intertextuality/intersubjectivity. Obviously I am offering these categories not as definitive but as general tendencies within the field as scholars attempted to deal with the convergence of texts and theories and the resultant dilemma I outlined above. Moreover, I am aware that many African Americanists theorize from a hybridity that combines two or all three of these metadiscourses:

   1. *Tropological/vernacular*: locates the ground for narrativizing African American literary tradition in textual revisionism. In *Signifying Monkey* (1980) Henry Louis Gates, Jr., argued that black writers read and revised each other's work, providing a linguistic and textual ground for black in-

tertextuality in a gesture that critiqued the category of "blackness" as, in and of itself, adequate as the basis for the relationship between and among African American texts. Similarly, Houston Baker in *Blues, Ideology, and Afro-American Literature* (1984) theorized African American literary tradition (and by extension, American literary history) through the figure of "blues" as a vernacular trope for African American textuality. At bottom, this approach seeks an "indigenous," vernacular trope or controlling metaphor as a descriptor for black literary tradition.[12]

2. *Familial*: uses figures from the "family plot" of psychoanalysis as the basis for constructing a literary historical lineage for black women writers. Tropes of "sisterhood" or "matriliny" form the core of feminist and black feminist correctives to Harold Bloom's Oedipalization of literary tradition in *The Anxiety of Influence*. Examples include Diane Sadoff's "Black Matrilineage: The Case of Alice Walker and Zora Neale Hurston," Michael Awkward's *Inspiriting Influences*, Joanne Braxton's *Black Women Writing Autobiography*, in which Braxton writes that black women constitute a "mystic sisterhood" (1), and Mae G. Henderson's designation of black women's intertextuality and intersubjectivity as "testimonial (familial)" in "Speaking in Tongues."

3. *Social/ideological*: understands relationships between African American women's texts as a function of the writers' responses to prevailing discourses and ideologies of "blackness" and/or "womanhood." The work of Hazel V. Carby in *Reconstructing Womanhood* (1987) de-essentialized the category of black womanhood as it was used in much black feminist criticism of the 1970s and early 1980s, refiguring black feminist criticism as "a problem, not a solution, a sign that should be interrogated, a locus of contradictions" (15). Houston Baker's *Blues* could be included here, as he structures his literary history around African American writers' negotiations of the "economic deportation" that began with U.S. chattel slavery. Also, though Awkward and Henderson make use of "familial" metaphors as a part of their theorizing, each also locates the basis of black women's intertextuality as a set of responses to social forces, what Henderson calls "multi-metalevel negotiations" resulting from African American women's social positionality.

Clearly, each of these metanarratives has its own explanatory power, and each, in its own way, has contributed to my understanding of the problems and possibilities of theorizing early black women's literary tradition. The central critique of the applicability of Gatesian revisionism for a narrative of African American women's literary tradition was framed by Hortense Spillers in 1985, as she characterized African American women's literature within a dialectic of "Cross-Currents, Discontinuities."[13] In situating black women's intertextuality within "a matrix of literary discontinuities" (251), Spillers pointed to the lack of an unbroken textual and linguistic lineage from the early writers to contemporary novelists and poets. Taking Spillers's critique seriously, recent scholarship on African American women writers has tended to focus more specifically on a single period of African American women's literary history rather than to attempt a totalizing narrative to fit all of black women's literary production. Two important examples in this regard are Frances Smith Foster's *Written by Herself*, which sketches the cultural historical parameters for black women's writing from 1746 to 1892 and Claudia Tate's *Domestic Allegories of Political Desire*, which looks at black women's domestic fiction at the turn of the twentieth century.

In *Spiritual Interrogations* I have chosen both to specialize within a focused historical period—in this case pre-Emancipation—and to continue Gates's project of documenting direct textual revisionism among African American writers. Thus I have uncovered in the writings of Wheatley and Ann Plato, Jarena Lee and Rebecca Cox Jackson, two instances of direct revisionism that make Gates's paradigm compelling and useful. I have found, however, that earlier conceptualizations of vernacular and "blues" need to be adapted and revised to fit the writers under discussion. Thus I reformulate vernacularity according to the specific demands of the writers' historical and geographical conditions and posit a "spirituals matrix," rather than the "blues matrix" offered by Baker, as a more accurate figure for the unique historical and critical displacements of the pre-Emancipation period.

Baker, among others, has noted that the term "vernacular" derives from the Latin designation of "a slave born on the master's estate" (*Blues* 6). Applied to a North American context, vernacular, then, originates from the position of the subject vis-à-vis "master narratives" of race, class, and gender. Yet in *Workings of the Spirit* Baker's treatment of African American women writers reveals a conceptualization of the vernacular that exceeds social positionality. Baker laments the "daughter's departure" from her southern, matrilinear, vernacular "roots" (note the slippage into familial signifiers) as a retreat to a culturally "sterile" U.S. North: "a nineteenth-century black women's vernacular southern culture in the heroism of its economic survival, and then in the resonances of its quilts, gardens, conjuration, supper-getting-ready songs, churched melodies, woven baskets at Charleston wharves, and culinary magnificence, is a *great absence* in the texts of the escaped, northern daughters *as authors*" (30). While Baker is talking here about southern-born black women who journeyed north in the late nineteenth and early twentieth centuries, specifically Harriet Jacobs, Pauline Hopkins,

Frances Harper, Anna Julia Cooper, Nella Larsen, and Jessie Fauset, his remarks have serious consequences for the writers in this study whose location above the Mason-Dixon Line I attempted to account for earlier. Baker's formulation depends on a particular chronotopic configuration in which South/North figure as presence/absence, vernacular/domesticated, theoretical/essential. This association of the vernacular with a specific region and cultural mode of production delimits the applicability of the term for African American women writers whose northernness can be figured only as a "great absence."

Similarly, Henry Louis Gates, although he insists on the vernacular as tropological in *Signifying Monkey*, does not completely succeed in divorcing the term from an insistence on specific linguistic practice, what Gates calls "blackness of the tongue" (*Signifying Monkey* 92). Indeed, so insistent is Gates on representations of black speech as constituting "a sign of black difference" that he actually locates the beginnings of black vernacular representations in a parody of Wheatley's letters in a derogatory racist broadside titled "Dreadful Riot on Negro Hill," which was circulated as early as 1816. A caption under its visual representation of a feisty black woman fighting off a mob of white males reads, "Copy of an intercepted Letter from PHILLIS to her Sister in the Country, describing the late Riot on NEGRO HILL" (91). As Gates writes, "Scholars do not believe that Wheatley's letters to Arbour [*sic*] Tanner were published until 1863–64, thereby raising a host of fascinating questions about how someone else could have been so remarkably familiar with the originals" (90). Yet in referring to this document as a example of "black difference," curiously, Gates implies that the broadside is more "vernacular" than Wheatley's own neoclassical verse written in standard idiom. This tendency to conflate vernacular with representations of "dialect" while maintaining an emphasis on its structural and tropological properties raises serious questions for pre-Emancipation writers. As Donald B. Gibson reminds us, "standard idiom" was part of nineteenth-century writers' strategy of self-representation. "There was no value in the stock of the vernacular," he writes; "nothing could be achieved by claiming it as valuable in the mid-nineteenth century" ("Response to Gates" 47). Wahneemah Lubiano provides a clarifying note in "But Compared to What?": "African-American vernacular is *not* necessarily synonymous with Black English or any form of Black dialect (rural or urban). . . . African-American vernacular is an attitude toward language, a language dynamic, and a technique of language use" (279 n. 19).

I go on at some length about this because of the tendency to equate vernacularity with authenticity, which threatens to dismiss much of the early black writers' work as somehow "inauthentic." Ironically, early attempts to articulate a vernacular theory for creating narratives of African American literary tradition threatened to exclude the plethora of texts that were being rescued from the archives as "weighed in the balance and found wanting."

The etymology Baker offers, which casts vernacularity as social positionality and thus a condition of relations of power, and Lubiano's idea of an "attitude toward language" are steps toward a way of talking about cultural specificity in African American textuality while at the same time resisting the dependence on specific regional sites and linguistic expressivity. A vernacular, in my formulation, is an index to the sites of domination and resistance within a sociocultural sphere and therefore is not reducible to merely linguistic constructs. In this sense, the vernacular records the "hidden transcripts" that mark the site(s) of resistance in a specific cultural sphere.[14] Thus the search for only externally recognizable textual signs fails adequately to contextualize the relations of power inhering in cultural forms of resistance. To say, therefore, that throughout the global history of the oppression and domination of African Americans there have been and continue to be *many vernacular expressions*, each adapted to particular historical, geographical, and social conditions of African American resistance, is to open up the sign of culture to include the metalinguistic, theorizing apparatus of the text rather than to limit the use of the term to description of a particular linguistic pattern.

In "Black Matrilineage: The Case of Alice Walker and Zora Neale Hurston," Diane Sadoff examines Walker's revision of Hurston and offers an alternative paradigm to the Bloomian "anxiety of influence," arguing that "race and class oppression intensify the black woman writer's need to discover an untroubled matrilineal heritage" (211). This desire for matriliny, moreover, demands a "cover[ing] over" (211) of black women's ambivalence about this very object of desire. In a similar vein, Michael Awkward argues that the process of revisionism in the tradition of twentieth-century African American women's novels is characterized by the

> sense of bonding, of energetic explorations for and embrasure of black female precursorial figures, which distinguishes the Afro-American women's novels . . . from competitive black male intertextual relations. Instead of an anxiety of influence, in other words, . . . these novels constitute a textual system characterized by what I call "inspiriting influences." (7–8)

For Awkward, even when a later writer's agenda is critical of or antithetical to that of a precursor, the sense of "bonding" and "embrasure" remains the primary motive of revisionist strategies. In this sense, Awkward's model of African American women's tradition accords with

Sadoff's premise that black women writers mask over their ambivalence about matriliny and sisterhood.

Similarly, Mae G. Henderson's hermeneutics in "Speaking in Tongues" distinguishes between testimonial (familial) and competitive (public) discourses. Henderson writes:

> black women writers enter into testimonial discourse with black men as blacks, with white women as women, and with black women as black women. At the same time, they enter into a competitive discourse with black men as women, with white women as blacks, and with white men as black women. (20)

The abstraction of categories of race and gender here obscures the understanding of differences within any of these four "subgroups." As such, "black women"/"white men"/"black men"/"white women" remain static, undifferentiated blocks. Specifically, what such a formula cannot account for is the ways in which black women's writings fail to form a neat lineage of only testimonial utterances. That is, I want to hold out the possibility that black women's revisionist strategies can occur within a dialectic of testimonial/competitive utterances, a prism that Henderson reserves for discourses between black women and black men/white women.[15]

I find myself uncomfortable, however, with revisionist paradigms based on feminist psychoanalytics which posit a "female" psyche that is dichotomous to Freudian models of male Oedipal competition. Such an opposition only strengthens essentialist notions of "womanhood" and "femininity" and, to the extent that they are based on Gender as an abstract and unmediated category of identity rather than on actual interactions between women, threatens to reify narratives of intertextual Matrilineage and Sisterhood into "natural" relations of black women's intersubjectivity. As Hazel Carby points out in *Reconstructing Womanhood*, notions of "sisterhood" between black and white women that are rendered problematic when ideologies of race as well as gender are taken into account also impose comparable difficulties on the search for sisterhood and generational alliance between black women writers.[16]

While the focus on the social and the ideological negotiations of black women writers has worked to destabilize essentialist notions of black womanhood, however, the "social" often becomes such an all-encompassing category that it masks or mutes the importance of culture to these texts. Moreover, while feminist and black feminist literary critics have written at length about the interconnective relationship between race and gender, the relationship among race, gender, and culture has not been as clearly articulated. Indeed, the slippage among these collective designations and their problematical relationship to Euramerican psychoanalytic theories of subjectivity and identity have caused the various crises surrounding the word "race" and its deconstruction. A social designation, newly liberated from its biological overtones, "race" does not always coincide with the collectives that it purports culturally and geographically (one might include economically) to designate. Yet in the effort to de-essentialize, the significance of the overlap among these conceptual categories has been minimized. The study of pre-Emancipation African American culture and literature is significant because it is here that we can trace the beginnings of African American notions of community or "peoplehood," to catch, if you will, African American cultural production in the very act of *performing* community.

A focus on cultural production as community performance produces, in turn, a new formulation of gender as well. Thus in arguing that gender as a socially constructed category of identity is insufficient in and of itself as an analytical prism through which to understand black women's subjectivity, I mean to locate black women's subjectivity not only within socially constructed racial boundaries but within an African American cultural context, a context generally treated as a gender-neutral terrain. The retrieval of this cultural context involves an examination of African American community, as community signifies a collective identification that mediates the gendered dialectic of society and family. Theories of the "social" that underlie "cultural studies" and theories of the "familial" that serve as the foundation for psychoanalytic approaches to language converge through the rhetorical figure of "community," which necessitates the recovery of the cultural aspects of black women's utterances. Karla F. C. Holloway's observation that "race has a cultural presence" in literature by black women (11) helps to refigure the terms of black women's subjectivity away from race as a stable and transhistorical category of identity, and toward culture and community as dynamic, complex, and constitutive of black women's intertextuality.[17]

One of the difficulties with analyses based on social and ideological contructs, while they recover the importance of power relations as central to textual analysis, has often been a problem with the subject and agency. Sherry B. Ortner's distinction between "constructionism" on the one hand "in which cultural categories, or historical subjects, or forms of subjectivity are—passive voice—made" and "making" on the other hand, the question of "how actors 'enact,' 'resist,' or 'negotiate' the world as given, and in so doing 'make' the world" (*Making Gender* 1) is useful for the reconsideration of issues of culture, gender, and agency. In discussing the "anti-subject or anti-agent poststructuralism" that produced readings of "a discursively constructed position that cannot recognize its own constructedness," Ortner notes that "the denial of the intentional subject, and of 'agency,' both misreads and works against the intellectual and political interests of women, minorities, postcolonial, and other subaltern subjects" (8). Thus, she writes,

> Studies of the ways in which some set of "texts"—media productions, liter-
> ary creations, medical writings, religious discourses, and so on—"con-
> structs" categories, identities, or subject positions, are incomplete and mis-
> leading unless they ask to what degree those texts successfully impose
> themselves on real people (and *which people*) in real time. Similarly, studies
> of the ways in which people resist, negotiate, or appropriate some feature
> of their world are also inadequate and misleading without careful analysis
> of the cultural meanings and structural arrangements that construct and
> constrain their "agency," and that limit the transformative potential of all
> such intentionalized activity. (2)

Questions of agency, intentionality, and empowerment are central to the study of pre-Emancipation black women writers precisely because the writers themselves are so conscious of their positionality. Indeed, one of the things that was most striking to me as I began to study black women writers of this historical period was the seriousness with which they regarded their authorship. The blossoming of black female literary societies in the early nineteenth century in which black women gathered to submit poems, anonymously, to be read and critiqued by the group is but one indication of the seriousness with which these women approached literary authorship. Thus to Foucault's famous interrogative at the end of "What Is an Author?"—"what matter who's speaking?"—the women who signed themselves as authors of poetry, fiction, autobiography, essays, and political speeches of this era in African American literary history gather as a collective witness to the importance of the author not just as a function of textuality but as a specific embodiment (of "real people . . . in real time," to quote Ortner) of a subjectivity that comes into being by virtue of its investment in authorship as a position of agency and empowerment. Thus though black women have been "'buked," "scorned," and "talked about," the narrative of black women's authorship in America records black women's "talkin' back."[18]

THE SAVING CHANGE

Significantly, the struggle for empowerment, agency, and subjectivity within a cultural and communal frame of reference is nowhere as evident as in black women's negotiations with prevailing *religious* discourses. These negotiations occur within African American women's appropriation and transformation of Protestantism as expressed by white northern

Christian hegemony that surfaced during the First and Second Great Awakenings in America, and in their struggles with emerging independent African American denominations and expressions of African American Christianity. Albert Raboteau discusses the complexity of slaves' "acceptance" of Christianity in the eighteenth century in *Slave Religion*:

> Adapting to the foreign culture of the Europeans meant for the African not the total abandonment of their own cosmologies but, rather, a process of integrating the unfamiliar reference to the familiar. Catechesis moved in two directions. The slaves were taught the prayers, doctrines, and rites of Christianity, but as the missionaries realized, the slaves had to somehow understand the meaning of Christian belief and ritual if instruction was to become more than mere parroting. And here the whites had only limited control. For the slaves brought their cultural past to the task of translating and interpreting the doctrinal words and ritual gestures of Christianity. Therefore the meaning which the missionary wished the slaves to receive and the meaning which the slaves actually found (or, better, made) were not the same. (126)

David W. Wills, in arguing for inclusion of "the encounter of black and white" in accounts of American religious history that have traditionally focused on a dialectical narrative of "pluralism" versus "Puritanism," writes that

> numerically significant Christianization of the slave population only began after 1760 and did not really come to full tide until after 1830, by which time most American blacks were native born. While some blacks at the time of their capture and enslavement were Muslims, the vast majority were adherents of some form of African traditional religion—and it is presumably as such that they lived and died in America. (Wills 14)

Wills lays out the parameters of the continuum of black religious experience in America before Emancipation. That the dates of the beginnings of African American literary tradition coincide with the periods of intensification of conversion is instructive. Clearly African American women and men seized on the discourse of conversion as a fundamental means for self-expression.

In a letter to her black woman friend, fellow slave, and confidante Obour Tanner, written in Boston on May 19, 1772, Wheatley refers to conversion to Christianity as "the saving change." After addressing Obour as "dear sister," Wheatley writes,

> I greatly rejoice with you in that realizing view, and I hope experience, of the saving change which you so emphatically describe. Happy were it for us if we could arrive to that evangelical Repentance, and the true holiness of

heart which you mention [in your letter of February 6th]. Inexpressibly happy should we be could we have a due sense of the beauties and excellence of the crucified Saviour. (Shields 164)

That this phrase appears in a letter, written to mediate the distance between Wheatley in Boston and Obour Tanner in Newport, Rhode Island, makes it all the more fitting. For the two women, both brought from Africa to serve in America as slaves, religious conversion provided a common experience and the language of Christianity provided a common language in America (through the medium of written English, of course) that mediated other cultural/discursive differences which may have existed in their places of origin. It is this sense of the language of conversion as a common lexical, syntactic, and semantic domain that I wish to invoke here,[19] a rhetorical meeting place that occasioned the correspondence between Wheatley and Tanner, a surprising feat in and of itself given the difficulties of their lives as eighteenth-century slave women.

Conversion, or what Wheatley calls "the saving change," operates as an important dialectical movement, calling forth, as it does, both the continuity of salvation and the transformation of radical change. Thus the experience of Christian conversion demands a fundamental displacement, figured by its "from . . . to" syntax, "from sinner to saint." One changes in order to preserve/conserve one's soul, which becomes consecrated to another place (heaven). Thus conversion signals both a departure and an arrival, an eternal continuity of the soul, even as it demands a discontinuity, a break in the course of one's sinful life: "If anyone be in Christ, he is a new creation. Old things are passed away, behold, all things are become new" (2 Cor. 5:17). The rebirth of Christian salvation is a transgression against the "natural" order of things, a turning away from the narrative of life, written by Adam and Eve via the Fall to a narrative of grace, written by Christ, the Word of God.

While on the one hand, it is easy to characterize African American conversions to Christianity as part of an acculturation process that denied them their own culturally distinct subjectivity, it is also easy to see why so many African Americans seized upon this discourse, especially after the First and Second Great Awakenings made such language so widely acceptable. For individuals socially "cursed" with a racialized and othered subjectivity, conversion represented one of the few discourses, and certainly the most prominent, holding the promise of a radical change in subjectivity. If one could move "from sinner to saint," she/he could also move "from slave to free," "from bondage to freedom." Thus conversion functions in early black women's literature both as an event and as a process for the revisioning of community.[20]

THE EARLIEST BLACK WOMEN'S WRITING COMMUNITY

Miss Obour Tanner, Worcester
favd by Cumberland

> Boston May 10, 1779

Dr. Obour,—By this opportunity I have the pleasure to inform you that I
am well and hope you are so; tho' I have been silent, I have not been un-
mindful of you, but a variety of hindrances was the cause of my not writing
to you. But in time to come I hope our correspondence will revive—and
revive in better times—pray write me soon, for I long to hear from you—
you may depend on constant replies—I wish you much happiness and am

> Dr. Obour, your friend & sister
> Phillis [Wheatley] Peters

> And then I think I will compose,
>   And thus myself engage—
> To try to please young ladies minds,
>   Which are about my age.

> The greatest word that I can say,—
>   I think to please, will be,
> To try and get your learning young,
>   And write it back to me.
>   *(Ann Plato, "Advice to Young Ladies" [1841])*

In "Moving On down the Line," Hortense Spillers defines "community" as "both a *groping* and a *given*":

> We can either read "community" as homogeneous memory and experi-
> ence, laying claim to a collective "voice" and rendering an apparently
> unified and uniform Narrative, or we might think of it as a content whose
> time and meaning are "discovered," but a meaning, in any case, that has
> not already been decided. In other words, "community," in the latter in-
> stance, becomes *potentiality*; an unfolding to be *attended*. (89)

This dialectical movement sets the parameters for what Spillers elsewhere designates "the community of black women writing in the United
States," a collective shaped by "the palpable and continuing urgency of
black women writing themselves into history" ("Cross-Currents" 249).
Spillers's term "writing community" is helpful as a theoretical rubric
through which to attend the "unfolding" of early African American
women's literary production.[21] As a corrective to the term "tradition,"
"writing community" invokes the sense of a boundary or border (community) that remains actively and dynamically in the process of its own

renegotiation (writing). Indeed, under the sign of "tradition," the argument for including early African American women's texts within various canons (American, African American, even African American women's literature) has rested on the concept of "firstness." Phillis Wheatley, the "first" black/woman to publish a book of poetry. Ann Plato, the "first" to publish a book of essays. Harriet E. Wilson, the "first" to publish a novel. Maria W. Stewart, the "first black woman political writer."[22] Appearing as a series of unrelated beginnings, early black women's texts have often been celebrated as separate and isolated publishing "events." The term "writing community," then, helps us to revision the emergence of African American women's authorship as a collective "event" that changed forever the "master narrative" of American authorship even as African American women transgressed the race, class, and gender boundaries of American literary production.

In the passages from Wheatley and Plato at the beginning of this section, each woman, in her own way and in her own era, articulates the need for a reconfiguration of the history of black women's literary production before Emancipation. Clearly neither Wheatley at the end of the eighteenth century nor Plato in the middle of the nineteenth could assume a large, literate audience of black women as readers of their texts. The power relations inherent in proscriptions of race, gender, and class produced the "variety of hindrances" that sought to relegate black women to silence and isolation. Yet the notion of a *potential* community of black women readers (and writers) that would, in Wheatley's words, "revive in better times" grounds the seriousness with which these women invested in conceptions of authorship.

It is fitting, then, that early black women's writing community begins with Phillis Wheatley's seven-year correspondence with Obour Tanner, her confidante and a fellow enslaved African woman.[23] Not only do these seven surviving letters necessitate a revision of the notion of a Phillis Wheatley completely isolated from other black women in community, they also serve as a paradigm for the problematics and possibilities of early black women's writing community. In this broken, one-sided narrative in which letters are often sent back, delayed, or not received, large gaps in time—sometimes as much as four years—mark the desire for response with an ever-present deferral. Hand-delivered by a third party (usually male), the letters are prone to violation and interception.[24] Perhaps more important, each letter is sent "favd by" someone, and "in care of," which marks the problematics of ownership for black women slaves, a qualification that framed even their most intimate attempts to communicate with each other. The sense of surveillance that collapses the distinction between public and private confers on this correspondence the possibility of an audience larger than the letters' original addressee. As

William Robinson writes, "despite the threat of penalties, colonial American privacy of the mail was hardly guaranteed; it would have been even less so with letters written by blacks" (*Phillis Wheatley and Her Writings* 25). Thus the letters bear witness to the violence done to black women's bodies, lives, and texts.

In "The Problem of Speech Genres," Bakhtin theorizes the "utterance" as an act of speaking or writing that may range in length from a single word to a multivolume novel (or even a writer's entire oeuvre). Bounded by "*the change in speaking subjects*" (*Speech Genres* 71), the utterance is characterized by "*the possibility of responding to it*" (76). Thus all utterances (acts of speaking/writing) are dialogized by the desire for "active responsive understanding" from an actual or potential "other." Crucial for my purposes here is Bakhtin's concept of the "addressivity" of the utterance (95). Speakers come to voice not only out of the desire for response but also by a "dialogic turn" that confers on the utterance "the quality of turning to someone" (99). The utterance is determined, then, by an addressee "*for whose sake . . . it is actually created.*" "From the very beginning," writes Bakhtin, "the speaker expects a response from them, an active responsive understanding. The entire utterance is constructed, as it were, in anticipation of encountering this response" (94).

The role of the "other" accords with Mae Henderson's theory of black women's subjectivity and discourse as distinguished by "the privileging (rather than repressing) of 'the other in ourselves'" (19). The lines from Phillis Wheatley and Ann Plato prefigure these critical responses. In her last letter to Obour Tanner, Wheatley implores her friend to "pray write me soon," as "self" expression and the desire for response from an "other" proceed dialogically from epistolarity. Similarly, Ann Plato's twenty-four-line poem "Advice to Young Ladies" functions as an "open letter" to her female students in the segregated African Free School in Hartford, Connecticut. Plato's advice to her black female readers to get their "learning young" (through her own efforts as a teacher?) is a call to create a circle of correspondents who will be able to "write . . . back," thus completing the circuit of desire. Early black women's community was clearly "a community conscious of itself" (Spillers, "Cross-Currents" 250). "Mindful" of each other, their collective formulation of the meaning of their authorship posits black female authorship as a subjectivity of desire.

SPIRITUALS MATRIX

For the study of pre-Emancipation African American women's writing community, then, I posit a "spirituals matrix," rather than the "blues matrix" offered by Baker in *Blues, Ideology, and Afro-American Literature*, as more appropriate to the specificity of their social, cultural, and textual negotiations, their particular vernacularity. Not only do virtually all scholars on the spirituals identify the pre-Emancipation period as the historical era of the composition of the majority of the songs, but the spirituals themselves encode the very problematics of representation, performativity, and inaccessibility of narratives of "origins" that characterize the scholarship of pre-Emancipation African American literature. In this sense, the spirituals stand in for a multidirectional African American desire figured as a deferred search for community even as they project that desire elsewhere.

I take up the issue of spirituals and pre-Emancipation African American subjectivity in chapter 7. Suffice it to say here that a spirituals matrix proceeds from the deconstruction of oppositions of sacred/secular, political/religious, social/spiritual that plague much thinking around spirituals even as it disrupts the binaries of African/Euramerican, functional/aesthetic. Moreover, because the written texts of spirituals were recorded decades after the "originary" composition of the songs, the spirituals participate in the overall difficulties of historicity that mark the "rediscovered" literary texts. As performed texts, moreover, they point to the need for new formulations of intertextuality that can go beyond traditional assumptions about the way written texts inform one another. What spirituals ultimately perform, as I will argue below, is a desire for community and communal longing that configures a displaced African American subjectivity. In the chapters that follow, the desire/search for community emerges as a primary narrative in the writings of Phillis Wheatley, Ann Plato, Jarena Lee, and Rebecca Cox Jackson, the four women who form the "writing community" I explore in this book. Indeed, each, in her own way and in her own time, *is* writing community, inscribing her own sense of communal boundaries within the realm of desire, sometimes in harmony, other times at odds, with the larger project of African American community formation.

Diaspora Subjectivity and Transatlantic Crossings: Phillis Wheatley's Poetics of Recovery

> My project rises from delight, not
> disappointment. It rises from what I know about
> the ways writers transform aspects of their social
> grounding into aspects of language, and the ways
> they tell other stories, fight secret wars, limn out
> all sorts of debates blanketed in their text. And
> rises from my certainty that writers always know,
> at some level, that they do this.
> (*Toni Morrison,* Playing in the Dark)

> [P]eople of color have always theorized—but
> in forms quite different from the Western
> form of abstract logic.
> (*Barbara Christian, "The Race for Theory"*)

TONI Morrison's *Playing in the Dark: Whiteness and the Literary Imagination* might seem an unlikely critical text with which to open a discussion of eighteenth-century slave poet Phillis Wheatley. After all, Morrison's project, which she describes as "unencumbered by dreams of subversion or rallying gestures at fortress walls" (3), materializes through her readings of white Americans writers' construction and use of "a sometimes allegorical, sometimes metaphorical, but always choked Africanist presence" (17), a psychical/discursive process Morrison refers to as "American Africanism." Yet at the very outset of *Playing in the Dark*, Morrison defines her critical project as one that (she tells us three times) "rises" from overlapping concerns of subjectivity ("aspects of . . . social grounding"), utterance ("aspects of . . . language"), and epistemology ("what I know"; "my certainty that writers always know. . . ."). Such a project does not hold itself to binaries of American/African American or, indeed, even writer/critic, and I turn to Morrison precisely because her project enables a theorizing positionality that renders meaningless these conventional battle lines. As Morrison writes, "I want to draw a map, so to speak, of a critical geography and use that map to open as much space for discovery, intellectual adventure, and close exploration as did the original charting of the New World—without the mandate for conquest" (3).

Similarly, Barbara Christian's brilliant if often misunderstood observation that "people of color have always theorized—but in forms quite different from the Western form of abstract logic" ("The Race for Theory" 38) raises precisely this issue of epistemology and culture. Using the verbal formation "theorize" instead of the abstract nominative "theory," Christian locates the culture-specific theorizing of African Americans in narrative, stories, riddles, and proverbs. Often misinterpreted as "antitheory," Christian's theorizing understands African American thought as a radically Other (and other-ed, dismissed, discredited) epistemology. Like Morrison, she deconstructs the oppositions praxis/theory, writer/critic, performer/thinker. It is thus that a discourse which I will call "African Americanism" rises out of the shadows of these formulations. Both Christian's understanding of an alternative theorizing cultural presence and Morrison's writerly "certainty" signal a discourse that shadows—contours, if you will—the discourse of American Africanism.

Given Morrison's premise that "literary blackness" and "literary whiteness" are mutually dependent and mutually constituting, her title could well read, "Playing in the Dark (/Light): Whiteness (/Blackness) and the Literary Imagination." Such a deconstruction, however, does not render meaningless the notion of a discourse of African Americanism that is distinct from yet related to American Africanism. Morrison points to the presence of African Americanism as a discourse (albeit unnamed) when she writes:

> The principal reason these matters loom large for me is that I do not have quite the same access to these traditionally useful constructs of blackness. Neither blackness nor "people of color" stimulates in me notions of excessive, limitless love, anarchy, or routine dread. I cannot rely on these metaphorical shortcuts because I am a black writer struggling with and through a language that can powerfully evoke and enforce hidden signs of racial superiority, cultural hegemony, and dismissive "othering" of people and language which are by no means marginal or already and completely known and knowable in my work. My vulnerability would lie in romanticizing blackness rather than demonizing it; vilifying whiteness rather than reifying it. (x–xi)

African Americanism as a discourse derives its power from its self-reflexivity, its self-consciousness about both the possibilities and the risks in written language. This self-reflexivity derives from an African artistic and performing heritage which informs the writerly consciousness that is the basis of African American interpretive and theorizing practices. It derives, as well, from the ability of the diasporic African American subject to see what is supposed to remain unseen: the subtle but destructive mechanism of American Africanism. Characterized by "significant and underscored omissions, startling contradictions, heavily nuanced conflicts," American Africanism produces a national literature whose signfying traits are "in fact responses to a dark, abiding, signing Africanist presence" (Morrison 6, 9). Morrison's shift of the terms of "call and response" here is significant. For if white American identification is refigured as a "response" to a (largely created) "Africanist call," by what means, then, do Africans in America come to recognize (re-know) themselves? If the national literature is founded on "responses to . . . Africanist presence," what could be the African(/American) response to this response?

If "whiteness" comes into being as a reaction to the presence of "blackness," then African Americanism must be more than simply a reaction to that reaction. In fact, it is a vantage point—Du Bois called it "double consciousness"—that sees the construction of whiteness, catches it, if you will, in its reflexive posture vis-à-vis its construction of a discourse of blackness as a discourse of difference. Unlike "African Assimilationism," in which "American means white, and Africanist people struggle to make the term applicable to themselves with ethnicity and hyphen after hyphen after hyphen" (Morrison 47), African Americanism is not an exercise in psychical/discursive application but represents the creative insistence of an African American theorizing heritage in which African writers in the Americas come to "tell other stories, fight secret wars, limn out all sorts of debates blanketed in their texts." Morrison's description of the revelatory potential of African Americanist theorizing—a revelation that occurs to her when she begins reading "as a writer"—is illuminating: "It is as if I had been looking at a fishbowl . . . and suddenly I saw the bowl, the structure that transparently (and invisibly) permits the ordered life it contains to exist in the larger world. In other words, I began to rely on my knowledge of how books get written, how language arrives . . ." (17).

The language of "arrival" here is instructive since it is precisely the terms of African arrival to the New World that construct the dynamics of African American subjectivity and discourse which underlie Wheatley's work. Born in Africa, captured, enslaved, and transported via the notorious transatlantic crossing known as the Middle Passage, Phillis Wheatley was sold in Boston in 1761 to John Wheatley as a personal servant to his wife, Susannah. Yet with the publication of *Poems on Various Subjects Religious and Moral* in London in 1773, Wheatley became the first African and only the second woman in America to publish a book of poetry.

The arrival of both her (captive) body and her text forces an interroga-tion of the terms of American literary production, for only in "a highly and historically racialized society" (Morrison 4) such as the United States would the intertwined issues of subjectivity, utterance, and episte-mology become tied so firmly to debates over Wheatley's Africanness. Indeed, issues of subjectivity (Who was Phillis Wheatley?), utterance (What did she write?), and epistemology (Did she know—could she have known—what she was doing?) have been central to Wheatley com-mentary almost from the beginning.[1] And all three questions are bound up in the discourse of what Morrison calls "American Africanism."

Indeed, the first two questions and the relationship between them have drawn much attention from critics such as Houston Baker, Henry Louis Gates, Jr., Alice Walker, June Jordan, and, more recently, Sondra O'Neale, Russell Reising, Phillip Richards, and Frances Smith Foster.[2] The question of epistemology, however, has remained politely unasked. And yet assumptions about this issue—did she know what she was doing?—have shaped critical perception of the relationship between who she was and what she wrote. In the discourse and criticism sur-rounding Phillis Wheatley and her poetry, this question goes far beyond notions of authorial intent. As is made clear by the prefatory material in *Poems on Various Subjects Religious and Moral*—the letter of attestation and "To the Publick," which form the "authenticating apparatus" of the text—the very fact of her authorship was subject to suspicion and inter-rogation by her (white and male) contemporaries. The current critical bent in Wheatley studies is to focus on (and marvel at) her "mastery" of Western discourse, either as evidence of cultural "assimilation" or as semiotic "trafficking" in representations of whiteness.[3] However, the question of epistemology is answered by Wheatley herself at the end of *Poems*, an ending overlooked in criticism in favor of the prefatory mate-rial. After the ode "Farewel to America," which would seem a "natural" ending for *Poems*, Wheatley includes "A Rebus by I. B." and "An An-swer to the *Rebus* by the Author of These POEMS." This inclusion is nei-ther frivolous nor gratuitous but represents Wheatley's own answer to the letter of attestation (or, indeed, to the question such a letter raises—did she know what she was doing?). In "An Answer to the *Rebus*," Wheatley actually solves the versified riddle of one of the authenticators. In a gesture of self-authentication, Wheatley responds to the issue of epistemology by demonstrating that she can, indeed, crack the codes of Western discourse. And her decoding encodes the point of entry for an African Americanist theorizing.

In this chapter, I revisit the subject of Phillis Wheatley's relationship to a displaced Africanity through the recovery of her poetics. Thus I en-vision this chapter as a naming ritual.[4] As John S. Mbiti writes in *African*

Religions and Philosophy, in traditional West African societies, "Some names describe the personality of the individual, or [her] character, or some key events in [her] life. There is no stop to the giving of names in many African societies, so that a person can acquire a sizable collection of names by the time [she] becomes an old [woman]" (115). Since Phillis Wheatley's original name, which would have been bestowed in a communal ritual as early as her first week of life, is unrecoverable, I will begin by tracing the history of her misnamings—beginning with "Wheatley," the patriarchal name of the family that bought her, and "Phillis" the name of the slave ship that brought her to Boston.[5] Ultimately, however, what "names" her, marks her most clearly, is her survival of the Middle Passage, an "event" whose constituent parts (capture, enslavement, transport, sale) and results (catechism, conversion, poetic authorship) are explored and developed in Wheatley's own poetic utterance, a writerly-theorizing explication that is representative of her deepening awareness of the meaning of her own displacement. These naming events, in fact, constitute the "metaoccasion" for a body of work often dismissed as merely "occasional" verse.[6] The recovery of Wheatley's "writerly self" is crucial to the revisioning of the meaning of her poetics. Thus a good deal of this chapter is devoted to restoring a sense of the care with which Wheatley revised her own poems and the ways in which those revisions help us to retrace the development of her thinking about issues of power, knowledge, and cultural identity. Indeed, issues of subjectivity, poetic utterance, and epistemology are issues Wheatley herself was concerned with and articulate about. True to her theorizing heritage, Wheatley is both writer and theorizer of African Americanism, a discourse she helped to invent.

DIASPORA SUBJECTIVITY

In *Between Slavery and Freedom*, Bill E. Lawson writes of the "functional lexical gap" evidenced by the lack of an appropriate collective nomenclature for descendants of Africans enslaved in the Americas. Noting that "the language we use to frame a group's political and social status can have an impact on the public policy regarding that group," Lawson concludes that "our moral/political vocabulary is morally unsatisfactory and inadequate for characterizing the plight of present-day black Americans" (McGary and Lawson 72). Lawson's important observation about collective designation has its beginnings in the ritual misnamings of African peoples that characterized the transatlantic slave trade. Further, this "conceptual" and "lexical" gap (77) has had a direct impact on the perception and reception of Phillis Wheatley as an enslaved African woman and a poet. As June Jordan posed it in "The Difficult Miracle," "How could there be black poets in America? It was not natural and she was the first" (23).

While Jordan's appeal to "nature" might be off-putting to those concerned with de-essentializing "race," her question expresses the problematic of African American authorship as it is based on a subjectivity of displacement. Part of the difficulty arises from the discourse of American Africanism, which Morrison links to the beginnings of an "American" national identity: "the formation of the nation necessitated coded language and purposeful restriction to deal with the racial disingenuousness and moral frailty at its heart" (6). It is thus that terms like "black," "poet," and "America" become coded and conceptually shackled as part of a discourse which seeks to jettison "black" from the equation. Henry Louis Gates, Jr., has demonstrated how Wheatley's poetry became embroiled in prevailing discourses of black intellectual inferiority. He and others have discussed the presence of the "authenticating documents" at the beginning of *Poems on Various Subjects Religious and Moral,* including the frontispiece portrait of Wheatley by Scipio Moorhead, as evidence of the discourse of racial inferiority. What remains to be examined is the matrix of gender and culture in which this discourse of race and racialization occurs.

Questions of social, cultural, and racial positionality and origins have plagued the discourse surrounding Phillis Wheatley almost from the initial publication of *Poems on Various Subjects Religious and Moral* in 1773, an event that assured Wheatley, as the first African and only the second woman in America to publish a book of poems, a lasting place in American and African American literary history. Wheatley's "originary" position, however, has often attracted more critical commentary than her poetry. M. A. Richmond's conclusion, "it is the tragedy rather than the poetry of Phillis Wheatley that has the more enduring relevance for American life" (66), is exemplary of the type of dismissal Wheatley's work has suffered. While more recent critics have taken a variety of historical, anthropological, and discursive approaches to Wheatley's work, the emphasis remains on her "tragic" life rather than the poems themselves. June Jordan and Alice Walker, offering a black feminist corrective to the customary elision of Wheatley's gender, have revisioned Wheatley's life not as "tragedy" but as "miracle," yet the focus of their analyses is on her originary or "foremother" status rather than her poetry.[7]

The confusion over the cultural, racial, and social trajectories of identity and discourse becomes complicated even further by the problem of psychical processes and poetic production, memory and poetic utterance. Such a knot of discourses appears in the very first biography of

Phillis Wheatley, published in 1834, a half-century after the poet's death, by Margaretta Matilda Odell, a self-styled "collateral descendant" of the Wheatleys.[8] The text appeared anonymously under the title *Memoir and Poems of Phillis Wheatley. A Native African and a Slave*, a title that creates the expectation of a relationship between life and work, identity and language, that the anecdotal, gap-ridden biographical narrative continually frustrates. Odell's central "thesis" is that Wheatley's "literary efforts were altogether the natural workings of her own mind" (18), a gesture of "authentication" that situates the African woman writer in America within discourses of black and female intellectual inferiority.[9] The *Memoir* inscribes, ultimately, one writer's memory of another writer's memories, as a significant portion of the text is devoted to a quasi-scientific explanation of what Odell supposes to be a defect of Wheatley's mind:

> [Phillis] does not seem to have preserved any remembrance of the place of her nativity, or of her parents, excepting the simple circumstance that her mother *poured out water before the sun at his rising*—in reference, no doubt, to an ancient African custom. The memories of most children reach back to a much earlier period than their seventh year; but there are some circumstances . . . which would induce us to suppose, that in the case of Phillis, this faculty did not equal the other powers of her mind. (12–13)

I will return to the issue of Odell's misreading of what are probably ritual libations for the ancestors as some form of "ancient" sun worship. My concern here is with the assumption that Wheatley's ability to learn English and Latin, to master literature, the Bible, geography, and astronomy well enough in nine short years to publish a book-length volume of poetry displaced a "normal" capacity for early childhood memories.[10] Odell's memory of Wheatley's lack of (certain) memories constructs the notion of a "life" that the title (*Memoir*) promises, even as the subtitle, *A Native African and a Slave* portrays Wheatley as a "Native African" with virtually no remembrance of Africa, a "Slave" whose very poems are used to underscore the fact of this erasure.

While many of the "facts" of Odell's *Memoir* have subsequently been proven false, the portrait of Wheatley's near-amnesia about her African past has since become cliché, used by scholars to prove everything from the wretchedness of enslavement to the much-held view of the total "white-washing" of Wheatley resulting, the theory goes, in a body of poetry with no racial consciousness. The image remains of a Phillis Wheatley completely passive and powerless, if not oblivious, to the forces around her, rather than a young black woman with a "standpoint"[11] on her own oppression.

Morrison's analysis in *Playing in the Dark* helps put to rest the notion
of a "raceless" Phillis Wheatley when she notes that "for both black and
white writers, in a wholly racialized society, there is no escape from racially inflected language, and the work writers do to unhobble the imagination from the demands of that language is complicated, interesting,
and definitive" (12–13). Here the debate becomes not whether
Wheatley was African/black enough in her poems but what kind of Africanity (what theories of blackness) her work enacts and enables. And for
me the answer is similar to Morrison's own description of her Africanist
Americanist work: "The kind of work I have always wanted to do requires me to learn how to maneuver ways to free up the language from
its sometimes sinister, frequently lazy, almost always predictable em-
ployment of racially informed and determined chains" (xi).

The Language of Survivorship

The slippage in the Wheatley discourse blurring the binaries memory/
psyche, slave/social position, African/cultural evidences a crisis around
the word "race" that deconstruction and de-essentialization have failed
adequately to address. If, in the eighteenth century, the concept of race
resulted from what Ali Mazrui calls "the dis-Africanisation of the diaspora,"[12] then the racialization of African peoples involved not only a
dis-Africanizing but an un-Americanizing as well,[13] all of which bears
directly on Wheatley's situation in Boston on the eve of the American
Revolution. That Wheatley consistently refers to herself as "Afric[an]"
or "Ethiop[ian]" in her poetry rather than "slave," "black," or, indeed
"American" represents an act of self-naming that transgresses the racialized boundaries which sought to constrict African American subjectivity.[14] Thus Wheatley's self-designations keep ever in view "the crucial
marker of difference in a US Real—the vital sign of 'Africanity'" (Spillers, "Who Cuts the Border?" 11).

Second, while Sondra O'Neale urges in "A Slave's Subtle Civil War"
that "any evaluation of Phillis Wheatley must consider her status as a
slave" (14), I propose to go beyond the nominative "slave," which denotes a racialized status or condition based on the notion of inherent
(and inheritable) African inferiority, to refigure Wheatley as a Middle
Passage survivor.[15] The weeks-to-months-long voyage across the Atlantic from the West African coast, often to the West Indies, and finally to
North America, inscribes the condition of diaspora subjectivity as geocultural displacement. In the European-American scheme of things, Africans were positioned in a no-win situation (individually and collec-

tively) between enslavement and death. Thus the survival of African peoples who crossed on the Middle Passage, a survival mandated by the enslavers, became not an "event" to be celebrated but, in the dialectic imposed by this discourse, yet another mark of African inferiority and thus "proof" of their enslavability. In the Iberian colonies, early attempts to enslave indigenous peoples had failed owing to harsh labor demands and lack of immunity to European diseases. The transfer of their labor functions to imported and enslaved Africans led to European beliefs that "the work output of one African was equal to four to eight Indians" (Reynolds 60).

The belief that Africans were physically and thus genetically fit for slavery recast their physical survival of the harsh conditions of the Middle Passage as a sign of mental, moral, and cultural weakness and docility. Indeed, their physical survival was mandated by the captors, as the captives were regularly forced to eat, exercise, and so forth. The only sign of "honor" recognized by the Europeans, suicide, meant self-annihilation. An English traveler in 1746 wrote of an African-born slave: "If he must be broke, either from Obstinacy, or, which I am more apt to suppose, from *Greatness of Soul*, will require . . . hard Discipline . . . you would really be surprized at their Perseverance; . . . they oft die before they can be conquer'd" (qtd. in Blassingame 12). Companies that insured slavers against accident and mishap counted as "natural death" disease and "also when the captive destroys himself through despair, which often happens" (qtd. in Reynolds 50).

A language of African survivorship calls to mind the survival of Africanity and African structures within New World spaces.[16] As Ngugi Wa Thiong'o writes, "you can destroy a people's culture completely only by destroying a people themselves" (45). Survivorship also signals generational survival, as one is survived by one's descendants. The issue of ancestors and remembrance will become crucial to an understanding of Wheatley's embracing of the elegiac genre. Finally, it points to the survival of black texts despite centuries of neglect and hostility. This is especially important in Wheatley studies, as drafts and variants of her poetry are still being recovered.[17] Connotations of survivorship—black bodies, African cultures, and black texts—converge in the figure and poetics of Phillis Wheatley.

Wheatley appears on the auction block in Boston in 1761 at a kind of crisis point of the transatlantic slave trade. Not only does her lifespan (1752?–84) encompass the peak years of the trade, but her presence in New England serves as a reminder that in the eighteenth century, the New England colonies were "the greatest slave-trading section of America" (Greene 24). As Philip D. Curtin's seminal study *The Atlantic Slave Trade: A Census* shows, an estimated 9,566,100 Africans landed in the

Americas between 1502 and the mid–nineteenth century, 399,000 of them in British mainland North America. Moreover, the trade peaked in the eighteenth century (1741–1810) with 80 percent landed in the century and a half between 1701 and 1850. As sensational as these numbers appear, "the cost of the slave trade in human life was many times the number of slaves landed in America" (Curtin 275).[18]

In "Mama's Baby, Papa's Maybe" Hortense Spillers meditates on the instability of African categories of identity in "the socio-political order of the New World": "That order, with its human sequence written in blood, *represents* for its African and indigenous peoples a scene of *actual* mutilation, dismemberment, and exile. First of all, their New World, diasporic plight marked a *theft of the body*—a willful and violent (and unimaginable from this distance) severing of the captive body from its motive will, its active desire" (67). The horror of this description of bodily theft is only magnified when we consider the African Sacred Cosmos, whose worldview theorizes subjectivity in terms of not individual and nuclear family units but extended family, community, and land/environment.[19] Theologian Dwight Hopkins describes this "theological anthropology" as follows: "To be human meant to stand in connection with the larger community of the invisible ancestors and God and, of course, the visible community and family" (18). Thus with her transportation to America, Wheatley's very (black female) body marks her as a truncated part of a whole community and kin network. While the specifics of that community are unrecoverable, what we do recover is her own critical and interpretive displacements in which Wheatley writes/rewrites the Middle Passage in her poems.

WRITING THE MIDDLE PASSAGE

The Language of Displacement

The Middle Passage as the scene of psychic and communal fracture reinscribes black women's subjectivity at the metalevel of the utterance, as diaspora subjectivity authorizes a "claiming residence" in language (Holloway 63), a "making [one's] self at home" within the space of the text (June Jordan 26). Dispossessed as black women writers are of memory, culture, and history, their "possession of the *word*" is, fundamentally, "a cultural and gendered legacy" (Holloway 27). Thus we can reread Wheatley's memory of her mother's morning libations as a "(cultural) mooring" that initiates a series of African American female "(spiritual) metaphors" (Holloway 1). Moreover, insofar as this is a religious memory, Wheatley's own religiosity—enacted in her conversion to Christianity—repeats, however unconsciously, her mother's spiritual ritual, inadvertently, perhaps, laying claim to a legacy at once African and female. True to the displacements signaled by diaspora subjectivity, Wheatley's poetics of recovery will lead us simultaneously backward, to the African community from which she was prematurely severed, and forward, to the community of black women writers prefigured by her correspondence with Obour Tanner, a fellow female slave, one of the few black women of her era as Christian and as literate as she.[20] It is through this poetics of recovery that Wheatley challenges and revises the American Africanist notions inhering in the colonial discourse which surrounds her. Far from "assimilating" this discourse,[21] Wheatley both perceives its ideological form and configuration within the domain of sociopolitical relations of power and challenges its premises by displaying its constructedness as ideology. In Morrison's phrasing, she sees the "fishbowl" within which the oceanic discourse of African enslavement is contained, and through her bold poetics, she invents a discursive strategy for breaking the glass.

Significantly, Holloway writes that "spiritual and psychic fracture" is represented textually by the black woman writer's manipulation of "alternative spaces" (117), a moving "between worlds" (114) that stages the displacement of the diaspora subject. No reading of the poetry of Phillis Wheatley would be complete that did not account for her most famous and oft-anthologized poem, "On Being Brought From Africa to America." In this poem, Wheatley establishes the parameters for her own self-naming and self-positioning as poet, African American woman, diaspora subject. I quote the poem in its entirety:

> 'Twas mercy brought me from my *Pagan* land,
> Taught my benighted soul to understand
> That there's a God, that there's a *Saviour* too:
> Once I redemption neither sought nor knew.
> Some view our sable race with scornful eye,
> "Their colour is a diabolic die."
> Remember, *Christians*, *Negroes*, black as *Cain*,
> May be refin'd and join th'angelic train.

A terse, eight-line poem in a single stanza, "On Being Brought" appears to be a seamless whole even as its surface-level meaning is presented as a rational and unified argument ("'Twas mercy brought me from my *Pagan* land"). However, line 4—"Once I redemption neither sought nor knew"—creates a rupture that structurally breaks the poem in two.

From this structural fracture, a poem emerges that is *about* spiritual and cultural fracturing. As June Jordan observes, the single word "once" suggests that "[o]nce I existed beyond and without these terms under consideration. *Once I existed on other than your terms*" (26). If the "once" brings to consciousness some primal memory, some originary moment and place, then its positioning at the end of the "conversion narrative" part of the poem represents a critical realignment of the terms of narrativity.[22] The narrative frame "on being brought *from* Africa *to* America" is temporally displaced as the first half of the poem ends, as it were, at the beginning.

The "once" signifies not only another time but another place, representing a realignment of space as well. In the context of this utterance, the realignment of the place of originary memory forms a hinge; it provides a transition to the second quatrain, which brings the poem from the individual and psychical to the social and cultural. In the second half of the poem, the autobiographical "I" becomes renegotiated in what Julia Kristeva calls "the metamorphoses of the 'we'" (220). That is, it "reproduces itself" (Henriques et al. 227) within a social/cultural matrix that multiplies the very terms of its subjectivity. The "I" of the first half of the poem joins communally with its socially copositioned others to become "our sable race" (line 5). Even more dizzying is Wheatley's appropriation of the "gaze" of the Other(s)[23] and the voicing of the Other's racializing discourse ("'Their colour is a diabolic die,'" line 6). What emerges from this new position (as "other" of an utterance represented within the frame of her own poem) is what Mae Henderson refers to as the distinguishing feature of black women's writing: "the privileging (rather than repressing) of 'the other in ourselves'" (19).

These critical shifts renegotiate space as (past, present, and future) community. Yet owing to the dictates of diaspora subjectivity, space/community is multiple rather than singular, as the "I" is inscribed within three interlocking communal structures. First, following from the "once" in line 4, the "I" is embedded within the ancestral space of "My *Pagan* land," complete with the possessive pronoun. This "cultural mooring" will become significant in the later discussion of this poem's critique of American Africanist ideology. Second, it is repositioned within "our sable race," constructed as a community of "others" via the white gaze that perceives black skin as "a diabolic die." Finally, the "I" is located once again with the bi(non)racial "angelic train" that ends the poem. This multiple communal structure effaces both present *time*—as the poem moves from the originary "once" to the eschatalogical "angelic train"—and present *space*: "America," the designated point of arrival in the poem's title, which is refigured as a mere way station along the poet's real journey from Africa to Heaven. Heaven as "alternative space" (Holloway) marks the very dispersal of the diaspora subject, as it is specifically not Africa and, more important in Wheatley's context, *not America*.

Arrival/Departure

In order fully to appreciate the achievement of this poem's African Americanist theorizing, we must compare it to four lines from "To the University of Cambridge in New-England." Following a conventional two-line invocation to the Muses, Wheatley writes:

> 'Twas not long since I left my native shore
> The Land of errors and *Egyptian* gloom:
> Father of mercy, 'twas thy gracious hand
> Brought me in safety from those dark abodes.
>
> (Lines 3–6)

This passage establishes the context of "On Being Brought," which revises—in the sense of "repetition and difference" (Gates, *Signifying Monkey* 64)—this passage from "Cambridge" in terms of their relative placements in the narrative line of *Poems*. The narrativity of the volume is especially important to the reading of the elegies. Of importance now is the fact that "On Being Brought" appears to be a revision of an earlier poem identified in Wheatley's book proposal of February 29, 1772, as "Thoughts on being brought from Africa to America" and scheduled to appear tenth in the originally proposed volume.[24] The version of "Cambridge" printed in the 1773 *Poems* also underwent substantial revision from an earlier draft subtitled "Wrote in 1767" (when Wheatley was just fourteen) whose variant is extant. Scheduled to be placed fourth in the original proposal, the poem that was finally printed must have been composed between April 1772 and August 6, 1773,[25] when *Poems* was printed in London. Owing to the recovery of manuscript drafts and other variants of Wheatley's poetry, we now have a sense of her revision practices.[26] Thus it is reasonable to assume that the poem listed in the proposal as "Thoughts on being brought from Africa to America" underwent revisions by the time it appeared in *Poems* as "On Being Brought."

What all this establishes is that Wheatley was a meticulous reviser of her own work. Not only do "Cambridge" and "On Being Brought" represent, in their final published forms, the development of Wheatley's thinking about her captivity and enslavement, the order in which they appear in *Poems* makes "On Being Brought" a "revision" of "Cambridge" within the context of the volume. To chart the development of Wheatley's thought on her own displacement to America, I will compare the 1767 variant of "Cambridge" to the 1773 version in *Poems* and demonstrate how the four lines about her transport from Africa were revised. Then I will return to the important relationship between them as they appear in *Poems* to construct a complete narrative of captivity, Middle Passage, and enslavement.

In the 1767 version, the relevant lines are:

> 'Twas but e'en now I left my native shore
> The sable Land of error's darkest night
> There, sacred Nine! for you no place was found.
> Parent of mercy, 'twas thy Powerful hand
> Brought me in safety from the dark abode.
>
> (Lines 3–7; Shields 196)

It is important to keep in mind that Wheatley was about fourteen when this poem was composed.[27] Shields claims that "Wheatley made few major alterations" between this version and the 1773 final version. I disagree. What appear to be "minor" revisions in the later version of "Cambridge" reveal a sharpening and development of Wheatley's thought on her experience of the Middle Passage.[28] The change from " 'Twas but e'en now" to " 'Twas not long since," for example, represents the advance of six years. The most obvious change is the omission of the line about the Muses, which appears as line 5 of the 1767 version. Indeed, it is an omission of a line about Africa's lack ("There, sacred Nine! for you no place was found"). It is chiefly through this line that Africa is cast in a negative light as lacking the inspiration for poetry. When the line is contrasted with the poem's first two lines, "While an intrinsic ardor bids me write / the muse doth promise to assist my pen,"[29] an important contradiction emerges that favors the poet's present location (in literate America) as the location for poetic expression and sensibility. Its omission in the 1773 poem suggests a change in Wheatley's visioning of Africa and her poetic heritage.

The next line of the 1767 "Cambridge" describes the poet's "native shore" as "the sable Land of error's darkest night." This line and the reference to the poet's gratefulness at being rescued from "the dark abode" have been taken to mean that Wheatley sees Africa as the stereotypical "dark continent" of American Africanism and thus to evince self-hatred and self-denial. Yet Wheatley here capitalizes "Land" and in describing it as "sable" is not necessarily invoking a discourse of inferiority. Wheatley's use of "sable" as an adjective for land and people ("our sable race") can be understood apart from American Africanist racialized proscriptions. It is only through the gaze of the White Other who racializes black peoples under the sign of inferiority (" 'Their colour is a diabolic die' ") that "sable race" is transformed into a socially constructed negativity. Recall Morrison: "Neither blackness nor 'people of color' stimulates in me notions of excessive, limitless love, anarchy, or routine dread" (x).

I am not arguing for the absence of a discourse of African inferiority in the 1767 "Cambridge." Indeed, such a discourse exists; it is not to be found, however, in the fact of "blackness," but in what Wheatley calls "error." In line 4 of the 1767 version, "error's" is a possessive. In the 1773 version, the entire line is rewritten as "the land of errors, and *Egyptian* gloom" (line 4). Addressed to Harvard divinity students, "Cambridge" is, after all, about sin and redemption. Wheatley exhorts the divinity students to "let sin . . . / By you be shunn'd" (lines 23–24). But what, exactly, is the sin she refers to and for which Africa, her "native shore," serves as a particular kind of "stage"?

I want to make an argument here that the "sin" is slavery, conceived of by Wheatley (because she probably experienced it as such) as a global system of captivity and forced labor.[30] I base this argument first on the rewriting of "The sable Land of error's darkest night" to "The land of errors, and *Egyptian* gloom." The vagueness of the first version's notion of "error's" is specified in the final version by the phrase "*Egyptian* gloom." That is, in the final version, Wheatley means to signal the reader as to exactly what she means by "the land of errors." Whatever the impetus behind the choice of the adjective "sable," Wheatley's substitution of "*Egyptian*" is probably a response to her growing awareness of the racialization of the society around her, a factor that would definitely affect her (white) readers' response.

This point can be glossed by a famous passage in Wheatley's letter to the Native American Reverend Samson Occom dated February 11, 1774:

> Reverend and Honoured Sir,
>
>   I have this Day received your obliging kind Epistle, and am greatly satisfied with your Reasons respecting the Negroes, and think highly reasonable what you offer in Vindication of their natural Rights: those that invade them cannot be insensible that the divine light is chasing away the thick Darkness which broods over the Land of Africa; and the Chaos which has reigned so long, is converting into beautiful Order, and reveals more and more clearly, that glorious Dispensation of civil and religious Liberty, which are so inseparably united, that there is little or no enjoyment of one without the other: Otherwise, perhaps, the Israelites had been less solicitous for their Freedom from Egyptian slavery; I do not say they would have been contented without it by no Means, for in every human breast, God has implanted a Principle, which we call Love of Freedom; it is impatient of Oppression, and pants for Deliverance; and by Leave of our Modern Egyptians I will assert, that the same Principle lives in us. (Shields 176–77)

In keeping with colonial New England's relish for the epistolary genre, this letter was published in ten New England newspapers between March and April of 1774. The fact that it was intended as a public utterance helps explain the carefully worked out rhetorical structure that informs the letter. This passage follows the classic Wheatley pattern of beginning with statements straight out of the discourse of American Africanism only to *convert* that discourse to antislavery argument. By linking the story of African capture and enslavement to the Old Testament Israelites, she forces a link (one that transgresses "racial" and geographical boundaries) between white Anglo-Americans and the enslaving Egyptians.[31] Thus in using the phrase "*Egyptian* gloom" in "Cambridge," Wheatley is signifying the slaveholding tendency of Egypt, not its "blackness" or "Africanness." When I talk of georacial transgressions, I mean that Wheatley understands slavery as a *global* system, encompassing Africa, Europe, the Caribbean, and North America. It is also quite possible that her original captors were black.[32] What we get, then, is a discourse that cuts across the racial divide imposed by American Africanism. "Modern Egyptians" can be of any race or nationality, according to Wheatley. Similarly, "Love of Freedom" becomes the great equalizer in a world structured on "Enlightenment" hierarchies of the "Great Chain of Being." Her overall project is to unwrite, if you will, the discourse of blackness/Africanity as a discourse of difference. As she states in her poem "America," "Sometimes by Simile, a victory's won."

Following a mild exhortation about sin to "Let hateful vice so baneful to the Soul, / Be still avoided" (lines 26–27), the conclusion of the 1767 "Cambridge" reads:

> Suppress the sable monster in its growth,
> Ye blooming plants of human race, divine
> An Ethiop tells you, tis your greatest foe
> Its transient sweetness turns to endless pain,
> And brings eternal ruin on the Soul.
>
> (Lines 28–32)

In the 1773 revision, following a stronger imperative to "shun" sin and evil, we find these lines:

> Suppress the deadly serpent in its egg.
> Ye blooming plants of human race divine,
> An *Ethiop* tells you 'tis your greatest foe;
> Its transient sweetness turns to endless pain,
> And in immense perdition sinks the soul.
>
> (Lines 26–30)

By changing "sable monster" to "deadly serpent," Wheatley raises the "error" of slavery to the theological status of Original Sin. The reference to the Fall in line 17 is thus emphasized, as the serpent recalls the Garden of Eden. In this way, Africa, the poet's "native shore," becomes the scene of man's Fall into "error" via slavery.

It could be argued that "sable monster" is a more precise designation for the slave trade than "deadly serpent," which connotes a more abstract notion of sin and temptation. Wheatley's use of the more abstract term in the final version supports my view that she would have felt "*Egyptian* gloom" to be specific enough to carry the antislavery message home, especially to a Bible-reading New England public. There is, however, another reference that would have signified the transatlantic slave trade to that audience: the mention of sin as "transient sweetness" that "turns to endless pain." In the eighteenth century the intended readers would have understood this as a reference to the "sweet" industries of sugar, rum, and molasses, which specifically connected New England to the slave trade. The New England distilleries, in fact, were among the most dependent on the traffic in African bodies: "Most of the so-called 'middle passages' terminated in the Caribbean, where the slaves were exchanged for specie, bills, and return cargoes of sugar or molasses."[33] Wheatley had experienced firsthand the brutalities of a system that literally traded human beings for the sugar and molasses so vital to the rum industry.

Finally, the matter of the "dark abodes," a phrase that appears to be a mere repetition of American Africanist discourse. First, it is singular ("dark abode") in the 1767 version and plural in the final draft. Second, in the final version "land" is singular while "abodes" is plural; thus the "dark abodes" cannot signify Africa (as it does in the first version). The entire couplet reads: "Father of mercy, 'twas thy gracious hand / Brought me in safety from those dark abodes" (lines 5–6). The key words here are "in safety." Wheatley is offering a prayer of thanksgiving (a direct address to God the "Father" as opposed to the third-person reference "'Twas mercy brought me . . . " of "On Being Brought") for her survival of the hazardous journey of the Middle Passage. She is not, as some have assumed, thankful for slavery, but for her safety. Here, the "dark abodes" could signify nothing but the hateful and unsanitary ship's holds where the majority of enslaved Africans spent the bulk of their time during their crossing, chained together, deprived of light, air, decent food, and water. Scholars whose interest in the slave trade is medical and historical report that "at least one in three Africans died between the time they were removed from their homeland and the time they were unloaded in the West Indies of the Americas."[34] Not only would Wheatley have witnessed an incredible amount of suffering and death, but "in most cases, the seamen were allowed to have sexual intercourse with the females. Officers were always permitted access to the women" (Reynolds 50–51). The age of the victim would have been little protection against possible assault. By the time Phillis Wheatley stood on the auction block in Boston, she was wearing only a tattered piece of carpet over her frail body. In supplying these details, I am trying to include what had to be excluded from Wheatley's poems. By carefully placing a few key signifiers ("dark abodes," "transient sweetness," etc.), Wheatley is able to write her experience of the Middle Passage in the only way she could.

Race, Power/Knowledge

All of this serves as the context for the first line of "On Being Brought From Africa to America"—" 'Twas mercy brought me from my *Pagan* land." My argument has been based on the observation that what appear to be "minor" revisions in the later version of "Cambridge" reveal a sharpening and development in Wheatley's thinking about the meaning of her experience of slavery and Middle Passage over the six intervening years. In this sense, "On Being Brought" represents her highest poetic achievement, especially if we appreciate it as a continuation of the narrative developed in the initial four lines of "Cambridge." For the "Cambridge" lines end precisely where "On Being Brought" begins. "Father of mercy, 'twas they gracious hand / Brought me in safety from those dark abodes" becomes "Twas mercy brought me from my *Pagan* land." If, as I have argued, the appeal to "safety" and "dark abodes" calls up the weeks-to-months-long horror of the Middle Passage, "On Being Brought" picks up where the Middle Passage ends, that is, at the point of arrival. It is the task of its eight lines, then, to chronicle the remaining part of Wheatley's "journey": specifically, the twin processes of racialization and acculturation.

Crucially, if ironically, during the six years between the first draft of "Cambridge" and the publication of *Poems,* which contains both the final draft of that poem and "On Being Brought From Africa to America," Wheatley was baptized in the Old South Meeting House of Boston (1771). This accounts for the changes in "Cambridge" from "Parent of mercy, 'twas thy powerful hand" (line 6, 1767 version) to "Father of mercy, 'twas thy gracious hand" (line 5, 1773 version). The more personal (and patriarchal) epithet "Father" is associated with "grace" rather than "power," a clear indication of a Judeo-Christian orientation toward divinity. Her baptism would also explain why Wheatley's critique of slavery as sin gains theological coherence in the final version. Yet—and here is the great irony—her reading of Africa is less pejorative in the second "Cambridge" than in the first. In other words, it is *after* Wheatley becomes converted to Christianity, a religion often associated with the theological justification for enslavement of African peoples as well as a major component of American Africanism, that her views about

Africa and her own Africanness become more empathic. She moves, then, *through* the discourse of Christianity, from a repetition of American Africanism to its critique.

"On Being Brought" presents Wheatley with a new set of issues beyond the apparent presence/absence of the Muses in Africa and thankfulness for having been spared on the Middle Passage. By abandoning the personalized "Father of mercy 'twas thy gracious hand" in favor of the more abstract " 'Twas mercy brought me," Wheatley opens the way to subject the "doctrine of merciful enslavement" to a more intense interrogation. To thank God for one's physical safety is one thing; to appear grateful for one's captivity and enslavement is quite another. God and Mercy, which are equated in "Cambridge," must be read as two separate and distinct entities or forces in "On Being Brought." If a Judeo-Christian conceptualization of God as "Saviour" retains the personal connections witnessed (and witnessed to) in the thanksgiving prayer of "Cambridge," "Mercy" in Wheatley's poetics cannot be conceived of apart from what Foucault calls the "power/knowledge axis."[35] That "mercy" *teaches*—"*Taught* my benighted soul to *understand*"; "Once I redemption neither sought *nor knew*"—foregrounds issues of epistemology within a terrain of global relations of power.

Structural shifts, multiple postionings, and temporal/spatial displacements discussed above serve to underscore the passive construction of the poem's title: "on *being brought*." The signifier "mercy" as the real subject (the agent of the passive voice) emerges as a site of interrogation and contestation. "Mercy" as it signifies in a Western discourse that sanctions the commercial exploitation of black bodies as a means of saving souls can only be a positive agent within the ideological construction of Enlightenment rationale. The confiation of conversion and enslavement is thus posited as an ideological discourse whose signifying power is problematized by the very terms of its othering. Ironically, it is the very apparatus of the slave trade, the transporting of black bodies from Africa, that most threatens the balance of power created and maintained by European hegemony. However much white slave owners insist on seeing black skin as "a *diabolic* die," the transportation of slaves from Africa assures that "Negros, black as Cain / May be refin'd and join th'angelic train" (lines 7–8).[36]

What "On Being Brought" ultimately encodes is the system of racialization in progress. With the displacement of African bodies from their homelands and the meanings and definitions associated with their land came the transformation of Africans into "Negros." Wheatley encodes this process of racialization in the tension created from the first four lines to the last four lines of this poem. If the trajectory of subjectivity, the "I" emerging as "Our"/" 'their,' " creates a sense of continuity between the two sections, the issue of Africans' becoming "Negros" is more complicated.

TRANSATLANTIC CROSSINGS

It is important to remember that Wheatley's use of multiple positionings and displacements in "On Being Brought From Africa to America" inscribes diaspora subjectivity as a metalevel, structural component of poetic utterance. Scholars probing Wheatley's poems for overt references to the slave traffic have focused on literal fragments and representations upon which to base their arguments for or against Wheatley's "blackness" or political alliances. Yet they have consistently managed to overlook the very poems in which Wheatley reinscribes the slave trade over and over again. In addition to "On Being Brought" and the four lines of "Cambridge" discussed above, in which she figures her own transport to America, transatlantic crossings recur as a motif in *Poems*: "Ode to Neptune," which chronicles Susannah Wheatley's voyage to England (76–77); "To a Lady on Her Coming to North-America with her Son for the Recovery of Her Health" (78–79); "To a Gentleman on his Voyage to *Great-Britain* for the Recovery of His Health" (88–89); and "A Farewel to America," in which Wheatley versifies her own reverse Middle Passage in a provisional "ending" to the volume (119–20). The ports of call are familiar—Europe (England), the West Indies (Jamaica), and North America (Boston), as well as the "Pagan land" of Africa. Taken together, these poems trace and retrace what Spillers calls "the triangulation of a particular mapping."[37] It was during the eighteenth century that England perfected the "triangular" trade route. Lorenzo Johnston Greene describes it:

> From New England's many ports trim, sturdy ships, built from their own forests, carried to the West Indies much needed food and other commodities. . . . When the captains of these vessels were able to exchange their cargoes for rum, they would next proceed to Africa. There they were transported to the West Indies, where they disposed of them for rum, sugar, molasses and other tropical products or for bills of exchange. (24–25)

The association of this trade route with the geometrical figure of the triangle was clear even in the eighteenth century. Moreover, art historian Albert Boime has noted that the triangle was popular in British and American art in the eighteenth and nineteenth centuries, a popularity he attributes to the slave trade (15–46).

Also of importance is the recurring theme of "recovery" that these poems enact. As Wheatley chronicles the multiple crossings of those in ill health (including her own voyage to England in 1772 on the advice of a physician), she recovers, simultaneously, the triangular route of the Atlantic slave trade, her own Middle Passage experience, and the eighteenth-century discourse of environmentalism whose "race-place ideologies" underwrote Enlightenment ideas about place and subjectivity.

Weathering the Middle Passage

I want to focus on one particular transatlantic poem, "To a Lady on Her Coming to North-America with her Son for the Recovery of Her Health," a poem overlooked in all literary assessments of Wheatley owing, in large part, to its "occasional" nature. I select this poem among the others on the same theme for three reasons. First, read alongside "On Being Brought From Africa to America" and "A Farewel to America," poems in which Wheatley represents her own transatlantic crossings, "To a Lady on Her Coming to North-America" functions as an inversion of the Middle Passage and provides a forum for Wheatley's continued, if implicit, critique of the slave trade and its founding ideologies about climate and environment, which attempted to map race and subjectivity onto geographical space. Second, a diasporic reading of this poem reveals Wheatley's inscriptions of psychic fracture as a desire for communal wholeness, a desire that is represented by the focus on family and kin networks in the poem. This structuration of poetic desire will become crucial for an understanding of the funeral elegies. Third, because the principle character and addressee of the poem is a white "Lady," Wheatley anticipates, long before women's movements, the black feminist critique of how black and white women are differently located, a difference within the sign of "gender" that establishes the uniqueness of her own historically located black female body. Moreover, in locating black and white women within geocultural fields of Africanity/Europeanness, Wheatley underscores the epistemological dimension of gender within the field of culture and community.

Though the title of the poem mentions only the site of destination, "North-America," the poem begins on "*Jamaica's* fervid shore" (line 3). Here, the movements of the white lady are in accord with those of the invoked Goddess; indeed, the white woman and the Goddess of the sea are one as the stanza unfolds:

> See from *Jamaica's* fervid shore she moves,
> Like the fair mother of the blooming loves,
> When from above the *Goddess* with her hand
> Fans the soft breeze, and lights upon the land;

Thus she on *Neptune's* wat'ry realm reclin'd
Appear'd, and thus invites the ling'ring wind.

(Lines 3–8)

The "she" who reclines "on *Neptune's* wat'ry realm" is deliberately am-
biguous, as Wheatley conflates the image of the lady and the image of
the Goddess. The mood is one of leisure and control—"blooming
loves" (line 4); "ling'ring wind" (line 8)—emphasizing the languidness
of motion. We have no hint here of the "dark abodes" that marked African passage in the ship's holds. Ingeniously, this imagistic sequence rep-
licates poetically the movement of ships across the sea through the use
of the *-ing* constructions and the alliterative sequences ("from *Jamaica's*
fervid shore she moves"; "and lights upon the land"; "on *Neptune's*
wat'ry realm reclin'd"), which re-create the sound and motion of
waves.[38] Yet these images must be appreciated within the same representational field that inscribes the white lady within an economy of luxury,
leisure, and (Goddess-like) power.

Directly after the description, Wheatley takes on the character of the
Lady/Goddess by representing her speaking:

"Arise ye winds, *America* explore,
"Waft me, ye gales, from this malignant shore;
"The *Northern* milder climes I long to greet,
"There hope that health will my arrival meet."

(Lines 9–12)

That the speech genres[39] of the Lady/Goddess are represented as commands and expressions of her desire is significant, especially when we
recall that this poem follows "Ode to Neptune," the subject of which is
the transatlantic voyage of Susannah Wheatley, her mistress. Indeed,
many of the same types of phrasings of leisure appear in the poem subtitled "On Mrs. W——'s Voyage to England": "While my *Susannah*
skims the wat'ry way" (line 6); "The blue-ey'd daughters of the sea /
With sweeter cadence glide along" (lines 8–9).[40] Again, goddess(es) of
the sea, here described significantly as "blue-ey'd," are equated with
white womanhood, itself viewed as protected and indulged, frail and
commanding. In Wheatley's capturing of what she perceived as characteristic of "ladies'" speech, desire—"I long" (line 11), "there hope"
(line 12)—is inextricably bound with commands: "arise" (line 9), "waft
me" (line 10). As in "On Being Brought From Africa to America," it is
through the device of appropriating both the other's gaze and the
other's discourse that Wheatley opens a space for a critique.

The emphasis on climate is particularly important here as it repeats
the discourse of environmentalism prevalent in the eighteenth century,

which read the subjectivity of persons (behavior, moral character, intellect, and reason) as a function of environment. The signifying power of environmental discourse underwrote and justified the slave trade, as Africans' lack of morality and intellect was thought to result from their tropical location. According to this logic, the transportation of Africans to North America (via slavery!) would improve their overall "character."[41]

Thus Jamaica is described negatively as the "fervid shore" in contrast to the "*Northern* milder climes" that represent, in several key senses, the scene of the lady's desire. Yet in giving voice to this other (and othering) discourse, Wheatley's repetition bears a crucial difference. If for the Lady the journey north signifies the "hope" of recovery, for Wheatley, the so-called milder climes meant the exact opposite. Through the ventriloquized speech of the white lady, Wheatley invites interrogation into her own position. In "On Imagination," one of Wheatley's most important odes, she contemplates a beautiful spring in the dead of a Boston winter only to break off the reverie because

> *Winter* austere forbids me to aspire,
> And northern tempests damp the rising fire;
> They chill the tides of *Fancy's* flowing sea.
>
> (Lines 50–52)

Recall in the discussion of the early draft of "Cambridge" the teenage Wheatley's identification of Boston (her present space) as the home of the Muses and thus of poetic reflection and imagination. Here, the coldness of "*Winter* austere" is depicted as a barrier to the "rising fire" of poetic inspiration. Another such passage appears in "A Farewel to America" where Wheatley writes:

> In vain for me the flow'rets rise,
>   And boast their gaudy pride,
> While here beneath the northern skies,
>   I mourn for health deny'd.
>
> (Lines 5–8)

If the surface-level meaning of "To a Lady on Her Coming to North-America" prompts a reading of a slave girl's homage to a social "superior," the reflexivity of African Americanist discourse reinserts Wheatley's own history/memory into spaces mapped out (by quotation marks) for an-Other.

Bakhtin writes of the use of quotation marks in "The Problem of Speech Genres":

> Intonation that isolates others' speech (in written speech, designated by quotation marks) is a special phenomenon: it is as though the *change of*

speaking subjects has been internalized. The *boundaries* created by this change are weakened here and of a special sort. The speaker's expression penetrates through these boundaries and spreads to the other's speech, which is transmitted in ironic, indignant, sympathetic, or reverential tones. (*Speech Genres* 93)

While Bakhtin allows that the "judgment call" of tonality is to be determined by the "context that frames the other's speech by means of the extraverbal situation that suggests the appropriate expression" (93), such a framework does not help us here. Not only does Wheatley's use of quotations emphasize rather than "weaken" boundaries between self and other, but they encode a discursive mechanism that is designed precisely to introduce into Western language a responsive tonality that is socially inappropriate for an enslaved African subject. What is "internalized" for Wheatley is both the discourse of American Africanism and its constructedness, its boundaries, if you will, boundaries that Wheatley is free to exploit owing to her own positionality as the other of its claims to subjecthood. And it is through the voicing of the Other's claims of African otherness that an African/poetic "self" is fashioned.

The multiplication of perspectives at work in Wheatley's appropriated "I" of this poem shifts the terms of signification by rendering the signifiers of Western cultural spaces unstable. Wheatley relativizes the meanings mapped onto Jamaica/North-America by shifting the referents of health/dis-ease, recovery/loss. In the process, all signifiers become suspect. The white lady's very (European) presence on "*Jamaica's* fervid shore" becomes a sign to be interrogated; she comes to represent during the course of the poem a sign of power—slavery and colonialism—even as her illness and dis-ease recall the sense of "frailty" that will later blossom into the nineteenth-century U.S. Cult of True Womanhood.[42] For Wheatley, in order to recover *her* story, her memory of Middle Passage—which might, indeed, have included a stopover in the West Indies[43]—she must take on the perspective of the colonizing/enslaving other within its leisure economy. In fact, it is Wheatley's appropriation of this Other that exposes its position of leisure, domination, and privilege. Indeed, immediately after the lady's speech, Wheatley inserts herself (as poet) into the poem:

> Soon as she spoke in my ideal view
> The winds assented, and the vessel flew.

(Lines 13–14)

Not only does this couplet effectively underscore the quotation marks of the passage cited above, it actually highlights the representational nature of the utterance before it. The lady is once more "she" as the "I" emerges to remind us of the poet's ultimate control of the scene. The response of the vessel is thus a response to the poet's imaginative power ("in my ideal view"), which usurps the lady's ventriloquized commands ("Arise, ye winds"; "Waft me, ye gales").

The Language of Kinship

The syntactic chain of signification *from* Jamaica *to* North-America is momentarily displaced by a doubling back to the scene of the West Indies as the poem shifts again to direct address:

> Madam your spouse bereft of wife and son,
> In the grove's dark recesses pours his moan;
> Each branch, wide-spreading to the ambient sky,
> Forgets its verdure and submits to die.
>
> (Lines 15–18)

The motif of broken kin networks is heightened by images of death ("bereft," "submits to die") and the displacement of familial signifiers— "spouse," "wife," "son"—held in suspension by the figure of transatlantic crossing. A tension is created by a journey aimed at recovering the mother's health that simultaneously results in the loss of familial connection and the threat to the family line; the lady journeys "with her son," taking with her the assurance of the continuation of the patriarchal line.

Structurally the remaining sixteen lines of the poem are spaced in one long stanza, a departure from the pattern of short stanzas with their shifts in time and place. Once again, the poet reasserts herself:

> From thence I turn, and leave the sultry plain,
> And swift pursue thy passage o'er the main.
>
> (Lines 19–20)

Again we are reminded that it is the poet's vision, the poet's representation, which controls the discourse. Chronicling the arrival of the lady's ship to "the *Philadelphian* port" (line 22), the poetic "I" emerges again: "Thence I attend you to *Bostonia's* arms" (line 23). Unlike "On Being Brought From Africa to America," in which "America" is designated in the title only to remain unnamed in the poem proper, here the "North-America" of the poem's title is further specified, gaining in concreteness. The verb "attend" signifies doubly as it recalls both Wheatley's poetic control and her servant status within the space of Boston. The figures of poet and slave thus converge for the first time in the poem. If earlier the poet used her experience as servant to capture, ironically, the command genres of the white lady's speech, while ultimately usurping that control through her poetic imagination, "attend" brings the two back together again by exploiting the ironic tension between poetic/imaginative attention and the figure of the attendant servant. And it is with this conflation that the poet's own position becomes a site of contestation and critique within the poem.

Landed in Boston, the lady immediately reestablishes connections with others as "gen'rous friendship ev'ry bosom warms" (line 24). Similarly, of Susannah's arrival in England in "Ode to Neptune," Wheatley writes that "Thy welcome smiles in ev'ry eye" (line 16). Wheatley's own emergence from the "dark abodes" of the ship's holds would have drawn a crowd, but for a much different reason. Having "attended" the lady along her journey and into another circle of loved ones, the poet, in effect, retreats as the mood switches from the imperative and the indicative to the subjunctive:

> may health again,
> Bloom on thy cheek, and bound in every vein!
> Then back return to gladden ev'ry heart.
>
> (Lines 25–27)

The difference is clearly one of space, not only the distinction of the "sultry plain" from the "Northern . . . climes" with their attendant racist ideologies, but the difference between land and sea, groundedness in social reality and positionality versus an oceanic imagination that assumes the freedom to exercise poetic control. And here, while the poet is able to navigate the representation of the lady's journey to Boston, she cannot follow her on the "return." Her status as a slave, reinscribed through the verb "attend," is a startling reminder of her limited social position. And the constraint of that position is figured most prominently through the disconnection from kin and family. For Africans, the loss of community ties was the single most defining horror of the Middle Passage and New World enslavement, for they had lost the ability to be "human-in-community" (Hopkins 18). This facet of African dehumanization would have been grasped immediately, before the comprehension of market relations or, indeed, even the "chattel principle."[44]

Stripped, herself, of kinship ties, the poet can only figure the lady's return (which is itself ironic) as a future projection—a scene to which she has no access in her own personal history:

> Then back return to gladden ev'ry heart
> And give your spouse his soul's far dearer part;
> Receiv'd again with what a sweet surprise,
> The tear in transport starting from his eyes!
> While his attendant son with blooming grace

Springs to his father's ever dear embrace.
With shouts of joy *Jamaica's* rocks resound,
With shouts of joy the country rings around.

(Lines 27–34)

The sentimentality of this passage (long before the convention of literary sentimentalism) attests to the poet's lack of access to its vision. The redundancy of the phrases "back return" (line 27), "receiv'd again" (line 29) underscores the sense of "belonging" that is the lady's privilege, as she is implicated in white Western global domination. She is, the poem suggests, "at home" even in a geographical area for which she is represented as constitutionally unsuited. The poem ends, by returning full circle—spouses are reunited, generational continuity is restored and assured, and nature reverberates with regeneration as "rocks resound / with shouts of joy" (lines 33–34). This interconnection of family, generation, nature, and nation ("the country rings around") is the very matrix of relations whose absence marks the African subject of the diaspora as a subject of desire. If the poem began with the white lady's spoken desire for health in the "*Northern* milder climes," it ends with the poet's (unspoken) desire for interconnection with family, kin, community, and land.

Unlike the earlier changes of scene, here the poet is conspicuously absent. "The country rings around" in a closed circle that will not admit the poet, who must remain in attendant suspension in Boston. As in "On Being Brought," the subject matter announced in the title is indeed displaced. For the poem does not finally relate the story of a Lady coming to North America "for the Recovery of Her Health." Rather, a poem purportedly about the recovery of physical well-being is actually about the recovery of space figured as kinship and signified by the ability to return. Able to "claim residence" through the presence of kinship ties in Jamaica *and* America, the white lady becomes the sign of a colonial discourse wherein her very transatlantic movement, retracing one of the most important legs of the triangular slave trade route, marks her as the purveyor of power and domination. What is reestablished upon her return to Jamaica is a patriarchal lineage: an "attendant son" rushes back "to his *father's* dear embrace" (lines 30, 31). Earlier scenes of separation and death give way to reunion as rebirth and the promise of fecundity. The wife's sexual yielding ("give your spouse his soul's far dearer part") represents her role as a vessel of reproduction, while the son's "blooming grace"—his male seed—promises the continuation of the male family line and name. Thus what is recovered here, through a reading of Wheatley's own poetics of recovery, is the assurance of the continuance of white male hegemony.

The circularity of this ideological construction is premised on the freedom of return, the one power that Wheatley does not have at her disposal, imaginatively or otherwise. Here the central tension emerges between the poems of Others' (voluntary) transatlantic crossings and Wheatley's own experiences with ocean voyages—"On Being Brought" and "A Farewel to America." One of the last poems in the volume, "A Farewel to America" represents a kind of "last word" on the liminality of diaspora subjectivity and transatlantic crossings. If in "On Being Brought From Africa to America" the destination of the title is effaced and displaced onto the Christian Heaven, in "Farewel" the return to the point of origin (again "America") is also problematized.

Unlike the Lady/Goddess whose journey (in the physical, psychical, and social senses) is cyclical, the "I" of "Farewel" has no real place to which to return. Arrived in England, the poet begins to conjure up the image of a return trip:

> For thee, *Britannia*, I resign
>   *New England's* smiling fields;
> To view again her charms divine,
>   What joy the prospect yields!

(Lines 41–44)

Yet the (rather insincere) image is broken immediately by an agonizing reference to "Temptation":

> But thou! Temptation hence away,
>   With all thy fatal train
> Nor once seduce my soul away,
>   By thine enchanting strain.
>
> Thrice happy they, whose heav'nly shield
>   Secures their soul from harms,
> And fell *Temptation* on the field
>   Of all its pow'r disarms!

(Lines 45–52)

The temptation here is the temptation to stay in England, to bid a final "farewell to America." Beginning with the Somerset case in 1772, slaves brought to British soil (especially Christian slaves) could be considered free on a writ of habeas corpus.[45] As in the cases of James Albert Gronnoisaw and Olaudah Equiano, Wheatley's status as a Christian coupled with early British antislavery sentiment would have rendered this an optimal opportunity to escape. Yet while Gronnoisaw and Equiano did avail themselves of the protection of British soil, Wheatley's situation is more complex. First, there is her conviction that to escape would be to

lose her soul (she writes of "seduction" here). Second, her gender
would have made it much more difficult to escape and to support herself
once "free." Equiano and other black males (who far outnumbered females in England's poor but sizable black population) had the maritime
industry available to them, an industry closed to women. And the scar-
city of domestic labor situations owing to competition with white peas-
ant women is attested to in Mary Prince's narrative. Mary Prince also
paid the supreme price for "freedom": separation from her husband,
who remained in the West Indies with little hope of ever reestablishing
those marital ties.[46] Third, since Wheatley's voyage to England was
prompted by failing health, she would have been in a tenuous position
to contemplate a life of productive manual labor. And last, the "hidden
agenda" of Wheatley's trip (given the discussion of climate above, it is
difficult to imagine Wheatley's really buying the idea that damp, cold
England would make her well) was to oversee the publication of *Poems*
and to secure patronage, both of which ends were accomplished.
Though the temptation to stay would have been great, Wheatley must
have perceived that her future lay in the poems she had so carefully prepared and revised, and she put her faith in them as the ticket to her freedom. Indeed, she was freed by the Wheatleys sometime after her return
to Boston.

And of course, the "return" to Boston is a return to the place of displacement, foreclosing the possibility of a narrative that could come full
circle. A clue as to how Wheatley and other diaspora subjects and Middle Passage survivors must have felt about a "return" to their African
homelands is provided in a short narrative appended to *The History of
Mary Prince*, entitled "Narrative of Louis Asa-Asa, a Captured African,"
in 1816. Evidently asked about his plans to stay in England rather than
return to Africa, Asa-Asa answers: "I am very happy to be in England, as
far as I am very well;—but I have no friend belonging to me, but
God. . . . I should like much to see my friends again, but I do not wish
to go back to them: for if I go back to my own country, I might be taken
as a slave again. I would rather stay here, where I am free, than go back
to my country to be sold" (Gates, *Classic Slave Narratives* 242). For
Asa-Asa and other Africans displaced through the slave traffic, their
homeland carries with it memories of the scene of initial rupture and
separation. Indeed, given Asa-Asa's description earlier in his narrative of
the decimation of his village, including the murder and capture of many
of his relatives, it is easy to see why many Africans would have lost the
faith that there was anyplace/anyone to return to.

Wheatley did come close to a return to her native land as she was
being recruited by the Reverend Samuel Hopkins to accompany

two other converted Africans on a missionary journey to Africa. Wheatley's response is provocative, the classic response of the diaspora subject:

> But why do you hon'd sir, wish those poor men so much trouble as to carry me so long a voyage? Upon my arrival, how like a Barbarian shou'd I look to the Natives; I promise that my tongue shall be quiet / for a strong reason indeed / being an utter stranger to the language. . . . (Shields 184)

"The Too Advent'rous Strain": Slavery, Conversion, and Poetic Empowerment in Phillis Wheatley's Elegies

IN 1772, Phillis Wheatley underwent what Henry Louis Gates calls "one of the oddest oral examinations on record" as eighteen prominent Boston merchants, clergymen, judges, and other community pillars met to determine the validity of her claims to poetic authorship. As Gates imagines the scene, the examination would have prompted questions about Greek and Latin, classical mythology, and the works of Alexander Pope and John Milton (*"Race," Writing and Difference* 7–8). Yet Wheatley would have encountered a similar situation the previous year when she had stood before the Congregationalist members of Boston's Old South Meeting House, and God, to be examined for her piety and her knowledge of slave catechism. Here she would have been tested on her willingness to confess, among other things, that Africans "were enslaved because they had sinned against God and that God, not their masters, had enslaved them" (Greene 286).[1]

Yet as we are poised to sketch a scenario wherein Wheatley is circumscribed by "the conflict between coercion to speak and silence" (Fogel 196), the text of *Poems on Various Subjects Religious and Moral* (1773), with "Phillis Wheatley" as author, offers the possibility of a counternarrative. The agency signaled by her authorship represents a break in a series of events—capture, enslavement, catechism, conversion—that promised a narrative of passivity and powerlessness. While *Poems* clearly bears the traces of its author's constricted social space and slave status— recall that the very name on the title page derives from a combination of the name of the slaving vessel, the *Phillis*, that brought her to Boston and the surname of the man who owned her[2]—it bears, as well, the traces of a poet's active struggle with the discourses of Puritan theology and literary convention.

This chapter examines the terms of that struggle within the literary domain of a specific genre, the Puritan funeral elegy, as Wheatley's "diaspora subjectivity" (see chapter 2) demands the "re-accentuation" (Bakhtin, *Speech Genres* 80) of the elegiac genre. By inscribing within the elegiac her own African American female subjectivity, Wheatley lays claim to a discursive practice that refigures the self/other terms of subjectivity and literary utterance.

As I argued in chapter 2, critical assessments of both Wheatley and her poetry have traditionally been based on categorical and ahistorical formulations of "race" and on spotty readings of her poetic canon. Thus in refiguring Wheatley as a Middle Passage survivor and diaspora subject, I argued for a reading of her poetics based on "recovery" as historical paradigm, psychoanalytic construction, and literary critical intervention. Thus part of the recovery process involved the reclaiming of Wheatley's "occasional poetry," poetry often dismissed as "coerced speech" and thus outside the domain of "genuine" poetic art. In like vein, no group of poems in Wheatley's oeuvre has been more universally denigrated than the funeral elegies. Failing to grasp the significance of slavery and conversion as "metaoccasions" that inform Wheatley's poetics, critics have accused her of being a "mere" occasional poet, churning out on demand elegies with no lasting literary value. It is precisely in these occasional poems, the funeral elegies, however, that Wheatley's struggle for poetic agency emerges.

Over one-third of Wheatley's surviving corpus consists of funeral elegies. Fourteen appeared in *Poems on Various Subjects Religious and Moral* published in London in 1773, including revised versions of six elegies that appeared as broadsides and in newspapers between 1770 and 1773. Six other elegies are now extant. There are now nine known variants from broadsides, newspapers, periodicals, and manuscripts in Wheatley's own hand. From a 1779 proposal written by Wheatley for a second volume of her writings, we learn of another nine elegies that were slated for this volume but have yet to be recovered in manuscript. Modern critics have lamented the fact that Wheatley wrote so many elegies, treating them as material to pass over in favor of the more "artistic" odes; the sheer volume of the funeral elegies, however, makes them difficult to ignore. While recent critics have begun to treat these poems more seriously,[3] the central question—why is it that Wheatley returned to this form so often that it became her primary vehicle for poetic expression?—has gone unanswered.

There are, of course, the literary conventional, material, and economic answers: the popularity of the funeral poems in the "elegy-making age" of colonial America (Loggins 22), Wheatley's need for patronage from white benefactors like the Countess of Huntingdon, the attention elicited by her first elegy on the Methodist evangelist George Whitefield, which increased the "demand" for her elegiac verses. Yet I would argue that when a writer "invests" so heavily in a form, as did Wheatley in the funeral elegy, there are equally compelling psychosocial forces at issue.[4] Clearly, something was at stake for Wheatley that underlies her compulsion for elegiac expression. Before turning to the elegies themselves, I first want to explore Wheatley's engagment with discourses of slave conversion and catechism, as her articulations of poetic empowerment redefine the terms of salvation and ultimate power and redemption.

SLAVERY, CONVERSION, AND POETIC EMPOWERMENT

Recalling Wheatley's reported memory of her mother's morning libations, which I discussed in chapter 2, we must understand that the meanings Wheatley created out of this fragment of cultural memory are to be found in her negotiations with prevailing *religious* discourses. For within *Poems on Various Subjects Religious and Moral,* Christianity and slavery are represented in dialogical relation to each other. In "On Being Brought From Africa to America," for example, Wheatley clearly "reads" her captivity through the language of Christian conversion and Providence, the only available discourse that could help her make sense of her place in America. However, she also reads spiritual conversion through her experience of physical capture and ownership. If Christian conversion mandates that body and soul be conceptualized as distinct categories of being, with "soul" as the privileged category, Wheatley's experience as a black woman slave demands the recognition of the very body that Christian discourse would repudiate. Wheatley's desire to reconnect the captured (black female) body and the converted ("freed") soul leads to a poetics grounded in issues of power and empowerment.

From the beginning of the slave trade, "Christianity was viewed by the emerging nations of Western Christendom as a justification for the enslavement of Africans" (Raboteau 96). While the Spanish and Portuguese, under the banner of Roman Catholicism, began the process of baptizing slaves as soon as they disembarked on New World shores, in the Protestant English colonies the conversion of slaves was a contested issue through to the eighteenth century. English colonists found themselves in a theological dilemma where "the Christian commission to preach the gospel to all nations ran directly counter to the economic interests of the Christian slave owner" (98). A kind of unwritten British sentiment that only heathen could be rightfully enslaved led to the perception that "to baptize the slave meant that [the owner] would lose him," while at the same time "to withhold conversion would retard the spread of Christianity" (Greene 259). The opposition to converting slaves had economic, social, religious, and political overtones. C. Eric Lincoln argues that the implications of resistance were more important than the economic arguments. For Lincoln, the Puritan church was "a closed-membership organization" (*Black Church* 12): "The essential factor at work here was an Anglo-Saxon tribalism militated against the creation of opportunities for sharing the in-group experience [of Christianity] even temporarily, *even* for the propogation of faith" (14). Whatever the underlying cause, strategies ranging from the argument that blacks were beasts and had no souls, to petitions to the colonial legislatures to ensure that baptism did not lead to legal freedom, abounded in the eighteenth century. Yet it was Cotton Mather's pamphlet *The Negro Christianized: An Essay to Excite and Assist that Good Work the Instruction of Negro Servants in Christianity* (1706) that solved this dilemma.[5]

Mather devised a set of theological principles whereby "Christianity and slavery were not antithetical" (Greene 264). This depended on the conflation of God and slave master, and Mather went so far as to rewrite the Ten Commandments for the slave catechism, which replaced (for slaves only) the word "God" with "master" (Greene 286). The aim was to employ religion "as a device for making the slave content and submissive in his bondage, thereby protecting the master in the retention of his property" (285–86). As Mather put it, "Your Servants will be the *better Servants* for being *Christian Servants*" (64).

Designed as a "hard sell" to induce masters to offer religious instruction to slaves, Mather's treatise includes the catechism for slaves that in all probability was the text from which Wheatley was taught Euro-Christian precepts. Three specific features of this catechism are of interest for my purposes here. First, slaves were to be taught "that it is God who has caused them to be *Servants*" (69–70). Second, Mather maintains the absolute separation between the slave's body and soul throughout his text: "*Christianity* directs a *Slave*, upon his embracing the *Law of the Redeemer*, to satisfy himself, *that he is the Lords Free-man*, tho' he continues a *Slave*" (67). And again,

> Tho' they are to enjoy no *Earthly Goods* but the small Allowance that your Justice and Bounty shall see proper for them, yet they are become Heirs of God, and *Joint-Heirs* with the Lord Jesus Christ. Tho' they are your *Vassals*, and must with a profound subjection wait upon you, yet the *Angels* of God now take them under their Guardianship and vouchsafe to tend upon them. Oh! what you have done for them! . . . (64).

This logic is dependent on the maintenance of body and soul as separate categories. Third, Mather continually places the slave as an individual within the master's household as the Yankee brand of "family slavery" mandated. Indeed, the epigraph to *The Negro Christianized* is taken from Josh. 24:15: "As for me, and my House, we will serve the Lord." By constructing the slave as a mere part of the master's household, Mather denies slaves any sense of family or community of their own. Indeed, Mather conflates the notions of blacks as part of the family and as possessions: "You take them into your *Families*; you look on them as part of your *Possessions*; and you Expect from their Service, a Support, and perhaps an Increase, of your other *Possessions*" (60). These three ideological constructions of the discourse of slavery and conversion— God as Slave Trader (and Slave Trader as God), the separation of body and soul, and family slavery, are the major premises with which Wheatley grapples in "To Maecenas," the ode of invocation that begins *Poems on Various Subjects Religious and Moral.*

While most readings of "To Maecenas" have focused on the identity of Wheatley's Maecenas (both John Wheatley and the Countess of Huntingdon have been conjectured), "To Maecenas" also functions as one of Wheatley's clearest articulations of poetic power, As Cynthia J. Smith has pointed out, "Maecenas is addressed not as a provider of material support but as a sympathetic reader" (583). Smith reads the poem as evidence of Wheatley's concern about her imminent literary reception. Indeed, the volume was published in London under patronage of the Countess of Huntingdon precisely because the racial climate of Boston precluded its publication in the United States.

But if Wheatley invokes Maecenas as an "idealized reader" (Smith), she also inscribes herself as poet in a gesture of self-authentication that establishes the terms by which she will negotiate for poetic power throughout the volume. Houston Baker notes that Wheatley's reference to "the happier *Terence*" writes "her male precursor's African name . . . and body into the discourse of eighteenth-century heroics" (Baker and Redmond, *Afro-American Literary Study in the 1990's* 137). Mae Henderson's "Response" in that volume, however, offers an important corrective, namely, that Wheatley writes not only Terence but "*herself* and *her story* into *history*" (157). Thus Wheatley's act is one of "self-inscription" based on her "dialogic engagement with the various and multiple discourses of the other(s)" (157) as both a black and a woman.

Taken together, these readings offer a way into Wheatley's conceptualization of the reader-writer matrix as a potential site for poetic power and black female empowerment. Having lamented the "partial grace" shown to "one alone of *Afric's* sable race" (lines 39, 40), Wheatley resigns herself to the fact that history (as implicated by "canonicity") has failed to supply her with a black female literary foremother. It is at this point that she exclaims to Maecenas,

> I'll snatch a laurel from thine honor'd head,
> While you indulgent smile upon the deed.

> (Lines 46–47)

The word "indulgent" in line 47 has hampered a proper reading of this couplet. It is part of the domesticating strategy of Wheatley's poetics, designed to soften the powerful blow of line 46. Indeed, these two lines are in dialogic relation as each struggles for primacy of meaning. In line 46, the word "snatch," however, arrests our attention; the very abruptness of its sound produces a rupture, a clear break with the soft, lyrical sounds of the rest of the poem. Significantly, some form of the verb "to snatch" appears in two other places in *Poems*, and in each case, it is in a very different and contradictory context.

The word "snatch d" appears in a much-quoted passage from "To the Rt. Hon. William, Earl of Dartmouth":

> Should you, my lord, while you peruse my song,
> Wonder from whence my love of *Freedom* sprung,
> Whence flow these wishes for the common good,
> By feeling hearts alone best understood,
> I, young in life, by seeming cruel fate
> Was snatch'd from *Afric's* fancy'd happy seat:
> What pangs excruciating must molest,
> What sorrows labour in my parent's breast?
> Steel'd was that soul and by no misery mov'd
> That from a father seiz'd his babe beloved:
> Such, such my case. . . .
>
> (Lines 20–30)

The second appearance is in an elegy, "A Funeral Poem on the Death of C. E. an Infant of Twelve Months":

> The angels view him with delight unknown,
> Press his soft hand, and seat him on his throne;
> Then smiling thus. "To this divine abode,
> "The seat of saints, of seraphs, and of God,
> "Thrice welcome thou." The raptur'd babe replies,
> "Thanks to my God, who snatch'd me to the skies."
>
> (Lines 9–14)

Crucially, this sequence of utterances equates three figures: God, Slave Trader, and Poet. If, on the one hand, Wheatley subsumes all under the auspices of God's ultimate Providence (with portraits of the blissful dead and the Christianized slave), "the deed" ("To Maecenas," line 47) she owns for herself as Poet borders on the heretical. For Wheatley, poetic "trafficking" in bodies simultaneously involves trafficking in souls.[6] In order to appropriate the power of the Slave Trader in a bold reversal of power relations, reclaiming, as it were, her own body, she must simultaneously, and at great risk, appropriate a godlike power to deal in souls. The empowered black female Poet then, wills (and wields) poetic power at great risk. First, there is the risk that stems from her knowledge that, insofar as she is a slave poet writing at the beginning of black women's writing "tradition," her poetic deeds may have real material consequences for other enslaved Africans as well as for future black women writers.[7] Second, for a Puritan poet like Wheatley, there is the danger of blasphemy as her need for an empowered persona can slip at any moment into heretical discourse, which, in Wheatley's theology, threatens her immortal soul and promises to alienate her from the covenant of believers. Her challenge, then, is to create and enact a poetics through which she can appropriate the enormous amount of power she must have in order to speak at all while, at the same time, eliciting the blessings of her "idealized reader" who will "smile upon the deed."

Wheatley's equation of God and Slave Trader repeats Mather's formulation, while her addition of the Poet provides the loophole through which she will renegotiate its parameters. By inserting her poetic "self" into the formulation, Wheatley enacts a crucial displacement that mediates the terms by which the two figures will be metaphorically linked.

THE ELEGIAC SUBTEXT

Bakhtin's theory of literary genre as "form-shaping ideology," "a way of seeing," "a specific kind of creative activity embodying a specific sense of experience" (Morson and Emerson 282–83) is useful for a consideration of Wheatley's elegies. For the poet-as-elegist performs an important *social* mission: the function of consoling the bereaved family and community, a "social gesture" (Henson 11) that returns the broken collective to a sense of wholeness (present and future). It is this sense of an invisible community of believers predestined to be reunited in heaven upon which the Puritan elegy turns. In terms of signification, what I will call the "elegiac pact"[8] positions the poet as the maker of meaning. The bereaved readers come to the funeral elegy with a desire for comfort and a "referent" (belief in salvation) for which the elegist must provide the "signs" (corresponding details from the deceased's life). Yet in the process of providing solace to her readers, Wheatley runs directly into the more profound rupture of her own separation from her kin in Africa as she was "snatch'd" from her "parent's breast" ("To Dartmouth"). Thus it is within the communal genre of the elegy that Wheatley comes closest to expressing her own deeply felt isolation.

I will read the elegies according to their narrative placement in *Poems*, rather than as abstract groupings according to subject (deceased and/or bereaved) as is the usual practice.[9] This process allows us to read a narrative subtext that emerges from the *development* of Wheatley's increasing engagement with poetic power.

Significantly, the first sequence of elegies in *Poems* begins immediately after "On Being Brought From Africa to America," creating a kind of "dialogue" with the subjectivity of initial rupture. Five elegies are then "clustered" in rapid succession: "On the Death of the Rev. Dr. Sewell," "On the Death of the Rev. Mr. George Whitefield," "On the Death of a Young Lady of Five Years of Age," "On the Death of a Young Gentleman," and "To a Lady on the Death of Her Husband." These elegies establish the basic paradigm for Wheatley's articulation of loss/grief and, more important, the poet's role in providing solace and familial and communal healing.

Wheatley's revision of a couplet in "Sewell" is a fitting point of reference for the narrative subtext that unfolds in the elegies. In the version printed in *Poems*, we find the following couplet:

> "*Sewell* is dead." Swift-pinion'd *Fame* thus cry'd.
> "Is *Sewell* dead," my trembling tongue reply'd.
>
> (Lines 23–24)

This dialogue between *Fame* and Poet, complete with the chiasmic reversal within the quotations, establishes the similarity and difference between them. Like Fame, the poet's job is to publish the news of the subject's death. The poet, however, has a larger overall mission: to interrogate the bar dividing life/death and to insert herself as mediator and arbiter of grief/solace, loss/restoration. Further, in the manuscript variant of this poem (see Shields 203 ff.), the second line of the couplet reads "'Is *Sewell* dead,' my trembling heart reply'd" (line 24). The shift from "heart" to "tongue" is the movement from emotion to voice. That in the final version Wheatley places the emphasis on voice signals a growing awareness of the power inhering in the role of elegist. For within the elegy Wheatley indeed struggles to recover voices "silenced" by death.

Holloway writes of "frustrated speech" as a theme in contemporary black women's writings:

> In works that indicate this kind of frustration, speech is manipulated—inverted from its usual dimensions and replaced into other spheres (layers) of the text. It becomes liminal, translucent and subject to disarray, dislocation . . . and dispersion in the text. Only the recovery of voice restores the balance to the text between its voice and the voices collected into its rearticulated universe. (6)

The recovery of voice (and, I would argue, vision) is precisely what Wheatley's elegiac persona most desires. Bereavement is figured as the loss of sound and sight, material and sensory interactions with the deceased. Thus Wheatley writes in "Sewell":

> Hail, holy man, arriv'd th'immortal shore,
> Though we shall hear thy warning voice no more.
> Come let us all behold with wishful eyes
> The saint ascending to his native skies.
>
> (Lines 3–6)

Similarly, she writes of the departed "Whitefield,"

> We hear no more the music of thy tongue.
>
> > (Line 3)

> He leaves the earth for heav'n's unmeasur'd height,
> And worlds unknown receive him from our sight.
>
> > (Lines 12–13)

The representation of sight and sound, however, is the poet's stock in trade. In "On Imagination," Imagination/Fancy is figured as an "imperial queen" whose power resides in the ability to restore sensory images:

> Thy various works, imperial queen, we see,
> How bright their forms! how deck'd with pomp by thee!
> Thy wond'rous acts in beauteous order stand,
> And all attest how potent is thine hand.
>
> > (Lines 1–4)

Notwithstanding the power of imagination to invoke sensory images, in "Sewell," the poet can only assert that Sewell is "number'd with the happy dead" (line 2) and "arriv'd th'immortal shore" (line 3). Though poetic imagination can create spring out of winter as Wheatley's ode maintains, it cannot, in this early elegy, create a vision of heaven and the afterlife.

Similarly, in "On the Death of a Young Gentleman," the poet laments the powerlessness of the classical muse to transgress the boundary between life and death: "O could my muse thy seat on high behold" (line 7); "O could she hear what praise thine harp employs" (line 9). After contemplating "the anguish of the parents heart," she asks:

> What shall my sympathizing verse impart?
> Where is the balm to heal so deep a wound?
> Where shall a sov'reign remedy be found?
>
> > (Lines 16–18)

At the poem's end, Wheatley abandons the classical muse in favor of the more powerful "gracious Spirit":

> Look, gracious Spirit, from thine heav'nly bow'r,
> And thy full joys into their bosoms pour;
> The raging tempest of their grief control,
> And spread the dawn of glory through the soul,
> To eye the path the saint departed trod,
> And trace him to the bosom of his God.
>
> > (Lines 19–24)

If the muse cannot ascend "on high" (line 7), the Spirit is invoked to look down "from thine heav'nly bow'r" (line 19). Only Spirit (which is here distinct from God [24]) possesses the power "to eye the path" that leads over the mediating border which separates life and death.

By now a central contradiction should be evident. If the poet has the power of imagination that allows her to represent sensory experience, as "On Imagination" implies, why the need for restraint? The answer lies in Puritan theology, which mandates the attitude of "assured uncertainty" (Morgan) toward salvation and election. Interestingly, the subject of Wheatley's first elegy is George Whitefield, who, along with John Wesley, challenged Puritan hegemony during the Great Awakening (which climaxed in the 1740s and 1750s) by replacing the uncertainty of the doctrine of election with the "blessed assurance" of salvation through regeneration. Clearly such a theological mandate had great effect over a religious genre like the funeral elegy, which derived from the popularity of the Puritan funeral sermon. As Robert Henson notes, elegists had to be wary of the "risky embroidery on things not seen" (22).

Wheatley's membership in the conservative Old South Meeting House indicates that she was probably catechized along more traditional Puritan lines, especially given the controversy over religious instruction to slaves. However, as a result of the pervasiveness of Great Awakening sentiment and the "social earthquake" (Epstein 11) that ensued, a religious discourse was already in place that would allow Wheatley to challenge the doctrine of assurance, sanctioning her poetic transgressions into the invisible regions of heaven. There was for Wheatley, however, a more complicated dilemma. If, indeed, the important social function of the elegy allowed her to write herself into a community from which she was "othered" by race and slave status, to provide the images necessary to truly console that community of mourners would be tantamount to heresy and would, ironically, exclude her from the covenant of believers.

The subtext that develops in the elegies in *Poems on Various Subjects Religious and Moral* exploits this tension and stages a drama of ultimate power and empowerment. In "To a Lady and Her Children on the Death of Her Son and Their Brother," for example, Wheatley shows her awareness of the magnitude of such a transgression:

> But of celestial joys I sing in vain:
> Attempt not, muse, the too advent'rous strain.
>
> (Lines 21–22)

To claim assurance through (poetic) regeneration is to claim a privileged spiritual knowledge, the representation of which is evidence of heresy.

In "On the Death of a Young Lady of Five Years of Age," the poet ventures a bit further into forbidden terrain by envisioning the child "in her heav'nly home" (line 27). Yet the utterance remains on the plane of the desire to impart solace through the "sov'reign remedy" of poetic representation.

In "To a Clergyman on the Death of His Lady," however, the poet finally breaks through and for the first time not only envisions the deceased in heaven but represents her *speaking*. The poem begins with the word "Where," the repetition of which signals the poet's transgression into forbidden spaces:

> Where contemplation finds her sacred spring,
> Where heav'nly music makes the arches ring,
> Where virtue reigns unsully'd and divine,
> Where wisdom thron'd, and all the graces shine,
> There sits thy spouse amidst the radiant throng.
>
> (Lines 1–5)

The first transgression is one of vision, the poetic ability to conjure up a visual image of the deceased "amidst the radiant throng."

Even more daring, however, is the direct quotation from the deceased for which the poet sets the scene: "Thy spouse leans downward from th'empyreal sky" (line 16). For fourteen lines, Wheatley ventriloquizes the speech of the Other from an Other realm. In an earlier elegy, one written under the premise of poetic/theological restraint, Wheatley had urged the bereaved family to "let hope your grief control" ("On the Death of a Young Lady of Five Years of Age," line 27). Here, however, she urges the grieving clergyman to banish grief altogether:

> Then thou, dear man, no more with grief retire
> Let grief no longer damp devotional fire,
> But rise sublime, to equal bliss aspire.
>
> (Lines 33–35)

Having appropriated the "gracious Spirit" that enables her own poetic persona to "cross-over" into the Other regions, Wheatley now commands the clergyman to "rise" (line 35). But she goes further by asserting her poetic power to appropriate (and go beyond) the minister's function. It is the minister's role "t'unfold the oracles divine, / To sooth our woes" (lines 38–39), but Wheatley's newfound power as elegist replaces the minister's "talk" (line 41) with "the muse" who provides "a cordial" (line 41) of solace for him as grieving spouse.

Three other poems, which I will not take the time to read here, use the strategy of the speaking deceased: ""A Funeral Poem on the Death of C. E. an Infant of Twelve Months" (Shields 69–71), "On the Death of J. C. an Infant" (92–94), and "To the Honourable T. H. Esq; on the Death of his Daughter" (98–100). It is interesting to note that all of these poems involve the death of a woman or a small child. Moreover, Wheatley's anatomy of grief is physical—the physical senses fail, which provokes bodily responses (sighs, moans, tears abound in the elegies). This demands the *embodiment* of the resurrected deceased within the field of poetic representation.

"SELF" AS SPEAKING "OTHER"

> If she, this genius teenager, should, instead of
> writing verse to comfort a white man upon the
> death of his wife, or a white woman upon the
> death of her husband, or verse commemorating
> weirdly fabled white characters bereft of children
> diabolically dispersed, if she, instead, composed
> a poetry to speak her pain, to say her grief, to
> find her parents, or to stir her people into
> insurrection, what would we now know
> about God's darling girl, that Phillis?
> *(June Jordan, "The Difficult Miracle")*

June Jordan's lamentation on Wheatley's "choice" of subject matter in the elegies hinges on the concept of "self" as it encounters the domain of literary utterance. Jordan's "instead" (which reverberates with Alice Walker's rhetorical question "But how could this be otherwise?" in *Mothers' Gardens* 236) represents a desire for an alternative scenario. While I do not want to undermine the power and importance of feminist projects based on imagining "otherwise," I do want to interrogate Jordan's (and by extension Walker's) interrogative(s) by reading beneath its figurative economy as a means by which to return to Wheatley's own poetic utterance. While Jordan begins this passage with the conditional, ultimately her meditation relies on the notion of a stable self ("she") within a stable and identifiable racial/cultural community ("her people"). The suggestion that we do not "know" Wheatley effects a dismissal of her written utterances as somehow "other" than her own.

Yet Wheatley's subjectivity, as evidenced throughout her oeuvre and particularly in the elegies, is precisely that of one "diabolically dispersed." And it is here that we must recontextualize these poems within the frame of cultural memory and desire for community. The separation from her African roots becomes a kind of cultural "primal scene," an originary site of desire that fuels the elegiac compulsion. This scene is repeated over and over again in her work, played out on the terrain of poetic utterance.

Though the elegies are, indeed, written for specific occasions, expressions of someone else's grief, Wheatley is, tropologically, representationally, speaking her "self." Thus the device of having the deceased speak words of comfort to the loved ones left behind is a sort of self-ventriloquism, Wheatley speaking her self (*je*) as Other (*moi*).[10] As Michael Walsh writes of Lacanian mourning, "The death of a loved person constitutes a hole in the Real; like a psychosis, the work of mourning begins with a swarm of images rushing into the vacuum, and comes to rest in an acceptance comparable with the stabilization of the delusional metaphor" (81). Far from "delusional," Wheatley's elegies stage an important "spiritual interrogation" that serves to bring into focus a central facet of her diasporic religious experience—the desire to speak beyond the "grave" of separation to those she left behind for a "better" world ("'Twas mercy brought me from my pagan land").

Through religious discourse and the elegiac genre Wheatley's writings were to find a "home" in the imagination of Ann Plato. Thus a body of poetry shaped by the search for community and the ultimate deferral of communal belonging becomes a location for black women's writing community in the nineteenth century.

CHAPTER FOUR

"Social Piety" in Ann Plato's *Essays*

[T]he image of black women writing in isolation, across
time and space, is conduced toward radical revision.
(Hortense Spillers, "Cross-Currents, Discontinuities")

Nothing is absolutely dead: Every meaning will have
its homecoming festival.
*(M. M. Bakhtin, "Toward a Methodology for the
Human Sciences")*

IN HIS preface to Ann Plato's *Essays; Including Biographies and Miscellaneous Pieces in Prose and Poetry* (1841), the Reverend James W. C. Pennington, pastor of the black Talcott Street Congregational Church in
Hartford, Connecticut, provides the conventional authenticating statements about Plato's identity. Recalling the prefatory documents at the
beginning of Phillis Wheatley's *Poems on Various Subjects Religious and
Moral* (1773), Pennington's introduction enacts a curious reversal.
Wheatley's initial presentation "to the publick" as "NEGRO SERVANT TO
MR. JOHN WHEATLEY OF BOSTON" required a focus on her racial identity
to the exclusion of any commentary on her gender.[1] Race, however, and
not gender, provides the stumbling block for Pennington as he intro-
duces his young protégée "To the Reader." Pennington writes:

> I am not in the habit of introducing myself or others to notice by the adjec-
> tive of "colored" &c., but it seems proper that I should just say here, that
> my authoress is a colored lady, a member of my church, of pleasing piety
> and modest worth. (1)

Pennington's hesitation to pronounce the epithet "colored" leads to an
overemphasis on Plato's "feminine" attributes. If gender was the "unspeakable, unspoken"[2] of Wheatley's writings, then race becomes the
suppressed discourse of Plato's.

The shift from the recognition of Wheatley's race and the elision of
her gender to Pennington's acknowledgment of Plato's femininity and
his hesitation to name her race must therefore be historicized as a difference not only of time but of space (community) as well. This shift paral-
lels the difference between Wheatley's seat in the "Nigger Pews" of Old
South Meeting House and Plato's membership in the Talcott Street

Church under the pastorship of Pennington, "the fugitive blacksmith."[3] Thus the difference in community marks out the "*inter*cultural/racial and *intra*cultural/racial sites" (Henderson 24) that determine the boundaries within and between their written utterances. In either case, however, the barriers against the expression of race and gender as simultaneous markers of difference and domination construct black women's authorship as a realm of multiple transgressions.[4] As Mae Henderson describes it, the challenge to Wheatley and Plato in their separate milieus is "to speak at once to a diverse audience about [their] experience in a racist and sexist society where to be black and female is to be, so to speak, 'on trial.'"[5]

Ann Plato was probably born in Hartford, Connecticut, in the first quarter of the nineteenth century. While neither her birth nor her death appears to be recorded, internal evidence from her poems suggests that she, like Wheatley, was a teenager when *Essays* was published in 1841. Using a combination of the 1830 Census, the first census to enumerate free black heads of household, and early-nineteenth-century city directories of Hartford, we can deduce that her parents were most likely Henry and Deborah Plato of West Hartford. Henry Plato is listed in the 1830 Census as between twenty-four and thirty-six years of age and the head of a household of five (Piato apparently had at least one sibling, a brother who was an only son). The 1828 Hartford City Directory lists a Henry Plato, laborer, and Deborah Plato, seamstress, at 23 Elm Street, a street that follows the south bank of the "Little" or "Mill" River. Interestingly, Elm Street was also the location of Zion Methodist Episcopal Church where the second district of Hartford's Free African Schools was housed. It was here that Ann Plato taught until 1847.[6]

As I have already argued, the tendency among critics to focus on Wheatley's position at the beginning of African American and black women's literary traditions has often hampered the readings of the poems themselves. As such, this originary position has remained, to a large extent, "figurative," and the important work of determining specific intertextual relations between Wheatley's poetry and the work of later writers remains to be done. It is in the writings of Ann Plato that these textual continuities become evident, as Plato includes six lines, unacknowledged and slightly modified, from Wheatley's ode "On Recollection" within her poem "Lines, Written Upon Being Examined in School Studies for the Preparation of a Teacher."[7] However, Kenny J. Williams, in the Oxford edition of *Essays*, writes that "before it is assumed that Plato "copied" Wheatley or rushed into print in order to be considered as the direct descendant of Wheatley, it must be remembered that her poetry in many ways is more varied that the strictness of Wheatley's adherence to the neoclassical tradition" (xlix). Clearly the social position of Wheatley, writing as a Boston slave, differed markedly from that of

Plato, a free black schoolteacher in Hartford, Connecticut. Yet I would argue that the correspondences between them are equally compelling. They were both black women New Englanders, and both converted to Congregationalism at an early age, Wheatley at eighteen, Plato at thirteen. Both were highly educated, articulate women in a historical context which ensured that they would have few peers. And, for whatever reasons, Ann Plato read a copy of Wheatley's poems and became a poet herself.[8] What is needed here is not a curt dismissal of these connections through an appeal to causally related notions of "influence" but a way of theorizing black women's subjectivity, authorship, and writing community that will allow a historical dialogue to emerge between these texts and between their writers.[9]

FROM WHEATLEY TO PLATO

Unlike Wheatley—whose capture, enslavement, and transportation to America mark her as "diaspora subject"—Plato is lodged firmly within a culturally identifiable community. This difference between movement and stasis refigures the "from . . . to" formulation of conversion as a function of time rather than of space. In other words, Wheatley's poetics of recovery, as I have shown, highlights displacement as a textual strategy that reenacts the primary spiritual and cultural displacement of diaspora subjectivity. In Plato's case, by contrast, space remains static as Plato manipulates temporality to create what I call a language of (re)generation, one uniquely suited to her cultural location as emerging ideologies of gender within free black communities sought to constrict black women's public utterance.

In "From Wheatley to Douglass: The Politics of Displacement," Henry Louis Gates, Jr., argues that the line of descent from Phillis Wheatley to Frederick Douglass is one of displacement, involving "the cultural erasure of a female progenitor" in favor of the canonization of Douglass as the nineteenth century's "Representative [Black] Man" (48). As Gates has shown elsewhere, Wheatley "resurfaces" in the early nineteenth century as an object for abolitionist propaganda as her frontispiece image and her poems became reproduced within ideologies surrounding the debate over black intellectual inferiority (*Figures in Black*). Yet in a curious reenactment of the attestations that introduce *Poems*, Wheatley's gender remains in historical suspension. In "Wheatley to Douglass" Gates writes:

> Between 1773 and the middle of the nineteenth century, Phillis Wheatley virtually *was* the canon of black American letters. What's more, virtually all commentators thought so, and were proud of the fact. Her poems and letters, her book and books about her life, were reprinted widely, reviewed

prominently, and praised roundly as the work of the founding "genius" of African-American letters. Nowhere was she held in higher esteem than within abolitionist circles. (49)

Indeed, between Wheatley's death in 1784 and 1841 when Plato published her *Essays,* no fewer than ten reprintings of *Poems on Various Subjects Religious and Moral* appeared in the United States. In addition, Margaretta Matilda Odell's *Memoirs and Poems of Phillis Wheatley. A Native African and a Slave* was published anonymously in 1834, as was B. B. Thatcher's biography of the same title. Thatcher's text was issued in a second edition during the same year. In 1832, Garrison's *Liberator* began reprinting several of Wheatley's poems, beginning on February 11th and continuing through December 22d. Also in that year, *Freedom's Journal,* the black abolitionist paper, reprinted "To Maecenas" (February 11th) and "On Virtue" (February 18th). Excerpts of Wheatley's biography and poetry appeared in a rash of abolitionist books and tracts, many of the "facts" spurious and the details inaccurate and incomplete.

What is missing from Gates's account of Wheatley's "canonicity," however, is the perspective of free black Northerners themselves, an intracommunal response that shifts the emphasis from the interracial "gaze" of the (largely) white "abolitionist circles." Following gradual emancipation in the North, there was a dramatic rise in free black institutions, beginning with the Masons (New York) and the Free African Society (Philadelphia) in the late eighteenth century, and culminating in the establishment of black churches, the African Methodist Episcopal denomination, black mutual aid, education, literary, and debating societies, and the black press in the first third of the nineteenth century.[10] When the writings of these organizations are taken into account, the displacement of Phillis Wheatley in an emerging, self-consciously articulated African American literary "tradition" must be dated in the first decade of the nineteenth century, long before the appearance of Douglass's *Narrative.* Moreover, the attitude of nineteenth-century free black leaders toward Wheatley is not easily separated from their attitudes toward black women in general; and I would characterize that stance as, at best, ambivalent. This ambivalence manifests itself most clearly in the issue of black male authority, as free black institutions begin to fracture over the issue of black women's "proper place."

In an address to the New York African Society in 1809, William Hamilton ponders the difficulty of disproving the discourse of black intellectual inferiority. Looking back over the record of black achievement, he asks, "[I]s there aught to enkindle in us one spark of emulation: must not he who makes any considerable advances under present circumstances be almost a prodigy[?]" It is here that Hamilton turns to literature:

> Although the productions of Phillis Wheatley may not possess the requisitions necessary to stand the test of nice criticism, and she may be denied a stand in the rank of poets, yet does she possess some original ideas that would not disgrace the pen of the best poets.—Without naming others who have appeared in the interim of her and the present time, I hold in my hand a specimen of African genius. . . .
>
> This book contains an introductory address and an oration on the abolition of the slave trade, delivered in the African Church, the first of January eighteen hundred and eight; by two young men whom you are generally acquainted with: the address or frontispiece to the work is a flow of tasteful language, that would do credit to the best writers; the oration or primary work is not a run of eccentric vagaries, not now a sudden gust of passionate exclamation, and then as sudden calm and an inertness of expression, but a close adherence to the plane of the subject in hand, a warm and animating description of interesting scenes, together with an easy and graceful style. If we continue to produce specimens like these we shall soon put our enemies to the blush; abashed and confounded they shall quit the field, and no longer urge their superiority of souls. (In Porter, *Early Negro Writing* 36–37)

In what may well be one of the earliest examples of African American literary criticism, William Hamilton addressed an audience of free black men, organized, according to their motto, for "MUTUAL INTEREST, MUTUAL BENEFIT, AND MUTUAL RELIEF," and advocating an agenda for promoting black equality that is grounded in African American *literary* practice. What is interesting is that an organization founded for the alleviation of material, political, and economic distress in the segregated black communities of New York should find itself immersed in concerns for literary style and production. In fact, the production of African American literature began to flourish in just such a nexus of economic, social, political, and religious practices, all knotted together in the discourses and spaces of free black communities and institutions as they developed in the late eighteenth and early nineteenth centuries in America.

Yet Hamilton's battle cry for a literature to make the enemy "quit the field" turns on the displacement of Wheatley's poetry in favor of the text he "hold[s] in [his] hand." That this text is a work of published *oratory* is significant.[11] The genre of African American published oratory, beginning with the plethora of addresses and sermons delivered in celebrations of the abolition of the U.S. slave trade in 1808, dominated African American writing of the early national period.[12] Moreover, oratorical literature was clearly a gendered (black male) domain. Thus when Hamilton upholds (literally) the oratorical writings of Peter Williams as *the* "specimen" to be emulated in African American literary practice, he promotes a literary genre from which black women were necessarily excluded.

By the 1830s, editorials that sought to control black women's public speaking began to appear regularly in the columns of black newspapers and journals. Given to an anecdotal style wherever the subject of black women was concerned, stories of black women who were "too talkative" and thus undesirable marriage partners for black men were regular features of publications like *Freedom's Journal* and the *Colored American*.[13] For all the good black women could possibly do to overcome ideas about black inferiority, black male leaders seemed to think it best to keep them out of public discourse altogether, as their appearance as speakers was deemed too great a threat to black manhood. This public call for the silencing of black women is all the more ironic given the prominence of women like Maria W. Stewart, Sojourner Truth, and Frances Harper, among others, who were known for their effective public oratory.[14] Important for our purposes here is that Plato chose none of the generic options most available to her at the time; neither did she pursue public speaking, an arena already inhabited by Stewart, Truth, and Harper, or, indeed, the genre of spiritual autobiography at this time already pioneered by Jarena Lee. Her choice of poetry seems to be a deliberate claiming of the legacy of Wheatley, attempts to displace her "foremother" status notwithstanding.

In making the generic choices she did, Plato would become embroiled in intracommunal contestations over black women's role and black women's voice, all of which put pressure on her own creative utterances. In "Freedom's Yoke: Gender Conventions among Antebellum Free Blacks," James Oliver Horton argues that while female deference to male authority was universally applied in nineteenth-century American culture; "for black women deference was a racial imperative" (Horton 70). Because of overwhelming prejudice against free blacks as a class, black community leaders admonished their constituencies to act, as individuals, "for the good of the race" (73). This additional pressure constructed gender roles within the domain of racial politics. Thus black women felt compelled to show black men the proper "respect," for to do otherwise would be to uphold the practice of emasculation enacted under slavery. As Horton puts it, "Women knew what was and was not possible and respected their men within the context of realities of black life. In fact, that respect itself became an act of resistance" (59). "For the woman who chose duty to race over duty to sex," however, "there was ambivalence and personal tension" (68). And Horton concludes: "So long as black liberation meant the creation of a black patriarchy, black women could not themselves be liberated" (73).[15]

"SOCIAL PIETY": GENDERING COMMUNITY

Here I will return to the discussion of Pennington's preface with which this chapter began in order to interrogate his claim that Plato's work demonstrates "her social piety" ("To the Reader" xviii). First, the "publick" that serves as the addressee for the attestation of Wheatley's poems must be distinguished from the "reader" Pennington addresses in his introduction of Ann Plato. For all his worrying over the adjective "colored," Pennington clearly places Plato's "modest worth" as a black woman writer within the context of racial politics: "She [Plato] is willing to be judged by the candid, and even to run the hazard of being severely dealt with by the critic, in order to accomplish something for the credit of her people. . . . The fact is, this is the only way to show the fallacy of that stupid theory, that *nature has done nothing but fit us for slaves, and that art cannot unfit us for slavery!*" (xviii). Like William Hamilton, Pennington conceives of black authorship as service; thus he places Plato in a line of descent from others who "served in adversity" (Phillis Wheatley, Terence, Capitain, and Francis Williams) while "serving the world in high repute as poets" (xviii–xix).

Pennington talks at some length about the need of young writers for patronage: "our young authoress justly appeals to *us*, her own people, (though not exclusively,) to give her success. I say the appeal is *just*. And it is just because her success will, relatively, be our own" (xix). In discussing economic and financial "success," Pennington appeals "to us, her own people." Anticipating Harriet E. Wilson's appeal "to my colored brethren universally for patronage" in her preface to *Our Nig* in 1859,[16] Pennington notes that the financial success of *Essays* will lead to another kind of "success," which will "relatively, be our own." And he closes this paragraph with a pun: "But as Greece had a Plato why may we not have a Platoess?" (xx).

Yet Pennington's endorsement of Plato as an example of black equality is circumscribed by the intraracial emphasis on gender. The focus on black success takes on the perspective of the white gaze, the source of "that stupid theory that *nature has done nothing but fit us for slaves*." It is, however, the "ambiguously (non)hegemonic" (Henderson 20) black male gaze that seeks to constrain Plato's writings within the discourse Pennington articulates as "*social piety*" (xviii). Pennington praises Plato for having followed "her *renewed* turn of mind" (which suggests, possibly, that Plato was a relatively new convert to Christianity) and for placing religion first in her writings: "I know of nothing more praise-worthy than to see one of such promise come before the public, with the religion of Christ uppermost in her mind. It will be well for our cause when many such can be found among us" (xviii). Similarly, Pennington likens Plato to Phillis Wheatley because she "is passionately fond of reading, and delights in searching the Holy Scriptures" (xix). Plato's religiosity, according to Pennington, accounts for her "pleasing piety," a phrase that, like "social piety," represents a domestication of religion within the sphere of black male privilege, a proscription demanding the socialization of black women within a secondary religious and public sphere. Pennington is writing, ultimately, to assure his (particularly black male) readers that the writings which follow do not pose a threat to their authority.

It is against this backdrop of deference to black men as "racial imperative" that Ann Plato writes. Yet Plato's renegotiation of the role of religion and "piety" within her work relates dialogically to her redefinitions of the "social." For Plato has her own, separate agenda, her own "imperatives" (specifically "pedagogical" and "[re]generational") that will sanction her transgressions of the domestic sphere in key places within her writings.

Bakhtin writes that literary language results from the assimilation and appropriation of "speech genres" which occur within the social interactions of a given epoch. "We are given these speech genres in almost the same way that we are given our native language" (*Speech Genres* 78). Speech genres are diverse "because they differ depending on the situation, social position, and personal interrelations of the participants in the communication" (79). The diversity of speech communication in the realm of the social opens the way for a discussion of speech genres as gendered constructions, since, according to Bakhtin, "to learn to speak is to learn to construct utterances" (78).

As I have shown above, black male articulations of black communal subjectivity operated on the displacement and repression of black female voice. For example, the following pithy adage appeared in the *Colored American* on September 14, 1839: "Man talks to convince—Woman to persuade and please." This saying reproduces a gendered notion of speech within an intracultural frame of addressivity.[17] Black women, when not to remain silent altogether, are circumscribed within a speech construction that delimits the form of their speech by mandating its purpose. That man talks "to convince" confers upon black manhood a subject position assured of its conviction and rooted in its secured sense of self. The "other" in such a formulation exists as the object of the speech act, to be convinced and thus re-produced in line with the self-image of the speaker. For women, however, the goal to "persuade" and "please" constructs a speaker for whom the other's will is ever-present and ultimately determining of the worth of the utterance. Here, the other sits in judgment of the speaker's words, as black women's talk is figured as inherently intersubjective.

Black women's speech genres, defined by the presence of black male listeners/readers and as articulated within nineteenth-century black male discourse, must thus be marked by deferential signs that demonstrate the will to "please." These signs of deference can be seen at work in, for example, a letter written by a free black woman identified simply as "Matilda" that appeared in *Freedom's Journal* on August 10, 1827:

> Messrs. Editors,
> Will you allow a female to offer a few remarks upon a subject that you must allow to be all important?

The subject of Matilda's editorial is "the education of females." After delivering a strong and cogent argument in favor of formal education for black women, Matilda closes with more signs of deference: "I will not longer trespass on your time and patience. I merely throw out these hints, in order that some more able pen will take up the subject" (89). Matilda's letter is paradigmatic of the imperative "to please," which restrains her utterance by framing it within the speech genres allotted to black women by black men in the nineteenth century (note her opening request that the men "allow" her utterance). The injunction that women produce "pleasing" talk echoes Pennington's description of Plato's "pleasing piety and modest worth" as behavior indicative of her overall "social piety." Yet in one of her most provocative poems, "Advice to Young Ladies," Plato revises the notion of "pleasing" utterances by demarcating her own sense of audience, a drawing of black female boundaries that produces simultaneously a "closing of the ranks" of black women, generationally inscribed, and, paradoxically, a transgression of the boundaries of black women's speech genres that articulates her own pedagogical and (re)generational imperatives.

Bakhtin writes that "[speech] genres must be fully mastered in order to be manipulated freely."[18] Plato demonstrates her awareness and mastery of black women's "proper" speech communication by the repetition of the infinitive "to please" in the first three stanzas of "Advice to Young Ladies":

> Day after day I sit and write,
>   And thus the moments spend—
> The thought that occupies my mind,—
>   Compose to please my friend.
>
> And then I think I will compose,
>   And thus myself engage—

> To try to please young ladies minds,
>   Which are about my age.
>
> The greatest word that I can say,—
>   I think to please, will be,
> To try to get your learning young,
>   And write it back to me.
>
> (Lines 1–12)

Here Plato clearly takes on the goal of pleasing speech yet she reformulates it within the sphere of friendship, a circle of black womanhood that she will figure and refigure over and over in *Essays* (especially within the biographies of the four black women who died young). Having "specified" that her mission is to "[c]ompose to please my friend" (line 4), Plato constricts the addressivity of her utterance even further; she writes, she says, "[t]o try to please young ladies minds, / Which are about my age" (lines 7–8).[19] This poetic control over the addressee of her utterance is a challenge to black male ideologies of black women's constricted speech.

Yet while Plato critiques this ideological imperative by, significantly, limiting her audience, drawing ever tighter spatial and communal boundaries, the third stanza creates a generational alliance of black women who will "write . . . back" (12). While this line, in effect, closes the circle even further, it also subverts the boundaries erected by black male desire for hegemony by ensuring a literary tradition that refuses to be hedged in by its ideological parameters. Thus African American literary practice is (re)generated along an axis of gender that deconstructs the very notion of an-other who must be "pleased" (and appeased) through signs of deference.

Having invoked the need to "get your learning young," in "Advice to Young Ladies," Plato turns in the next stanza to the theme of religion:

> But this is not the only thing
>   That I can recommend;
> Religion is most needful for
>   To make in us a friend.
>
> At thirteen years I found a hope,
>   And did embrace the Lord;
> And since, I've found a blessing great,
>   Within his holy word.
>
> (Lines 13–20)

It is "religion" that cements this community of black women together and "make[s] in us a friend" (line 16). The juxtaposition of religion and education moves out into the concluding stanza, which (re)figures "desire" not as the will to produce socially pleasing utterances but as a generational will to pursue ambition:

> Perchance that we may ne'er fulfill,
>> The place of aged sires,
> But may it with God's holy will,
>> Be ever our desires.
>
> (Lines 21–24)

Here "God's will" is invoked as the sanction for black women's "desires" to take the places of the "aged sires" who represent the current (male) hegemony.

In her introduction to the Schomburg volume of *Essays*, Kenny J. Williams writes that "Plato's general philosophy seems to have been based upon a Christianity that relied heavily upon such concepts as obedience, devotion, unquestioned respect for authority" (xliv). Yet between the lines that display, indeed, a "social piety," we find an Ann Plato who is unapologetically ambitious, a "hidden transcript" (Scott) which produces a discourse that is precisely disobedient. Plato's use of generational tropes creates a language of (re)generation the aim of which is the transformation of the social realm. Karla Holloway characterizes "revision and the processes of transformation and generation" as "the substantive context of the black woman's text" (24). Like Wheatley's emphasis on transatlantic crossings, which recovers the discourse of slavery and the Middle Passage, Plato's generational subtext represents the return of a discourse repressed under slavery.

Holloway points out that black women's history is "a history of absence because slavery denied them the right to nurture, the physical and psychic assurance of generation, and a promise of cultural and generational continuity" (169). Moreover, this recovery of repressed continuity translates into specific strategies of representation within black women's texts:

> It is this complication of generational continuity that leads to *temporal displacements*, a strategy that is central to the texts in this tradition. These are recursive literatures, they recover history and subvert it; they assert the priority of time and then displace it; they offer the commonplace as reality and then assert the realm of the spirit as actuality. (171, my emphasis)

While black men privileged the reinscription of their (repressed) "'manhood rights'" (Horton 55) with the aim of creating a black patriarchy, black women focused, instead, on reclaiming generational continuity in its transformative potential. Indeed, Plato begins the volume with the essay "Religion," the first words of which figure religion in generational terms: "Religion is the daughter of Heaven—parent of our virtues, and source of all true felicity" (21).

The "aged sires" whom the young black women desire to replace in "Advice to Young Ladies" are recalled in an essay entitled "Reflections Upon the Close of Life":

> I stooped myself down over the grave of an aged sire. I said to him, tell me of this grave! Methought that he answered—"ask him who rose again for me." Noble sire, thou hast seen peace and war succeeding in their turn; the face of thy country undergoing many alterations; and the very city in which thou dwelt, rising in a manner new around thee.
>
> After all thou hast beheld, thine eyes are now closed forever. Thou wast becoming a stranger amidst a new succession of men. A race who knew thee not, had arisen to fill the earth. Thus passeth the world away: "and this great inn is by turns evacuated and replenished, by troops of succeeding pilgrims." (74)

The language of (re)generation here works to supplant the aged sire's gaze ("thou hast seen"; "thine eyes are now closed") with the "faces" of a new generation, "[a] race who knew thee not." Elsewhere in this same essay, Plato writes that "the generations that now exist must pass away; and more arise in their stead, to fill the places which they now occupy, and do effectual good" (73). Similarly in "Eminence From Obscurity," an essay that seeks to encourage black children born in poverty to strive for greatness, Plato concludes with the following direct address to her young readers: "Dear youth of my country, her pride and her hope, catch the spirit of well done Philanthropy. If you cannot surpass the great and the good who have gone before you, study their excellences, walk in their footsteps, and God give you grace to fill their places well, when they are mouldering into dust" (56).

As a member of a truly autonomous community of free blacks, Plato envisions the transformation of society as a function of time. Significantly, Plato's imperative to (re)generate cannot be separated from her overall pedagogical mission, a mission that subverts Pennington's portrait of her "modest worth." For her role as a teacher in the Hartford Free African School is, of course, indispensable to the regeneration of her community.[20] Thus in "Lines, Written Upon Being Examined in School Studies for the Preparation of a Teacher," Plato writes of the power of her new social position as she prays to God to "Teach me, O! Lord":

> To cultivate in every youthful mind,
> Habitual grace, and sentiments refined.
> Thus while I strive to govern human heart,
> May I the heavenly precepts still impart;

Oh! may each youthful bosom, catch the sacred fire,
And youthful mind to virtues throne aspire.

(Lines 8–13)

The recognition that to teach is "to govern human heart" (line 10) is the acknowledgment of the power of her position, a power that claims a gendered articulation of transgression against the constraints a rising black male patriarchy sought to construct.

FROM ELEGY TO (AUTO)BIOGRAPHY

Plato repeats Wheatley's strategies in the elegies—the speaking of self *as* other that recovers "(cultural) moorings" through "(spiritual) metaphors" (Holloway)—within four short prose biographies of black women who died very young. In these biographical sketches, Plato aims to set down in recorded memory the lives of her own generation of black women whom she sees passing away because of the material difficulties of free black women's lives.[21] If Wheatley took up residence in the elegaic genre to promote communal consolation, thus writing herself into the community's consciousness as empowered poet, Plato functions much more as community scribe. Through her participation as cultural scribe, however, she also articulates her own desire to be remembered, her own needs for recovered personal and communal history.

My designation of this strategy as (auto)biography derives from Bakhtin's theorizing that there is "no clear-cut, essentially necessary dividing line between autobiography and biography" (*Art and Answerability* 150). Refiguring biography as a value rather than a genre, Bakhtin writes that "[b]iographical value is capable of organizing not only the story of another's life, but also the experiencing of life itself and the story of one's own life, the form in which one sees and gives utterance to one's own life" (152). Just as Wheatley's appropriation of an Other's speech from an Other realm was her own metaphorical rendering of her culturally displaced subjectivity, Plato focuses on "the grave" as a site for her interrogations of memory, history, and (generational) continuity. Unlike Wheatley's desire to impart solace to those in grief, however, Plato's concern is with the inevitability and finality of death as the grave, in fact, "finalizes" the living utterance.[22] Thus Plato reflects "upon the close of life" even as she projects her own end as a means of determining the boundaries of her own subjectivity. This movement is precisely why the value of biography as elegiac (auto)biography so captured her imagination and provided such a consistent vehicle for her poetic and prosaic self-expression.

The "this-worldly" turning of Plato's poetics results from important changes within Congregationalism, as the Second Great Awakening of the 1830s and 1840s emphasized reform.[23] "Benevolence" replaced a "pessimistic other-worldliness" in favor of a belief that moral progress could be made in this world. The emphasis on "the immanence of God as Spirit in history" (Sernett, *Black Religion* 29) was particularly attractive to African Americans, who perhaps more than any other community needed a religious articulation grounded in social change. [24]

Plato's interrogation of the bar between life and death reverses Wheatley's earlier paradigm. Wheatley's transgressions—figured by her "adven'trous" poetic crossing beyond the boundaries of death, a "crossing over" that serves to represent an empowered black female authorship which ultimately calls into question all boundaries (black/white, male/female, master/slave, "Christians"/"Negros")—meets, in the work of Ann Plato, a determined refusal. And it is through Plato's near-heretical insistence on the finality and, often, injustice of death that she establishes herself as moral authority of the here-and-now. By emphasizing the bar between life and death, she underscores the social boundaries that produce gender, race, and class oppression.

An important poem in this sense is entitled, aptly, "The Grave":

> Who sleeps in silence 'neath this mound?
> 　Whose dust does here repose?
> Is it unholy, sinful ground,—
> 　And blood upon the rose?
>
> Does there a hero sleep beneath?
> 　Some chief of spotless fame?
> The flowrets here no fragrance breathe,
> 　No marble speaks his name!
>
> Does an historian's wither'd form,
> 　Here lie so dark and low?
> I hear no requiem but the storm,
> 　No mournful sound of wo.
>
> Is it a humble, Christian Child,
> 　Who free from care lies here?
> Around this spot, thus drear and wild—
> 　And not one friendly tear!
>
> No,—the dust that moulders here enshrin'd,
> 　Was here an infant heart,—
> A wreath by beauty's hand entwin'd
> 　Did love to it impart.
>
> The parents wept about its grave,
> 　And friends its loss did mourn;

> But tears could not their darling save,
> It died,—they thought it wrong.

The poem begins by emphasizing the anonymity of the deceased with an interrogative "[w]ho sleeps in silence 'neath this mound?" (line 1). Yet unlike Wheatley, who desires to bring the silent deceased to speech, Plato sustains a series of interrogatives for fully four stanzas (lines 1–16). Speech/sound is rendered in the negative as the poet tells us that "[n]o marble speaks his name!" (line 8); "I hear no requiem but the storm, / No mournful sound of wo" (lines 11–12). The last two stanzas begin with the poet's negative answer ("No!") to conjectures about the deceased's identity ("hero," "historian," "chief"). We are told, at last, that the grave covers "an infant heart," as the last stanza turns to the grieving parents and friends. Yet there is no desire to bring comfort to the mourners; rather, the poet's role here is to document the mourners' judgment that the death of the infant was "wrong."

Far from being "half-afraid musings on deathbeds and graveyards" (Loggins 248), Plato's writings figure as negotiations with discourses of moral authority. Moreover, as a composite "utterance," her reformulation of the elegiac as (auto)biographical discourse constitutes an "aesthetic of lived life" (Bakhtin, *Art and Answerability* 152), what Plato herself in "Education" calls "the science of living well" (27). Acutely attuned to the material deprivation that characterized free black life in the early nineteenth century, Plato insistently searches for "models" that will buoy up the black women and children of her community. And she turns, ultimately, to four black women who died in youth, making their "biographies" the centerpiece of the only volume of writings she ever published—though, as she writes in "Author's Farewell," she felt "anxious to compose / As much again" (121).

These four prose-elegies relate dialogically to the poems "Forget Me Not" (106–9) and "Author's Farewell," the last poem of the volume. (Auto)biographical discourse involves not only the "self" speaking as "other" but the meditation on one's own end as one projects subjectivity onto future space (here "the grave") in order to experience oneself *as* other. As Bakhtin writes, "my contemplation of my own life is no more than the anticipation of others' recollections about my life—of recollections by descendants or simply by family members and close relatives" (*Art and Answerability* 153). In this sense, (auto)biography concerns itself with the dialogical relations between art and life. As Plato writes in the biography of Eliza Loomis Sherman, "Let the young, in *forming their own characters*, be assiduous to secure the same sources of happiness, which cheered this lovely and exemplary young lady, and enabled her, during long decline, to comfort others with her own radiant countenance, and *to close her life like a music strain*" (86, my emphasis). The recurring premise of the four sketches is that one's lived life and peaceful death adhere to an aesthetic consistency. For Louisa Sebury, for example, "a solemn sense of divine things"(77) and early conversion lead to a death "like the fading of a serene Sabbath into the holy quiet of its evening" (79). And of Julia Ann Pell Plato writes simply that "her death was like her life; easy, unaffected, and pious" (82).

Thus the biographical sketches are written not so much to promote comfort as to position the reader as witness to the deathbed scene.[25] In positioning the reader within the space of the dying, Plato gives voice to the deathbed utterance either through direct quotation (82, 88, 89), by carefully selected biblical quotations (79, 86, 87), or with a song (89). For Plato, however, giving voice to the deceased is not as important as the questioning of the justice of their lives and their deaths. For example, she writes of Julia Ann Pell, who was born in Montville, Connecticut, in 1813, that "[s]he did not enjoy the privilege of living with her parents when a child. Her age did not exceed eight years, when she was sent to live with a family, where she served as an apprentice until she was eighteen. From thence she went to East Granby and lived some years in the family of the Pastor of that village" (80). In 1836 Pell "thought to benefit herself" by moving to Hartford, a show of agency reminiscent of Harriet E. Wilson's character Frado in her 1859 novel, *Our Nig; or, Sketches from the Life of a Free Black*. Of Eliza Loomis Sherman, Plato points out that "had she wished for shelter beneath a Georgian clime, that privilege would not have been granted her; on account of the laws" (85). Thus while we are called to witness the "favored, precious moments, when the *divine power* of religion breaks in upon us, dissolves the enchantment of the world, dissipates the mist of vain doubts and speculation, and raises a fervent aspiration, that whatever may be our allotment through life, we may die the death of the righteous, and the love of God be our portion forever!" (86) we are also called to witness the precariousness of life for free black women in the antebellum North. None of these four women lived beyond her "27th year" (83); the youngest died at seventeen. Living in a world where young black women such as herself routinely died before their thirtieth birthday, Plato situates her authorship as both a testament to the harsh conditions of free black life and the finality of death, and as a living monument, a series of epitaphic utterances aimed at restoring self and community through the hope of future generations.[26] Plato's ultimate fear is that she, and other black women like her, will be forgotten: "What if our tongues in silence sleep" ("Author's Farewell," line 15). Plato is far from forgotten; understanding the importance of her long-dormant speech has just begun.

"I Took a Text": Itinerancy, Community, and Intertextuality in Jarena Lee's Spiritual Narratives

IN 1844 Jarena Lee appealed to the book committee of the African Methodist Episcopal Church for permission to publish an expanded version of her 1836 narrative, *The Life and Religious Experience of Jarena Lee, A Coloured Lady, Giving an Account of Her Call to Preach the Gospel*. She was turned down. The all-male members of the Book Concern of the African Methodist Episcopal Church—which had been incorporated as the first African American denomination in Philadelphia in 1816—rejected the manuscript on the grounds that it was "written in such a manner that it is impossible to decipher much of the meaning contained in it."[1] Undaunted by this rejection, Lee financed the printing of her *Religious Experience and Journal of Mrs. Jarena Lee, Giving an Account of Her Call to Preach the Gospel* in 1849.[2] After all, thirteen years earlier she had published *Life* herself, paying thirty-eight dollars of her own money to have one thousand copies printed, and distributing the manuscript "at camp meetings and even on the street" (Andrews, *Sisters of the Spirit* 6).

Lee's stunning authority over her own texts—"written by herself" and published and distributed by herself—belies her social position as a poor black woman living in the first half of the nineteenth century. Born in Cape May, New Jersey, probably free, in 1784, a year after the death of thirty-one-year-old Phillis Wheatley, Lee was converted to Methodism at the age of twenty-one. During an itinerant ministry that began in 1822, she traveled thousands of miles, as far north as Canada, as far west as the "northwest territory" of Ohio, and south into the slave territories of Maryland. Lee's 1836 *Life and Religious Experience*, the first prose narrative published by a black woman, antedating African American women's slave narratives by over two decades, represents an early challenge to nineteenth-century religious institutions and literary convention. Beyond their originary status, however, Lee's spiritual journals mark the convergence of issues of text and context, culture and community, subjectivity and agency, as they initiate a multivalent and multidirectional intertextuality at the beginnings of African American women's autobiographical tradition.

Several key rhetorical figures structure Lee's spiritual writings as narratives that revision simultaneously Protestant morphologies of conversion and figurations of African American religious community. On the one hand, her texts speak to the structures of social domination of nominally free African Americans in the urban North; on the other hand, she gives voice to the politics of gender exclusion within an African American community still in the process of institution building and community formation. Specifically, Lee reinvests African American oral cultural forms of spirituals and preaching as overlapping narrative strategies of call and response through her deployment of figures that serve as tropes for the convergence of the world of the Spirit with social texts of power, domination, and resistance: (1) "taking a text" as the figure for gendered prohibitions against preaching from the Bible, the foundational text of Western cultural and literary expression; (2) "the pulpit," which serves for Lee as the metaphorical space for centralized power and agency; and (3) "the call" from God, which both represents a divinely sanctioned claim to access to ministerial vocations and also occasions the writing of her textual "response." Moreover, these figures are neither linear nor sequential in the texts but function as interlocking structural devices that often blur the boundaries between written and oral, textual and spatial. As "blurred genres,"[3] then, they mark, on a metalevel, the point of entry for new theorizing of African American women's literary tradition and cultural ways of telling.

In this chapter, I go beyond historical and thematic treatments of Lee's writings by scholars such as William Andrews, Frances Smith Foster, Joanne Braxton, Susan Houchins, and Jean Humez[4] to interrogate the structural and theoretical narrativizing within and around Lee's spiritual writings. Thus I begin by restoring the intertextual relationship between the two "editions" of her autobiography/journal and argue for the centrality of the longer and more densely written *Journal* in consideration of her work. From this intertextual reconstruction, I read the narratives as revisionings of the Ur-plot of American spiritual autobiography—Protestant morphologies of conversion—as a counternarrative about the search for religious community emerges to complicate the linearity of the "from . . . to" movement of Christian conversion. Moreover, the subplot of the search for religious community marks the point of entry for a consideration of the cultural specificity of African American religious practice. Thus I go on to read Lee's texts in the context of African American preaching, spirituals, and hymnody, a context in which the meaning of intertextuality as performance urges a reformulation of the ways in which we read the relationship between African American writing and African American cultural performativity. I end with a theoretical meditation that reads an important scene in Lee's autobiography in which she interrupts the preaching of a black male clergyman—an interruption that anticipates and theorizes a critique of Bakhtinian formulations of the operation of "speech genres" within literary texts.

ITINERANT TEXTS

> Power ceases in the instant of repose; it resides in
> the movement of transition from a past to a new
> state, in the shooting of the gulf, in the darting
> to an aim.
> (*Ralph Waldo Emerson, "Self-Reliance"*)

In his "Textual Note" to *Sisters of the Spirit*, the anthology of three nineteenth-century black women's autobiographies that rescued Lee's writing from the historical archives, William L. Andrews explains his rationale for reprinting the 1836 *Life and Religious Experience* rather than Lee's 1849 *Religious Experience and Journal*:

> This journal . . . reads much like a log of distances traveled, scriptural texts expounded, places visited, and numbers of people converted. Contemporary readers unused to the formulaic character of nineteenth-century ministerial journals and autobiographies are likely to find the added pages of the 1849 edition often tedious reading and rarely, if ever, revelatory of the inner character of the woman who wrote them. Because the added length of the 1849 edition does not offer us an appreciably expanded self-portrait of Jarena Lee, this volume reprints the first edition of Lee's autobiography.

The result of Andrews's editorial decision has been that critics have almost completely ignored the 1849 *Journal*, focusing most of their attention on the much leaner (and less intimidating) anthologized edition. Yet the later text incorporates important information about the *process* of Lee's writing and the connection between her itinerancy and textual production. Not only does the *Journal* include several metalevel discussions about its own history and composition, but encoded in the structure of repetitions that Andrews labels "formulaic" are condensed narrative events whose regularity is almost ritualistic. Understanding Lee's spiritual journal in the context of writing as (religious) ritual helps us to recover the theorizing ground of a narrative whose text-ness is foregrounded even as it is ultimately to give way to a traditional narrative of suffering and redemption.

The spiritual journal as a literary form is by no means unique to Jarena Lee. In several Christian faiths, the spiritual journal functioned as the

sign of the believer's consistent examination of her/his "inner life" in
the Spirit, especially important to a group like the American Puritans as
a way of assuaging their doubts about their own predestined "election."
By writing the *Journal*, however, Lee was being not only dutifully Christian but dutifully *Methodist*. At the end of the narrative, she writes that
her spiritual journal, "though much opposed . . . is certainly essential in
life, as Mr. Wesley wisely observes" (97). Drawing on the example of
John Wesley (1703–1791), the founder of Methodism, whose *Journals
of John Wesley* spurred many American Methodists to begin writing spiritual journals or pursue vigorous diary keeping,[5] Lee contextualizes her
personal struggle with the A.M.E. Book Concern by appealing to a
wider religious and generic convention that is denominationally specific.
Perhaps more important, during the nineteenth century, many of these
"private" spiritual journals were written "*with the hope of publication*"
(Kagle 51). For a black Methodist woman with ambitions to publish,
then, the spiritual journal was a literary form already sanctioned by
the founder of the denomination, and such authority would come in
handy for Lee as her text met with opposition from black male religious
leaders.[6]

Recalling her second ministerial visit in 1833 to the "scattered nations" of free blacks in Canada, several nascent congregations she is responsible for starting, Lee first mentions her desire to publish:

> I had, long before, felt a great anxiety to publish my religious experience
> and exercise to a dying world, but, laboring under the disadvantages of
> education, I thought it a favor to pay $5 to have *a portion of it* taken from
> the original of my own registering, and corrected for press. (*Journal* 66, my
> emphasis).

In other words, the edition we have come to know as the 1836 *Life and
Religious Experience* was, in fact, an excerpt from the *Journal*. When we
reconstruct *Life* as a "portion" of a larger writing, at the time of its publication (rather than as a complete work to which Lee penned a "se-
quel," as Andrews's "Textual Note" implies), the relationship between
the two "editions" becomes more complicated. Lee's intertextual reference, which embeds *Life* within *Journal*, not only produces a "text
within a text" effect but figures the writing and publication of the earlier
narrative as an *event* within the narrative line of the second text. The
earlier publication, indeed, shows up in the *Journal* in all its materiality,
its "bookness" a few pages later:

> [I] felt under much exercise to print a book, and I had some friends to
> encourage me, such as the Rev. R. R.—, and the Bishop, with others; and

every circumstance was so favorable that I finally succeeded, and when they were brought home, I sat down in the house and wondered how I should dispose of them; to sell them appears too much like merchandize. (77)

Significantly, this passage marks the break between the part of *Journal* written before the publication of *Life* in 1836 and the section that comes later. At the time when Lee parceled out "a portion" of her manuscript for publication, she had already written a manuscript over three times the length of what appears as *Life and Religious Experience*. By the time *Life* was published three years later, the manuscript was almost four times as long.[7] The economic references in the above two passages at least partially explain why such a small section of Lee's total writing was initially published. In a passage that appears at the end of both texts, she writes,

> But here I feel constrained to give over, as from the smallness of this pamphlet, *I cannot go through the whole of my journal, as it would probably make a volume of two hundred pages*, which, if the Lord be willing, may at some future day be published. (*Journal* 97, my emphasis).

The dilemma over how to "dispose" of her pamphlets results from the fact that she published *Life* at her own expense. The economic constraints she alludes to determined the boundaries of a text that critics read as if it were a complete whole. Indeed, the appearance of this same "conclusion," verbatim, at the end of the *Journal* could signal that even more of Lee's manuscript was written but never published. At the end of the paragraph quoted above, Lee writes that she is "something more than fifty years of age" (*Journal* 97). In 1836, she would have been fifty-three; in 1842 when the events of *Journal* end, fifty-nine. Yet in 1849 when *Journal* was published, again, at her own expense, Lee was already sixty-six. Given the kind of religious mandate that informs Lee's writings from their inception, at least fifteen years' worth of writings were probably completed and are now lost.

I began this section with a quotation from Lee's contemporary Emerson, because Emerson's formulation of a relationship between power and transition serves to highlight the importance of the compact, ritualistic entries of the longer *Journal* as central to any assessment of the narrativity of Lee's spiritual writings. I say this because the focus in the journal is precisely on the movement of Lee's body/text as she chronicles an exhausting list of dates, times, locations, audiences, and scriptural texts. From time to time Lee pauses long enough to relate a brief scene or memorable event, but the bulk of the journal is tightly compressed so that the preaching events give way to the transitions between them. Lee is, then, writing autobiography as chronicle.[8] Examples abound:

> The next day I hastened forward to the place of my mother who was happy to see me, and the happiness was mutual between us, with her I left my poor sickly boy while I departed to do my master's will. (19)

> "If they persecute you in one city, flee into another. . . . I hastened to Greenwich." (23)

If, on the one hand, these transitional phrases—many of which include scenes of Lee on foot, horseback, ship, and so forth—represent Lee as vulnerable, they are also the means by which she asserts her agency. In an era in which it was dangerous and transgressive for either African Americans or women to travel freely unaccompanied, Lee is signaling her ownership of her body by representing herself as an itinerant black and female subject.

CALL/RESPONSE

> My Lord He calls me,
> He calls me by the thunder,
> The trumpet sounds within-a my soul.
> (*"Steal Away," African American spiritual*)

In *The Life and Religious Experience of Jarena Lee, A Colored Lady, Giving an Account of Her Call to Preach the Gospel* (1836), the titular narrative line centers on Lee's "call" from God, for which both her bold itinerant ministry and her text(s) serve as "response." As William Andrews outlines in his introduction to the text, Lee's spiritual narrative follows the narrative line of traditional Christian morphologies of conversion: conviction of sin, justification from sin through belief in Jesus Christ, and, finally, sanctification, the state in which one's entire will is conformed to the will of God. Yet in the process of "giving an account of her call to preach the gospel," Lee's spiritual "call" from God is embedded within narratives of race, gender, and class in the psychosocial production of subjectivity. In the opening paragraphs of *Life* we are introduced to the reality of Lee's separation from her family "at the age of seven" (27), her being "bound out" to serve in a white family as a domestic—the first in a series of domestic labor situations—in addition to the search for holiness and salvation that marks this text as a "spiritual narrative." Lee's self-positioning as, in her words, a "poor colored female instrument" (37) within the first paragraph of her text refuses a split dividing the social, the historical, and the political from the spiritual call from God.

Lee is writing at the height of the Second Great Awakening that swept through the United States in the early nineteenth century, peaking in the 1830s and 1840s. She is writing, as well, at the beginnings of the formation of African American community consciousness in the North following gradual emancipation. The African American church was the primary institutional vehicle to register this collective consciousness in formation, serving not only as a spiritual center but as schoolhouse, meeting place for political gatherings, and even, in some cases, as the community's "insurance" agency.[9] The refusal of a split between religious and social, sacred and secular, is fundamental to African American religious culture.[10] An understanding of this basic concept illuminates the ways in which Lee constructs her text on the basis of the African American cultural forms of preaching and the spirituals that themselves deconstruct the opposition between worldly and otherworldly, political and spiritual.[11] Thus Lee's "call" and her (textual) "response" must be read within this context, a context that restores community as the mediating level of interaction and serves as the basis for Lee's "theorizing" about the relationship between spiritual experience and social identity.[12] Community as cultural performance mediates both the meaning Lee assigns to her "call" and the texture of her response(s), the multilayered, multidimensional narrativity that structures Lee's spiritual narrative in relation to the Anglo-Christian narrative paradigm of conversion. While the surface structure of Lee's text confirms such a narrative line, its communal and cultural subtext subverts (by revisioning) its linearity. Thus, in *Life and Religious Experience*, Lee *performs* community, even as her text draws our attention to community as an integral part of salvation, wholeness, and self-discovery.

It is out of this narrative of the search for religious community that the performing context of African American religious culture, a context which theorizes its own dynamic of intertextuality and revisionism, emerges as the basis for Lee's structuring of her written narratives. The play between oral and written—indeed, among spoken, sung, and written—forces a new way of talking about revision and intertext that can account for the cultural dimension of Lee's complex self-revisionings. By "self-revisioning" I mean not only the structuration of memory and desire that conditions any autobiographical utterance but the written prose strategy, invented by Lee, of multiply inscribing events in order to subvert hegemonic interpretations and intentionalities.

Significantly, this act of written textual subversion and resistance is accomplished through a complex maneuvering of African American oral cultural forms as part of written textual utterance. Folklorist Alan Dundes gives the term "meta-folklore" to the "shared and exchanged generic functions, or generic complementarity, in a group's folklore systems" (qtd. in Davis 37). Thus Lee's text constructs its metalevel structural mechanisms from the "sacred genres" of black culture, most notably black "sacred music": sermon, intonation, chanting, black hymns, spirituals, testimony, exhortation, tongues.[13]

Scholars date the composition of the bulk of African American spirituals in the late eighteenth and early nineteenth centuries, encompassing Lee's own life span (she was born in 1783) and her conversion experience.[14] In the history of the A.M.E. Church, even before African Methodism became an official denomination, Richard Allen compiled a hymn book in 1801, which ran through two editions.[15] In addition to spirituals (known at that time as "spiritual songs" and associated with camp meetings in which large numbers of African Americans, slave and free, took part), Allen's hymnal featured the "wandering refrain," verses tacked on to the end of many different traditional Methodist hymns, designed to allow for communal response.[16] The early African Methodist Episcopal church services were indeed spirited events. Before 1841, the year that Daniel Alexander Payne became bishop and the church took a more bourgeois approach to worship service, the A.M.E. style of worship included spirituals, spontaneous and antiphonal singing, and the ring shout, a holy dance adapted from African sacred dance ritual. Many of these elements became encoded as features of the Methodist camp meetings (spirituals were later referred to as "camp meeting hymns"), multiracial events during which large numbers of African Americans became converts to Christianity after the rise of Methodism in the United States. Throughout its early history, A.M.E. congregations were cited repeatedly by white Methodist visitors for singing "unorthodox hymns." That spirituals were a contested cultural form attests to their ability to critique and disrupt conventional narratives of piety and religiosity.[17]

As an itinerant minister and a participant in African American religious culture, Lee was undoubtedly familiar with spirituals. In her *Religious Experience and Journal*, she writes of a particular encounter with the spirituals at a camp meeting: "The people came from all parts, . . . and the display of God's power *commenced from singing*. I recollect a brother Camell standing under a tree singing, and the people drew nigh to hear him, and a large number were struck to the ground before preaching began, and signs and wonders followed" (45). As Jon Michael Spencer points out in *Protest and Praise*, "It is most likely that a substantial number of spirituals evolved via the preaching event of black worship" (225). Most scholars agree that the majority of spirituals probably originated "from extemporaneous sermonizing that crescendoed little by little to intoned utterance" (Spencer, *Protest and Praise* 225).

Journal is replete with verses and choruses of the songs made popular in the camp meetings, such that it reads almost like a hymnal interspersed with written narrative. The structure of the spirituals would have been intimately familiar to Lee, and, as she searched for a way to tell a complex and multifaceted life story succinctly (material conditions of poverty severely restricted the number of pages Lee could afford to have printed), the folk "genre" of the spirituals would have been available as an African American "artistic" model, one consistent with the unique demands of expressing African Americans' displaced subjectivity.

INTERTEXTUALITY AS SELF-REVISIONISM

True to the Anglo-Christian conversion narrative genre, Lee states her overarching premise in the first page of *Life and Religious Experience*: "the spirit of the Lord never entirely forsook me, but continued mercifully striving within me, until his gracious power converted my soul" (27). Significantly, her first communication with God takes place through revelation and outside of any formal religious structure. Her parents were "wholly ignorant of the knowledge of God" (27); thus when "the spirit of God moved in power through my conscience, and told me I was a wretched sinner" (27), it is a moment of pure revelation between God's spirit and Lee's soul. There are no mediating structures like Bibles, hymnbooks, preachers, churches, or missionaries involved.

The conversion narrative proper begins with the words "the manner of this great accomplishment was as follows" (27), and ends six pages later with the words "I have now passed through the account of my conviction, and also of my conversion to God; and shall next speak of the blessing of sanctification" (32–33). These self-conscious (and probably editorially interpolated)[18] temporal devices become the narrative frame that is simultaneously related and refuted. This framing positions social inscriptions of race, gender, and class—represented in the opening paragraph—and the direct communication from God to her "conscience" as *outside* the narrative of conversion, peripheral rather than central to the primary narrative frame. Yet within these narrative boundaries we find a series of events structured around Lee's search for a "church home"; Lee reinvents the traditional Anglo-Christian morphology of conversion by representing her conversion story as a search for religious community, culturally inscribed, even as the representations of the search for religious community transgress these narrative boundaries.[19] While God's "spirit" leads her through this period of religious seeking and "church shopping," Lee is motivated, as well, by the initial family rupture and the material conditions of nominally free and unsatisfying labor.

Lee's first experience with organized religious structures comes in 1804 when she attends the services of a Presbyterian missionary.[20] Lee's revelatory conviction is repeated and reaffirmed—this time, however, through exposure to a mediating text. She includes the first verse of a psalm that was "read" at this service, an Anglo-Protestant interpretation of Psalm 51 and the Fall in Genesis:

> Lord, I am vile, conceived in sin,
> Born unholy and unclean.
> Sprung from man, whose guilty fall
> Corrupts the race, and taints us all.[21]

Compare Ps. 51:1–5:

> Have mercy upon me, O God, according to thy loving-kindness: according unto the multitude of thy tender mercies blot out my transgressions. Wash me thoroughly from mine iniquity, and cleanse me from my sin. For I acknowledge my transgressions: and my sin is ever before me. Against thee, thee only, have I sinned, and done this evil in thy sight: that thou mightest be justified when thou speakest, and be clear when thou judgest. Behold, I was shapen in iniquity; and in sin did my mother conceive me. (KJV)

Couched in the rhetoric of traditional Christian penitence, the racial subtext of the verse is haunting: the sin (crime) for which Lee is convicted (convicts herself) is that she was "born unholy and unclean" to a corrupt "race" that is tainted (by skin color). (Recall Wheatley: "Their color is a diabolic die.") Thus a biblical psalm about the universal condition of human sin is rewritten by Anglo-Christian precepts that exploit the social meaning of blackness as a "taint" and "corruption." In addition, the versified psalm performs a (re)gendering of the biblical text by insisting on the paternity of fallen humanity, which erases the feminine "mother" in Psalms 51. These levels of mediation have profound social consequences for the means by which Christianity was presented to and adopted by African American women in the late eighteenth and early nineteenth centuries in America.

Lee's response to her first mediated contact with "Scriptures" is immediate and intense. "At the reading of the Psalms," she writes, "a renewed conviction darted into my soul" (27). Significantly, Lee is convicted at the very *words* of the psalm: "This description of my conviction struck me to my heart, and made me to feel in some measure, the weight of my sins, and sinful nature" (27). Read with respect to Lee's social position as an "abandoned" child whose blackness signifies in the

United States as the reason for her menial labor, Lee's guilt takes on a profound meaning. The narrativity of this scene is crucial: (1) Lee hears the words of the versified psalm; (2) she experiences conviction of sin; (3) she makes her first suicide attempt (28); (4) she suffers physical illness (28); (5) finally, she leaves her employer for Philadelphia (28). At this point, though Lee is personally convicted, she does not engage in religious community.

While in Philadelphia, Lee visits the congregation of Reverend Pilmore at St. Paul's Episcopal for "three months":

> While sitting under the ministrations of this man . . . it appeared that there was a wall between me and a communion with that people . . . and seemed to make this impression upon my mind, *this is not the people for you.*[22]

The search for religious instruction and a church "home" now becomes a search for community, for a "people." Lee was torn from her immediate family at an early age; "a people" becomes the construction of her desire. One day she asks a black cook working for her mistress about the Methodists. It is then that Lee goes to the African American church, Bethel A.M.E., and first hears Richard Allen preach (1808):

> During the labors of this man that afternoon, I had come to the conclusion, that *this is the people to which my heart unites,* and it so happened, that as soon as the service closed he invited such as felt a desire to flee the wrath to come, to unite on trial with them—I embraced the opportunity. (29, my emphasis)

Here, the religious service ends with Lee embracing the community, becoming united with worshipers at one of the first black churches in the country, soon to become the first black denomination in the United States.[23]

THE PREACHING CONTEXT

What is significant here, however, is the specificity of Lee's description. She is persuaded, she says, by Allen's "labors." The ambiguity of this phrase, which resonates with Lee's own gendered domestic labor situation and foreshadows the moment when she will take on the labors of itinerant preaching, is explicated later in the passage when, three weeks later, Lee experiences full conversion in the same church "*under preaching,* at the very outset of the *sermon*" (29, my emphasis). Through this important distinction between "preaching" and "sermon," Lee's cultural theorizing comes to the fore. Lee's acute awareness of the complex relationship between (preaching) performance and (sermon) text calls for a narrative analysis that can (re)articulate the theoretical propositions inherent in what Marcellus Blount calls "the preacherly text"; that is, narrative recontextualized as performance.[24] Lee writes that she is converted when "the text was barely pronounced" (29). Since Lee is converted not according to the "message" of the sermon as a formal literary entity but through the dynamic, communal, and contextual matrix[25] of African American preaching, conventional methods of analyzing intertextuality will avail us little here. As Gerald Davis points out in his study of the performed contemporary African American sermon, "African-American culture is still dynamically oral. While literary precepts and conventions are useful in framing approaches to the examination of the expressive products of oral cultures, in the final analysis, the scholar interested in these areas must look directly at the expressive systems for the answers he or she desires" (25).

Davis's remarks remind us that conventional literary methods of analysis of influence or discourse are inadequate to the study of a text like Lee's *Life and Religious Experience*. Moreover, Davis articulates the important difference between the sermon in print and in performance: "The minimal African-American sermonic phrase is highly irregular *when reduced to print*, but it is made regular and seemingly metrical *in performance* through the use of music and sound production principles" (25). In order to understand the context for Lee's sense of religious community and culture within conversion experience, then, we must refocus our attention, away from the African American *sermon* as a literary document and coherent whole, to African American *preaching* as what Gerald Davis calls the "sermon event."[26] Lee's "preacherly text," then, is a literary residue or remainder of a series of life-changing oral cultural events that the text points to as primary yet is powerless fully to represent. Thus the oral modes of African American preaching, singing, spirituals, hymnody, clapping, shouting, testifying, praying, speaking in tongues become an *excess* figured within the text by its structure of repetitions. The text's reliance on the reader's ability to restore paralinguistic signs constitutes its metalinguistic performance, its theorizing.[27] Thus when Lee writes that "this is the people to which my heart unites," "people" becomes her figure for a racial-cultural performing community.

African American preaching and singing are central to the complex structure of Lee's text. Lee's representation of her embrace of African Methodism theorizes via its rewriting of the conversion narrative as an implicit critique of mainline Christian styles of worship and their attendant (racist) ideologies. In his study of the performed contemporary African American sermon, Gerald Davis notes that "several important events precede the actual sermon performance" in the black church

(17). Sometimes referred to formally as the "praise service," singing, praying, testifying, Bible reading, announcements of upcoming events, and the like, precede the ascension of the preacher to the pulpit. In "lining-up" the congregation for the sermon, the praise service functions to focus "that portion of a congregation's energies that are voluntarily yielded to the preacher for the duration of the sermon" (17). The praise leader's or preacher's attempts at "lining-up" the congregation will determine the success or failure of the sermon itself:

> If the spoken and sung preparatory modes have been successful, the congregation's aural-oral mechanisms have been developed into a sermonic counterpointing instrument capable of several levels of spiritual expression. If the prepatory modes are unsuccessful, the preacher will likely spend a substantial portion of the time he would customarily devote to the delivery of his message to "raising the spirit" of his "dead church." (17)

The earliest surviving sermons from African American preachers date back to the beginning of the nineteenth century, when African American communities in the North congregated to celebrate the U.S. abolition of the transatlantic slave trade in 1808, the year in which Lee visits Bethel A.M.E. for the first time.[28] Some of these published oratorical tracts included a reprinting of the program or order of service to recreate for those who had been unable to attend because of domestic duties—or to enable those who had attended to recall—the eventness of the sermon, the sermon in context, the sermon as part of a larger service of communal celebration. This isochronic[29] portion of African American liturgy usually contains several or all of the following elements. This example is from *An Oration on the Abolition of the Slave Trade; Delivered in the African Church, in the City of New York, January 1, 1808*:

Order of Celebration of the Day:
Forenoon Service
1. A solemn address to Almighty God, by the Rev. Mr. Abraham Thompson
2. An appropriate anthem sung under the direction of William Hamilton
3. The act read with an introductory address by Henry Sipkins
4. The oration delivered by Peter Williams, jun.
5. An appropriate hymn, sung under the direction of William Hamilton
6. A solemn address to Almighty God, by Mr. Thomas Miller, sen.

Afternoon Service
1. An appropriate hymn, under the direction of William Hamilton
2. A prayer, by the Rev. Mr. June Scot.
3. An appropriate hymn
4. A sermon delivered by Mr. James Varick

5. A hymn

6. A prayer, by Mr. James Varick[30]

Lee's conversion at the very start of a sermon is possible because in African American religious ritual, the sermon is simply the climax in a series of spiritual events. Moreover, the basic structure of the service— hymn, prayer, hymn, sermon, hymn, prayer—oscillates between the spoken and the musical "word," so that hymns carry the authority of (spoken) sermons while sermons and prayers are "musicalized" through intonation and chanting, the "sermon surplus" Spencer identifies as the "preached word entrenched in musicality" (*Protest and Praise* 226). As flexible as such a structure is, it also carries within it antistructural elements such as spontaneous singing (songs not on the program, raised "from the floor" by a member of the congregation), testifying, shouting, clapping, stomping, "getting happy," speaking in tongues, and so forth, events that defy structuration because they arise from the direction of the Spirit. Indeed, the structural elements of African American liturgical performance are designed to elicit just such a spiritual response. Hymns, prayers, and other elements are selected and positioned in order to "raise the spirit" and "prepare the church" (Davis 16). That is, it is a structure whose intent is to produce antistructure. Isochronic events in time are constructed so as to produce links with "Almighty God" (who actually appears on the program above).

The emphasis on religious performance continues in Lee's text as she describes her conversion under Allen's preaching at Bethel A.M.E.:

> *That moment*, though hundreds were present, I did leap to my feet, and declare that God, for Christ's sake, had pardoned the sins of my soul . . . that day was the first when my heart had believed, and my tongue had made confession unto salvation—The first words uttered, a part of that song, which shall fill eternity with its sound, was *glory to God*. . . . During this the minister was silent, until my soul felt its duty *had been performed*, when he declared another witness of the power of Christ to forgive sins on earth, was manifest in my conversion. (29, my emphasis)

What might in other contexts look like a rude interruption of Allen's sermon when "the text was barely pronounced" (29) is here an acceptable part of the performing community. While Lee's soul "perform[s]," the minister is silent, shifting the "stage" from pulpit to pew.

Here, Lee subtly revises the earlier scene of conviction that led to her first suicide attempt and left her gravely ill. In contrast to the "hundreds" present for Allen's preaching, the Presbyterian missionary's ineffectiveness (and presumable lack of spirit) is commented on by the fact that "it was an afternoon meeting, but few were there" (27). Second, while the reading of the psalm produced an evident effect on Lee, who felt "struck to the heart" (27), there seems to have been no place in the Presbyterian service for the performance of that spiritual experience. Consequently, "not knowing how to run immediately to the Lord for help," Lee attempted suicide. Most important, however, the text of the psalm that convicted Lee, along with its racist subtext, is replaced by "that song, which shall fill eternity with its sound . . . *glory to God*" (29). Significantly, a prior text of conviction that equates sin with the "taint" of skin color (or a "corrupt" race) is literally stripped away in Lee's description of her conversion experience:

> That instant, it appeared to me, as if a garment, which had entirely enveloped my whole person, even to my fingers ends, split at the crown of my head, and was stripped away from me passing like a shadow, from my sight—when the glory of God seemed to cover me in its stead. (29)

This unwriting of a racialized Christian pre-text through the reinscription of her black skin as glorified and transfigured is not a whitening of Lee but a reassigning of the meaning of her blackness. Having been "clothed" in God's "salvation," Lee's (still) black skin is transformed from a sinful taint to a sign of God's glory. It has been, in Wheatley's words, "refin'd." And this act of rewriting appears via Lee's performance of her soul's "duty," an expressivity denied her in the Presbyterian service. The manifestation of her conversion through singing, exhorting, confession, and the accompanying body movements (she "leaps" to her feet) convicts the very text by which her conviction transpired. Thus the classic spiritual autobiographical narrative of conversion as proceeding *from* conviction *to* justification is subverted as, for Lee as an African American woman of the nineteenth century, conviction (via racist white "missionary" efforts) and justification (through the first contact with a culturally specific African Christianity) are represented as in tension, a tension that forces a rereading of the original moment of conviction according to the dictates of African cultural and communal worship practices and their attendant ideological constructions. "Arrival" thus refigures the meaning of "departure." Yet, paradoxically, it is the contradictory, back-and-forth impulses which characterize the stage of conviction that render such a rereading (and rewriting) possible. That is, Lee exploits the oscillating and conflicted repetitious structure of subjectivity under conviction, what she calls "merciful[ly] striving" (29), in order to write her own black female subjectivity into the discourse of conversion, even as her subjectivity is produced through these "contrary instincts."[31]

After explaining the method of her conversion "at the very outset of the sermon" and when "the text was barely pronounced" as I have explicated above, Lee quotes the text and the immediate response from "the centre of my heart": "The text was barely pronounced, which was: 'I perceive thy heart is not right in the sight of God' [Acts 8:21], where there appeared to my view, *one* sin; and this was *malice* against one particular individual, who had strove deeply to injure me, which I resented" (29). As quickly as the sin "appear[s]," it is erased through immediate and complete forgiveness. Lee writes, "At this discovery [of sin] I said, *Lord* I forgive *every* creature" (29).

Important for our purposes here, the focus on one particular sin, one particular individual, is characteristic of the style of Lee's structures of repetition. This self-revisionist strategy consistently strives to embody singularity ("that moment," "the day . . . ," "the hour of my deliverance," "my first awakening," "the instant," etc.) only to return to the singular moment, place, individual, and revision it from multiple perspectives within multiple narratives. We have seen how the account of justification forced a return to the account of conviction, rewriting the prior event. This time, the mention of "*one* sin" spirals the narrative backward even further in time to the opening page, where Lee recounts her first "sin" at the age of seven, an act of resistance against her first mistress, Mrs. Sharp:

> Not long after the commencement of my attendance on this lady, she had bid me do something respecting my work, which in a little while after, she asked me if I had done, when I replied, Yes— but this was not true.
> At this point, in my early history, the spirit of God moved in power through my conscience, and told me I was a wretched sinner. (27)

Between the tellings of these two incidents, an important inversion has taken place. In the later scene, the barely preached text convicts— that is, produces "sin" (via recollection)—and leads to immediate forgiveness. In the first instance, however, "sin" is performed, which leads to immediate and revelatory conviction. Having told Mrs. Sharp a sinful lie,[32] Lee immediately feels guilty:

> so great was the impression [of conviction], and so strong were the feelings of guilt, that I promised in my heart that I would not tell another lie.
> But notwithstanding this promise my heart grew harder. (27)

Lee's heart "hardens" toward Mrs. Sharp, yet at this point she continues to represent her lying as a guilt-producing spiritual transgression.

This spiritual guiltiness, however, is revisioned in the later scene when Lee recounts her sin of malice. After her verbal forgiveness of the transgression of others, she experiences complete forgiveness of her own transgressions: "I felt not only the sin of *malice* was pardoned, but all other sins were swept away together" (29). As with the juxtaposition of the conviction/justification narratives in which the taint of sin attached to blackness is stripped away via the representation of the glorified black female body, the ideology of obedience to white superiors is "swept away" here and new meaning assigned to the earlier event. Once again, Lee applies Christian precepts, in this case forgiveness ("forgive us our debts as we forgive our debtors"), in order to rewrite a prior narrative of spiritual deficiency according to social needs and desires. The lie to Mrs. Sharp, now forgiven, appears for what it really was: a simple act of resistance on the part of a seven-year-old who resented her treatment as a domestic servant.

These two bold rewritings of the underlying meanings attached to spiritual/social events and interactions informed and produced by conditions of social identity produced layers of narrative that work against the intent of the traditional Anglo-Christian morphology of conversion.

SPEAKING, SUBJECTIVITY, AND AGENCY

The boundaries of each concrete utterance as a unit of
speech communication are determined by a *change
of speaking subjects*, that is, a change of speakers. . . .
The speaker ends his utterance in order to relinquish
the floor to the other or to make room for the other's
active responsive understanding. The utterance is not
a conventional unit, but a real unit, clearly delimited
by the change of speaking subjects, which ends by
relinquishing the floor to the other as if with a silent
dixi perceived by the listeners (as a sign) that
the speaker has finished.
(M. M. Bakhtin, "The Problem of Speech Genres")

But to return to the subject of my call to preach.
Soon after this, as above related, the Rev. Brother
Williams was to preach at Bethel Church, where I
with others were assembled. He entered the pulpit,
gave out the hymn, which was sung, and then
addressed the throne of grace; took his text, passed
through the exordium, and commenced to expound
it. The text he took is Jonah, 2d. chap. 9th verse,—
"Salvation is of the Lord." But as he proceeded
to explain, he seemed to have lost the spirit; when

> in the same instant, I sprang, as by an altogether
> supernatural impulse, to my feet, when I was aided
> from above to give an exhortation on the very text
> which my brother Williams had taken.
> (*Jarena Lee,* Life and Religious Experience *[1836]*)

I begin this section with excerpts from Bakhtin's description of the "change of speaking subjects" and Jarena Lee's account of her bold interruption of a male clergyman's sermon in her 1836 spiritual autobiography *The Life and Religious Experience of Jarena Lee, A Coloured Lady, Giving an Account of Her Call to Preach the Gospel* because they represent alternative theories of the relationship between the act of speaking and subjectivity. In each case, change is signaled by a "sign" (from the speaker) that prompts a listener to respond. Yet as Bakhtin's implied listener seems poised to wait patiently for some predetermined moment of "closure," Lee, as listener-turned-speaker, assumes the agency to close off Brother Williams's spiritless talk. If, in "relinquishing the floor," Bakhtin's speaker emerges as subject through the shift from the "I" of his initial speech act to the silence that follows his utterance, signified by the "silent *dixi,*" Jarena Lee's subjectivity begins in the space between the "he" of Brother Williams's truncated sermon and the "I" that *springs* into being "in the same instant."

Of course the most obvious reading of such difference is a gendered one. Lee's interruption of Williams is set against the backdrop of black women's challenges to the all-male hierarchy of the African Methodist Episcopal Church, a contestation over black women's role in the church that structures the dynamic of conflict and resolution in Lee's narrative. Moreover, the gendered dimension of Bakhtin's speaker, who gains his subjectivity through the silence that follows his speech, must give way to the African American female's subjectivity, which is produced in the equally gendered "I" of her *spoken* challenge to patriarchal authority. What is less obvious, perhaps, is the cultural difference implicit in Lee's and Bakhtin's theorizing, as the gender difference becomes entwined within the difference between cultural epistemologies: dialogue and call-response.

Modeled on the dialogue as a "classic form" of speech communication (*Speech Genres* 72), Bakhtin's theory of speech genres restores "the active role of the *other*" to discussions of the process of speech communication (70). The boundary between utterances is thus a crucial domain in producing subjectivity, for it is at this moment that the speaker realizes that her/his entire speech act has been dialogized by the presence of other participants in the act of communication. It is only when the speech act becomes bounded, "finalized" as a completed utterance, that the subjectivity of the speaker emerges.[33] Thus the "change of speaking subjects" that is the essence of dialogue produces the subject in the site between speaking (self) and listening (other).

These two conditions of the utterance, the change of speakers and finalization, operate through "the speaker's *speech plan or speech will*" (77) made possible by a common cultural understanding between speaker and listener. This relationship is dialogic; the participation of the other in the sphere of communication dialogizes the utterance from its inception. At the same time, the utterance has the capacity "to determine directly the responsive position of the *other* speaker" (74). With the capacity to "evoke a response" the utterance creates relations between speakers even as it is created by those same relations. The speaker emerges as subject at the point where she/he is almost, but not quite "other," a point signaled by a pause that the speaker "designates and interprets" (74). It is through the concept of the "speech plan or speech will" that Bakhtin hopes to preserve agency. In order to avoid theorizing a subject that is determined *by* the other, Bakhtin must envision a speaker who retains the agency to control (albeit in dialogic fashion) the means by which her/his utterance is bounded.[34]

Two difficulties immediately present themselves within Bakhtin's formulation of speech and subjectivity. First, the cultural specificity of "the dialogue" as a paradigm for speech communication denies the existence of alternative paradigms in other cultural contexts. Second, a related issue, the power relations between speakers, while not incompatible with Bakhtin's theory, remain backgrounded rather than central to his thought.[35] Bahktin himself acknowledges cultural and contextual difference when he writes that the boundary signaled by the change of speaking subjects "varies in nature and acquires different forms in the heterogeneous spheres of human activity and life, depending on the functions of language and on the conditions and situations of communication" (72). Yet this nod toward heterogeneity and cultural difference is formulated as the "extraverbal context" (situation, setting, and "prehistory") of dialogue. From a perspective of Western hegemony, the dialogue is, indeed, the "classic form" of communication (recall, for example, the importance of dialogue in the philosophical writings of Plato). For subordinate groups and subjugated cultures, who have been denied dialogue with those in power and constructed not as cosubjects but as objects of commands and indoctrination, everyday speech communication may take a variety of different forms.[36]

Using African American women's quilting as a theoretical framework for African American women's history, Elsa Barkley Brown points to the cultural practice of "gumbo ya ya" (sometimes spelled "jambalaya"), a principle of language that connotes a polyrhythmic, multivocal style of expression. Brown writes:

> Luisah Teish, in *Jambalaya: The Natural Woman's Book of Personal Charms and Practical Rituals,* describes the practice of *gumbo ya ya,* which has been passed down among the women in her family. When she goes home to New Orleans to visit and is met by her family at the airport, she writes, "Before I can get a good look at my mother's face, people begin arranging themselves in the car. They begin to talk gumbo ya ya, and it goes on for 12 days. . . . Gumbo ya ya is a creole term that means 'Everybody talks at once.'" It is through *gumbo ya ya* that Teish learns everything that has happened in her family and community and she conveys the essential information about herself to the group. To an outsider, *gumbo ya ya* can only sound like chaos. How can anyone be listening to everyone else at once while they are also themselves speaking? But, as Teish describes it, this indeed is possible. In fact, the only time the conversation stops is when someone has asked a member of the group a question to which they do not respond—in other words everyone is hearing themselves and everyone else at once. (12–13)

Here boundaries are blurred yet somehow maintained (notice, for example, that conversation stops when someone fails to answer a question posed to her). Here, speaking/responding, and the resultant subjecthood(s) conferred by speech acts, are multidirectional and simultaneous. There is no clear point designated by the change of speakers to signal the emergence of subjectivity. In fact, "to an outsider," the women talking "gumbo ya ya" appear to be subjectless, not clearly definable, locatable, from any position except from within the cultural discursive circle. Gumbo ya ya represents a closing of the ranks, conferring from within its specific conversational matrix subjecthood that is communal rather than individual. In turn, it renders those outside the speaking circle mere objects, potential disruptions to be guarded against at all cost.

I chose this example because it represents the very point at which a new critical paradigm must emerge. African American women's cultural practices—encoded within the "speech genres" through which they theorize an empowered subjectivity, produced out of and by an overwhelming social "powerlessness"—leave behind texts that demand the centrality of concepts of domination and resistance in any act of analysis which strives to hear them.

In order to read (hear) the scene in which Jarena Lee interrupts the male preacher, we must go to the very margins of Bakhtin's discourse, a marginality that must be (re)positioned with respect to African American women's culture and discourse. In a parenthetical, Bakhtin writes:

(Any pause that is grammatical, calculated, or interpreted is possible only within the speech of a single speaker, i.e., within a single utterance. *Pauses between utterances are, of course, not grammatical but real. Such real pauses—psychological, or prompted by some external circumstance—can also interrupt a single utterance.*) (74)

Bakhtin recognizes interruption as a form of creating boundaries between utterances (as opposed to the speaker's plan or will) as a real sign of power and, traditionally, of domination. In the tradition of black women's struggle to establish and maintain a speaking/writing community, interruption expresses itself as a mode of domination and control that thwarts black women's attempts to connect with each other. (Recall the seven-year correspondence between Phillis Wheatley and her fellow enslaved African American friend, Obour Tanner, discussed in chapter 2).

bell hooks uses the term "talking back" to describe the act of "speaking as an equal to an authority figure" (5). It is not surprising, then, that Jarena Lee's entry into the genre of itinerant public discourse should hinge on a scene of interruption of an-Other's discourse. Black women called to preach in pre-Emancipation America could not wait for those who had power—in this case, free black males—to "relinquish the floor" to them. Their speech acts had to assume a violence as empowering as the violence enacted by the prohibitions against their voices. Lee's account of the interruption of Brother Williams represents nothing short of a hostile takeover, a seizing of the floor in the very face of authority. Subjectivity accrues, here, by virtue of Lee's ability to force a crisis of speaking subjects, a crisis that will eventually bring about a new formula for intersubjective utterance and restructure the means by which community functions and is designated. Lee's speech act is not "a symbolic declaration of war," as James C. Scott describes the opening statement of the "hidden transcript." It results, in fact, in the sanctioning of her call by none other than Reverend Richard Allen, the founder and pastor of Bethel A.M.E. This outcome, however, is not to be read as "co-optation" or an embrace of the status quo. For we must read Lee's speech act as that of one who seeks not to dismantle community but to effect communal change. Interruption in Lee's case does not aim to elect new voice(s) to a position of counterhegemony but seeks to create a heterophonous base for community, one that, ultimately, will do away with the need for hegemonic practices within the boundaries of collective subjectivity.

Rituals of Desire: Spirit, Culture, and Sexuality in the Writings of Rebecca Cox Jackson

TROUBLIN' THE WATERS

Wade in the water,
Wade in the water children,
Wade in the water,
God's gonna trouble the water.
(African American spiritual)

According to Rebecca Cox Jackson, on New Year's Day in 1857 Jarena Lee paid a visit to her home in Philadelphia. Lee was then seventy-three; Jackson was sixty-one.[1] The purpose of the trip was to heal a rupture that had occurred between the two women at least a quarter of a century earlier. As Jackson relates in her journal entry for that date:

> Sister Jarena Lee called to see me, under the influence of a very kind and friendly spirit. She spoke very lovingly, and I found that she was sincere. I was constrained to give God the glory, for when I looked back to the time and times that she was one of my most bitter persecutors, I said in my mind, "Is not this the Lord's doing? Is it not in answer to my prayer?" While I was casting these things in my mind she was saying to me, "Dear Sister, how well thee looks! Thee looks as well as thee used to! It is the Lord's doing! Bless his name!"[2]

Jackson represents this scene in clever call-and-response fashion, centering on the one point of fundamental agreement between the two women: the authority of God.[3] Jackson asks, in her mind, a rhetorical question, "Is not this the Lord's doing?" only to have Lee verbalize the response, "It is the Lord's doing!" Yet this seeming question and answer, appeal and affirmation, mask an important disjuncture: Jackson's unspoken "call" refers to Lee's visit and apparent sincerity; Lee's "response" refers to Jackson's apparent good health. There is the sense here of two women operating in different discursive registers, as will become clearer below. Suffice it to say at this point that harmony and discord coexist in this scene and form the dialectical prism which will govern Jackson's revision of Lee's *Life and Religious Experience* (1836) in her own writings.

Most commentators on Lee's and Jackson's lives and writings mention the two women together, often pointing out similarities in their religious experiences and writing styles.[4] What commentators have failed to examine, however, is the deliberate revision of Lee's 1836 narrative found in Jackson's spiritual writings.[5] William L. Andrews, and others, have long considered Jarena Lee's *Life and Religious Experience* to be paradigmatic of black women's spiritual narratives, yet specific revisionisms in later texts of this genre have gone unexamined. The case of Rebecca Cox Jackson and Jarena Lee represents a dialectic of difference occasioned by the mediation of abstract categories of identity—race, gender, class, sexuality—by very concrete, identifiable differences arising from their investments[6] in competing religious discourses.

Despite obstacles to her ministry throughout her preaching career, Jarena Lee remained connected to the African Methodist Episcopal denomination, though she had serious reservations about the increasing institutionalization of its structures.[7] Rebecca Cox Jackson, on the other hand, was raised in the A.M.E. faith, only to leave the denomination for the more radical communal life and doctrine of the Shakers. Jackson points out repeatedly in her journals that black churches were often the ones "closed" to her during her itinerancy, which began in 1833. While scholars generally interpret this exclusion as a function of Jackson's battle with A.M.E. male authority on the basis of gender alone, Jackson counts a leading black female preacher like Lee among her most powerful detractors. For in the 1830s, Jackson had begun to practice, and preach, celibacy as the only sign of salvation. Even other Holiness believers in sanctification and perfectionism found her teachings too radical. Though Jackson returned to Philadelphia in 1851 after a seven-year stay with the like-minded Shakers, she returned neither to African Methodism nor to the Holiness movement. Rather, she returned as one even more firmly committed to the doctrine of celibacy and determined to proselytize the Philadelphia black community to join in her lifestyle. Indeed, Lee's purported 1857 visit to Jackson would have brought her to the Philadelphia Out-Family that Jackson had established with her black woman protégée, Rebecca Perot, in "the Shaker Way."

In this chapter, I will explore Jackson's revisioning of the "search for community" narrative in Lee's 1836 text in the context of the differences between Shaker and Methodist theology with respect to gender, race, and sexuality. Yet these differences in theology and religious community point to alternative cultural locations as well. Thus I go on to look at the ways in which writing as ritual in Jarena Lee's *Journal*—

which, as I argued in chapter 5, is evidenced by a formulaic structure in the entries that focus on movement and transitions—takes on a different meaning in Jackson's dream visions. And it is here that the term "ritual" becomes tied to culture-specific practices of conjure, as Jackson continuously "marks" her text as ritual space. I look first at her conversion scene, in which biblical imagery of the giving of the Law at Mount Sinai is fused with imagery from Shango, a West African religious cult. From there, I lay the directional markers, which characterize so many of her dream visions and have thus far defied attempts at any meaningful interpretation, alongside the figures of cosmograms found in the Kongo region of Africa and on ritually marked spaces in the nineteenth-century United States.

Let me say at once that I am not trying to play anthropologist; neither am I arguing that Rebecca Cox Jackson was a "conjure woman." I do maintain, however, that the correspondences between these sets of signs cannot be ignored. I believe her conversions to Christianity and Shakerism to be authentic. I also think that in Jackson's time the presence of the traces of African religions/conjure would have been accessible as "folk customs" or beliefs that may not have retained specifically religious meanings. What is most significant in this analysis is how it points us, once again, across the Atlantic, back to the Middle Passage, back to the notion of arrival and desire that structures what I have been calling a diaspora or displaced subjectivity. Indeed, Rebecca Cox Jackson's ritual texts "trouble the waters" of our interpretive frameworks and intellectual assumptions about the relationships among subjectivity, culture, and spirituality.[8]

"GOD'S TRUE PEOPLE ON EARTH"

To return to the entry in Jackson's journal with which we began, several key differences between her religious beliefs and those of Jarena Lee can be discerned in the next paragraphs of the same journal entry:

> When she [Jarena Lee] got up to go, she said, "I do not know as I would do my duty if I should go away without a word of prayer. Sister, is thee willing?" "Well," I said, "it is our order to pray always." She replied, "That is good, too. But our Lord said to his disciples, 'Into whosoever house you enter, if you find it worthy, there leave your blessing.' And I find this house worthy. For I feel that the Spirit of the Lord is here." "Well," said I, "you can kneel, I cannot." "Well, thee can sit still, my dear," she said.
>
> So she sang a few verses and kneeled, and prayed a feeling prayer—and, I believe, a very sincere one. She prayed that the Lord might open the door

for me to preach the Gospel, and also prayed for a blessing on my household.

To my great surprise, when she was done I felt a gift to pray. And Mother blessed me with a weeping Spirit, and with love. When done, I rose and went to her and embraced and kissed her. (262–63)

The differences between Lee and Jackson represent no mere polite disagreement about doctrine and theology but a real clash of ideologies with powerful implications for their theories of identity and subjectivity. The embrace and kiss that end this seemingly harmonious scene barely veil the tension sown by fundamental religious discord. To the end, neither woman relinquishes her evangelical propensity to try to *convert* the other. (Indeed, the embrace and kiss represent the standard Shaker "Gift of Love" ceremony.) Lee prays and kneels out of "duty." Jackson can pray only after receiving a "surprise" gift from Holy Mother Wisdom.[9] For Lee, the commandment to pray is scriptural; for Jackson, it is a continual feature of the Shaker "order." Jackson's refusal to kneel—according to Jean Humez, who edited Jackson's writings—could refer to an arthritic condition or to the fact that she has not yet received a direct order from the Spirit to do so. It can also be interpreted, in this context, as a refusal to kneel to Lee's "God." Jackson's reference to "our order" (the Shakers) summons Lee's response to the word of "our Lord," yet the designation that customarily denotes an all-inclusive Christian brotherhood (or sisterhood) is here cast as a competing sense of community. It is precisely the contestation over definitions of community that is at stake here. It is the notion of community as a contested site that occasions Jackson's revision of Lee's text.

I argued in chapter 5 that the search for community emerged from the shadow of the conversion narrative of Lee's text as both a critique of notions of spiritual transcendence and as the register within which the cultural specificity of African American religiosity becomes encoded. In Lee's narrative of communal longing, the presence of an African American congregation—Bethel African Methodist Episcopal Church in Philadelphia under the leadership of Reverend Richard Allen—and a specific African American style of worship and preaching were the communal matrix for her own individual salvation experience.

Nothing could be further from the experience of Rebecca Cox Jackson, whose story of conversion and community inverts Lee's representational strategy. Jackson is converted in 1830, alone during a fierce thunderstorm (71–72). More important, Jackson states that she developed her practice of celibacy independently of the community of Shakers who would later confirm her beliefs during a visit to the Watervliet, New York, society in 1843. For Jackson, conversion can come only as a gift from God, individually and independently of an affirming and accepting communal structure. As James H. Evans points out in *Spiritual Empowerment in Afro-American Literature*, the A.M.E. church was to provide "a fund for [Jackson's] literary imagination as well as a foil for her emergent self" (58). Thus she recounts her persecution (by the very people that Jarena Lee came to embrace) in a section of her journal entitled "A VISION IN 1831, OF GOD'S TRUE PEOPLE ON EARTH, WHO LIVE IN CHRIST AND CHRIST IN THEM."[10] She writes:

> The Christian Church would be set before me, with all their Bishops and Elders, all living in the works of the first Adam. I saw nobody lived the life I was called to live. I then entreated to the Lord to tell me why it was that I was called to live a life that nobody lived on the earth. Then in answer to my request, "I have a people on earth that live the life that I have called you to live." (137)

Jackson's promise of a community is confirmed in a conversation with no less than *God himself.*

Here Jackson replaces the desire for a racial and cultural community with, in her scheme of things, a higher calling to spiritual fellowship. Shakers were careful to differentiate between "natural" relations and "spiritual" relations. Relations "of the flesh"—which included not only biological blood ties but male/female relations signified by sexual coition, with or without civil or religious sanction—were to be supplanted entirely by spiritual relations owing to the Shaker belief that the millennial church did not lie in the future or in heaven but had already been established *on earth.* Thus "family" yielded to the Shaker "Family" and communal lifestyle. As Henri Desroche writes in *The American Shakers*, Shaker theology required that "man's natural family be dissolved and disappear in the presence of Christ's Family, which in the eternal Kingdom of God is the basis of all social order" (83).

The radicalness of the Shaker Way can scarcely be overstated. Shakers were less concerned with developing a new doctrine or "church," though increasing opposition from non-Shakers in the 1820s and 1830s forced them to codify and defend their beliefs in writing, than they were committed to establishing an entirely new order of human relations, signaled by a new paradigm of relations between men and women: celibacy. Unlike other millennial denominations, Shakers believed that the Advent had already occurred, Christ's Second Coming being embodied in the form of Mother Ann Lee, the founder of the Shakers in America. Following Mother Ann Lee, they distinguished between "generational" relations, accomplished through sexual intercourse and physical birth, and relations of "regeneration," effected through spiritual rebirth.[11] The sign of regeneration was, in fact, celibacy, "the life" that Jackson laments had become her solitary practice at least twelve years before the crucial meeting with the Shakers. The renunciation of sex and the life of the flesh signals an embracing not only of the spirit but of an understanding of a totally new way of carrying out human relationships in the world.

Significantly, opposition to the Shakers in America centered less frequently on the "heresy" of their Four-Part Deity (God, Holy Spirit, Christ, Mother Ann Lee) than on the sense that the doctrine of celibacy threatened the ideology of the family, gender roles, and heterosexual relations, all considered "natural" by nineteenth-century standards: "People were outraged by what they thought of as the popery of celibacy, which threatened to break up families. But they were even more incensed at the idea of the full equality of women with men, which clearly struck at the roots of family and society, neither of which recognized anything approaching a legal autonomy of women" (Whitson 15). While the Shakers, and other dissenting sects, were often accused of a reactionary Catholicism, it is important to understand the difference between Shaker celibacy and pre-Reformation monasticism. Celibacy in the Shaker sense was not based on the medieval male fear of "contamination" by women, nor were the sect's celibate women forced into a paradigm of "chastity" as a prerequisite of "true womanhood." Rather, it constituted an "ascetic feminism" (Desroche); after all, Christ had returned, according to Shaker accounts, in the form of a woman. Most important, the restructuring of male-female sexual relations was based on the Shaker interpretation of *social* relations of power and dominance. As a Shaker writer explains "the meaning of the curse on Eve at the Fall" in one of the sect's own documents written in 1823,

> Thus the woman is not only subjected to the pains and sorrows of childbirth, but even in her conception she becomes subject to the libidinous passions of her husband. This slavish subjection is often carried to such a shocking extent, that many females have suffered an unnatural and premature death, in consequence of the unseasonable and excessive indulgence of this passion in man. This may indeed be a willing subjection on the part of the woman, and her passions may be even more debased than his; but whether her subjection be willing or unwilling, still this does not alter its servile nature, as respects the man's power of enforcing it, so long as he possesses that power, as her husband. (Qtd. in Humez, *Gifts of Power* [appendix] 332)

In her reading of Jackson's writings in *In Search of Our Mothers' Gardens*, Alice Walker responds to Jean Humez's claim that "perhaps had [Jackson] been born in the modern age, she would have been an open lesbian." After leaving the A.M.E. denomination, where she served for a time as an itinerant minister like Jarena Lee and others, Jackson met Rebecca Perot, and the two together moved to Watervliet to join the

Shaker Family. Rebecca Cox Jackson and Rebecca Perot lived together for over thirty-one years, the rest of Jackson's life, and Perot was often referred to as "Rebecca Jackson, Junior." Walker concludes that "there is nothing in these writings that seems to make Jackson [a lesbian]" (80); however, the absence of any direct evidence in this case is inconclusive. Among Shaker circles, such disregard for gender conventions— and even "gender switching" in nominatives like the "junior" applied to Rebecca Perot—within the context of Shaker theology, which so divorced material and spiritual, may not have raised an eyebrow. What we do know for certain is that Jackson embraced openly the doctrine of celibacy, and her choice of an openly unconventional, even liminal, sexuality brought her severe censure and persecution from the African American community. In the context of Lee and Jackson, such a doctrine (of celibacy) and worldview could be nothing but threatening to a denomination like the A.M.E Church, whose definition of black community relations and racial equality was predicated on the establishment of black men as heads of family, church, and community.

Given the Shaker redefinition of social relations into a duality of "natural" and "spiritual," a dualism that the significance of Jackson's presence in their community would come to problematize, the question becomes, what happens to race in such a formulation? Relations of blood and body are to be literally transcended in favor of spiritual connections. By extension, I would argue, race as it is biologically inscribed in skin color is categorically jettisoned. Jackson later experienced a wrenching conflict that left her torn between her desire to remain with the Shaker community and an equally strong desire to accomplish "a great work among my people," the free black community of Philadelphia. In this early writing, however, she is to know "her people" not by the color of their skin or even by their cultural expressive forms, but by the sign of celibacy.

In Lee's text, the search for religious community unfolds as a rapid series of interlocking, causally related events: a visit to Bethel, the hearing of Richard Allen's sermon, her decision to join the congregation "on trial," and her full religious conversion at a camp meeting. Importantly, Lee's sense of religious community is evidenced in her text by the *sounds* of black religious worship. By contrast, Jackson recognizes her religious community through the sense of *sight*. Early conversion and the religious practice of celibacy are thus followed by God's spoken promise of "a people" and then by a *vision* of that community presented to her "spiritual eyes":

> I saw in the distance flocks of kid, white as snow, on beautiful green grass. They laid close to the ground. Their forefeet were crossed and their chin rested on their forefeet. They were many miles apart. They all looked like

one kid yet I seen them distinct. And when I saw them, it was said to me, "These are my people. These live the life I have called you to live. And if you are faithful, I will bring you to see them." (137)

Usually, Jackson's dream visions are rather opaque and resist easy interpretation. In this case, however, uncharacteristically, the meaning is startling clear. The scene takes Jackson away from her urban Philadelphia to a pastoral setting, complete with "beautiful green grass." Indeed, the Shakers set up camp in the upstate New York "wilderness." The crossed forefeet of the kids represent the taking of the cross, which in Shaker terminology means the renouncing of the flesh. Whiteness here refers to spiritual purity rather than skin color, while the bowed kids represent humility. Jackson's own interpretation of this vision states that the kids' being "close to the ground" is the sign of "the state of the spirit of humiliation that they were called to live in daily, in order to live without sin" (138). The appearance of the flock as "one kid" yet "distinct" is a perfect description of the Shaker communal lifestyle. As Jackson would later describe her impressions of them on her first visit to Watervliet, "They all took their seats. They all set alike. They all were dressed alike. They all looked alike" (139). The nineteen Shaker communes at the time of Jackson's writing were, indeed, "many miles apart." More to the point, Jackson offers this peaceful pastoral scene as a stark contrast to the haughtiness of organized churches: "And I saw the state of the churches and their destruction, that they would all come down . . . and I testified against the churches" (137).

Appropriately, the next incident in Jackson's writing is entitled "MY FIRST VISIT TO NEW YORK AND TO SEE THE SHAKERS." Jackson claims to have known nothing of the Shakers: "I never heard that name but once, when I was young, and had only heard the name—I knowed not what it meant" (138). She then prays to God, "'If these be my people, make it known to me'" (138). Interestingly, the first person Jackson sees at the Shaker village is neither black nor female: "I saw an aged man in the front of the building. My spirit ran to him and embraced him in my arms as a father. I loved him as I loved nobody on earth. And it was said to me, 'These are my people'" (139). The Shaker demeanor and, significantly, *silent* style of worship seems, to Jackson, a perfect match for her own spiritual needs:

> They all seemed to look as if they were looking into the spiritual world. For the first time I saw a people sitting and looking like people that had come into a place prepared for the solemn worship of the true and living God, who is a Spirit and who will be worshipped in spirit and in truth. This people looked as though they were not of this world, but as if they were living to live forever.
>
> Here I saw why it was that I was moved upon always, when I went to

[Methodist class] meeting, to get right up and come out as soon as the
service was delivered, so that nobody could speak to me. And if they did, it
always wounded my spirit. I felt that we should always go to meeting in
prayer, and then go and kneel down in prayer and return thanks to God for
the blessed privilege. And here I was confirmed. (139)

Jackson finds the Shaker dance "very strange" (139) yet remains convinced by the voice that designated these her "people." After the service,
Jackson comes into possession of a book of Shaker writings delivered by a
man who was directed "by the Spirit" to give it to her. Told by the same
spirit to "open the book," Jackson receives the last bit of confirmation
she would need: "I opened on a part of my own experience. I opened at a
passage that condemned the works of the flesh in the regeneration, as it
was shown to me from heaven, and which no mortal had ever told me."
Jackson makes clear that this conjunction between her own spiritual practice and that of the Shakers means a redefinition of community:

I had suffered all manner of persecution and had kept the faith and daily
did the work that God required of me, though my only brother whom I
loved as my own soul turned against me. I chose rather to suffer at any time
than to offend him—but when I saw God, heard his voice, and understood
what his will was concerning me, I lost sight of my brother, husband, and
all of my people by nature, for I would not displease God to gratify my self
in anything, no, nor any other person on earth. Therefore the world, the
flesh, and the devil were all against me, and I stood alone in the earth. And
of the people, there were none with me even as there were none with Christ
when He stood in the Judgment. (42, my emphasis)

From what began as a search for religious community, Jackson seems
to have arrived at a place of ultimate isolation and radical individualism.
That is, her subjectivity comes into focus through others' being
"against" her. Yet this passage references her apparent isolation as the
point of entry for a specific connection to divinity, a God whom she sees,
hears, and understands. And it is within an exploration of Jackson's
revelatory connection with God, through her dense and mystifying
dreams and visions, that we uncover yet another layer of cultural practice—one that, ironically, may take us back to the inception of African
American religious practice, as the traces of neo-African conceptions of
humanity and divinity inhere in Jackson's use of the term "spirit."

SPIRIT AND CULTURE

In the introduction of *Gifts of Power*, editor Jean McMahon Humez
urges caution to the "modern reader" who would attempt to interpret

the meaning of Jackson's accounts of dreams and visionary experience "in historical context" (47). She writes:

> From the point of view of the modern reader, unfamiliar with Jackson's traditional sources, some of the most memorable items in her visionary vocabulary are among the most mysterious. In most of her dream accounts, for example, Jackson carefully locates the scene and describes movements by their geographical orientation. . . . Why the points of the compass are so essential in setting the scene in dreams we can only guess—is she thinking of the arms of a cross, the twelve gates of the City, the four winds of the earth? Her insistence on specifying directionality has the quality of ritual—nothing done for sacred reasons can be omitted in the performance. But what ritual? Is it part of a private mental world or part of a once public, though now obscure, cultural inheritance? (47–48)

What began as Humez's advocacy of a critical position of noninterpretation—of reverence for the unfamiliarity and mystery of "sacred literature" (47)—ends with a series of questions that suggest frustration. The back-and-forth movement of assertion and interrogation ("we can only guess"—"is she thinking of . . . ?"; "the quality of ritual"—"But what ritual?") stages a critical posture of talking to oneself that is entirely self-reflexive. That is, the series of questions pose an interrogation not so much of Jackson's writings as of Humez's epistemological boundaries. The reason for the interpretative difficulty is not only temporal/ historical, the function of being a "modern reader," but cultural as well. Humez's invocations of "the points of the compass" and "geography" betray a privileging of Western concerns for mapping, navigation, and ultimately conquest.[12] Having (mis)named the terms of Jackson's self-location, Humez encounters in the dreams and visions a mystery of essential Otherness. Nevertheless, her observation of the ritual nature of Jackson's visionary accounts, performed and reperformed in her texts, offers a way into a fuller discussion of the "traditional sources" and "cultural inheritance" behind Jackson's visionary writings. As Humez points out, an A.M.E. Church upbringing would have imparted to Jackson "a repertoire of visionary conventions" that are part of nineteenth-century African American oral culture. And the performativity of early black religious culture in particular meant that "much of the common vocabulary of dream symbol and visionary image would never have been written down at all" (47).

It is here, however, that the "vocabulary" and "conventions" of African American Christianity must come under closer scrutiny. As Charles Joyner writes, "the African American Christianity that developed [in America] was neither a dark version of the Christianity preached by slaveholders nor a continuation of African religion dis-

guised as Christianity" (19). Of the African American practice of conjure he writes,

> African cosmology maintained a subterranean existence outside of and in-
> imical to African-American Christianity. This element of slave religions
> continues to be *largely unknown and unknowable*. Documentation of voo-
> doo, or hoodoo (as African conjuration was called in the New World) is
> inevitably scanty, as such magical shamanism was practiced clandestinely.
> Still, sufficient evidence remains to testify to the existence of an under-
> ground stream of magical shamanism, not only throughout the slavery pe-
> riod, but long beyond. (324, my emphasis)[13]

Indeed, folklorist Zora Neale Hurston reported in 1934 in *Mules and
Men* that

> Hoodoo, or Voodoo, as pronounced by whites, is burning with a flame in
> America, with all the intensity of a suppressed religion. . . . It adapts itself
> like Christianity to its locale, reclaiming some of its borrowed characteris-
> tics to itself. Such as fire-worship as signified in the Christian church by the
> altar and candles. And the belief in the power of water to sanctify as in
> baptism.
>   Belief in magic is older than words. *So nobody knows* how it started. (193,
> my emphasis)

Hurston's statement is at once an argument for continuities of African
religious practices in the context of the New World as Hoodoo "adapts
itself . . . to its locale, reclaiming some of its borrowed characteristics to
itself," and an argument against any particular claims of origins—"so
nobody knows how it started" (103). Again we find ourselves face to
face with elements that displace Western regimes of knowledge, but
without offering, in return, a fully knowable alternative. In other words,
we find ourselves confronted, once again, with the positionality of diaspora subjectivity.

While it is outside the scope of this chapter to recount a history of
conjure in America or to mediate the controversies surrounding African
"survivals" and "syncretisms,"[14] I do intend to point to a possible direction future scholarship on Jackson—indeed, pre-Emancipation literature in general—may desire to take. It is my contention that the religious practice of conjure offers an alternative interpretive possibility for
the reading of Jackson's dreams and visions, although I make no claims
as to how Jackson came by conjurational signs, or about the meanings
she would have assigned to them. Moreover, I argue that Jackson is not
simply encoding certain elements and symbols of ritual into her visionary accounts, but that she is, in many ways, *performing ritual* within the
space of the text itself. Jackson's purpose in the accounts of her dream

visions is no less than to *embody* religious ritual within her narrative. This is why the visionary sequences differ so profoundly in her writings from the straight autobiographical narrative that they often interrupt or, more accurately, disrupt. They are, as Humez puts it, "the most memorable"; but beyond that, their very purpose in the text is to disrupt the reader's consciousness, to denaturalize and thus expand our notions of time and space,[15] as she performs literal and figurative stagings of "moving between worlds" (Holloway). If celibacy serves as a sign of liminal sexuality in Jackson's texts, similarly conjure would point to a liminal spirituality, one that frustrates, by design, our desire to fix or map, with certainty, textual signs onto either geographical space or interpretive grids.

"HE CALLS ME BY THE LIGHTNING"[16]

Jackson's journal opens with an account of her conversion during a fierce thunderstorm, a scene that lends itself to an alternative interpretive strategy. I quote the first paragraph in its entirety:

> In the year of 1830, July, I was wakened by Thunder and lightning at the break of day and the bed which had been my resting place in time of Thunder for five years was now taking away. About five years ago I was affected by Thunder and always after in time of Thunder and lightning I would have to go to bed because it made me so sick. Now my only place of rest is taking away and I rose up and walked the floor back and forth wringing my hands and crying under great fear. I heard it said to me, "this day thy soul is required of thee," and all my sins from my childhood rushed into my mind like an over swelling tide, and I expected every clap of thunder to launch my soul at the bar of God with all my sins that I had ever done. I have no language to declare my feelings.[17]

In *Shaker Spiritual Narrative*, Diane Sasson points out that "such imagery [of thunder and lightning] is unusual in Shaker testimony, autobiography, or song, but it frequently appears in black conversion narratives and black spirituals" (162).[18] She then goes on to interpret the scene in light of Old Testament uses of storms, clouds, winds, thunder, and lightning as images of God's manifest power. The Exodus account reads:

> And it came to pass on the third day in the morning, that there were thunders and lightnings, and a thick cloud upon the mount, and the voice of the trumpet exceedingly loud; so that all the people that was in the camp trembled. . . . And Mount Sinai was altogether on a smoke, because the Lord descended upon it in fire; and the smoke thereof ascended as the

smoke of a furnace, and the whole mountain quaked greatly. (Exod. 19:16, 18)

Jackson is "wakened by Thunder and lightning at the break of day" (71), a storm recalling the beginning of this biblical passage. Moreover, as Sasson explains, the thunderstorm refers to Yahweh, the God of Mount Sinai who called the formerly enslaved Hebrews "out of Egypt." Later in her text, Jackson twice mentions being called "out of Egypt."[19]

Clearly the Exodus story served as a kind of Ur-narrative in much early African American folk and religious practice.[20] Yet important elements of this dramatic opening conversion scene fall outside biblical writing. Theophus Smith uses the term "conjuring culture" to describe "the enduring cultural intention" of black American encounters with the Bible. Zora Neale Hurston puts it more directly when she writes in *Mules and Men* that the Bible was "the great conjure book in the world" (280). In other words, though the language and images may appear to be from the Bible, the ritual context points to various slippages in the signification that we would want to stabilize under the sign "biblical." The difference emerges when we consider that the stasis of the storm in Exodus contrasts sharply with Jackson's bold gesture of *letting the lightning into her house*. Indeed, the function of the display of thunder and lightning on Mount Sinai is precisely to draw and enforce a boundary between Yahweh and the people, between the human and the divine (Exod. 20:12, 18). And that sense of boundary or barrier, here understood as a natural phenomenon, which I will explicate below, is nowhere present in Jackson's account.

Having kneeled before God in the humility that characterizes Christian conviction of sin, Jackson writes: "My spirit was light, my heart was filled with love for God and all mankind. And the Lightning, which was a moment ago the messenger of death, was now the messenger of peace, joy, and consolation. And I rose from my knees, ran down the stairs, opened the door to *let the lightning in the house*, for it was like sheets of glory to my soul" (72) and "I opened all the windows in the house *to let the lightning in* for it was like streams of bright glory to my soul" (72). Sasson writes that with this gesture after her conversion "Jackson opens the doors of the house to let the lightning in, welcoming God's spirit into her soul. While thunder represents God's judgment, lightning signifies His grace" (162). Humez agrees that the moment of conversion is signaled by the moment "her phobia vanished" and Jackson "was suddenly able to rejoice in the presence and Lightning. Then and thereafter she regarded it as a welcome messenger from the divine, an instructive outpouring of God's energy" (*Gifts of Power* 15).

The question that remains is, why? Clearly Jackson's grafting of a New Testament morphology of conversion onto the Old Testament narrative of Exodus would lead to modifications in the basic story line. Yet some concept of the relationships among the natural, spiritual, and physical is operating here that goes beyond Christian understanding of an individual's "conversion." Jackson draws connections among her inner soul, natural elements, and her body's movements as the point of convergence: "I . . . walked the floor back and forth wringing my hands and crying under great fear" (71). And it is the kneeling of her body, the repositioning of her physical self in space—"I kneeled at the head of the garret stairs . . . down I kneeled" (72)—that quiets and "stills" the storm.

Layered upon imagery of Christian conversion and Mosaic lawgiving are elements suggesting the Yoruba god Shango. The mythic third king of Yoruba, Shango is the thunder god whose consort, Oya, is the whirlwind.[21] He is represented by the lightning bolt and in Oyo poetry "with flashing images" (Thompson 85). In ritual invocation of Shango, a masked priest "perambulate[s] the palace walls" and "gestures to heaven and then to earth, to heaven and earth again, and moves onto the next point of blessing" (Thompson 85). This establishes a ritual link between the worlds of heaven and earth as manifested in the presence of the ritual priest. Jackson points to a similar sense of convergence when she writes, "All this time it was a thundering and lightning as the heavens and earth were acoming together—so it seemed to me at the time" (71).

The question immediately arises as to how Jackson would have had access to any of this mythos within pre-Emancipation Philadelphia. Interestingly, William D. Piersen, in his history of blacks in colonial New England, found that "[i]n New England, black servants were taught as children that thunder was God's voice. . . . Such ideas would have seemed familiar enough to Africans acquainted with Shango, the Yoruba Thunder God who targeted adulterers, liars, and thieves for destruction" (79). Piersen's identification of the symbology of this African religious practice in the pre-Emancipation North is extremely important, part of the historical and geographical displacements I argued for in chapter 1.

Underlying much of this syncretism are conceptualizations of humanity, divinity, and their interrelation that differ from conventional Euramerican Protestant theology. To illustrate this and the significance it has for the reading of Jackson's conversion scene, I quote Robert Farris Thompson's version of the Shango myth in its entirety:

Once upon a time, as myth would have it, Shango was recklessly experimenting with a leaf that had the power to bring down lightning from the

skies and inadvertently caused the roof of the palace of Oyo to be set afire
with lightning. In the blaze his wife and children were killed. Half crazed
with grief and guilt, Shango went to a spot outside his royal capital and
hanged himself from the branches of an ayan tree. He then suffered the
consequences of playing arrogantly with God's fire, *and became lightning
itself. Like Eshu at the Cuban crossroads, in the lightning bolt Shango met
himself. He became an eternal moral presence*, rumbling in the clouds, outraged by impure human acts, targeting the homes of adulterers, liars and
thieves for destruction. (Thompson 85, my emphasis)

As "a tale of transformation of lightning into moral action" (Thompson
85), that of the mythical Shango embraces the concept of "conversion"
on a number of levels. First, unlike the remote thunder and lightning
announcing in the Old Testament the presence of Yahweh—God contacts people only through Moses and the tablets of Law—lightning in
the Shango myth is immediate and immanent. The result of Yahweh's
mediation—the Law—calls into being the *fact* of sin and transgression;
that is, creates the very notion of sin in the bringing of the Law. As I
mentioned earlier, it serves not only to mediate but to *separate* human
and divine:

> And Thou shalt set bounds unto the people round about, saying, Take
> heed to yourselves, *that ye go not up into the Mount, or touch the borders of
> it:* whosoever toucheth the Mount shall be surely put to death. (Exod.
> 20:12)

> And all the people saw the thunderings, and the lightenings, and the noise
> of the trumpet, and the mountain smoking: *and when the people saw it, they
> removed and stood afar off.* (Exod. 20:18)

By contrast, Shango's transgression does not come about as the result of
a legal text but is the consequence of his "bring[ing] down lightning
from the skies." Human in the role of the divine, appropriating divine
power, he recklessly produces the consequences of death and destruction. Again, it is not Shango's drawing near to God or transgressing
(physically) a boundary line set between human and divine, but it is his
actual misuse of a natural power (use of a supernatural power) that
brings about the unintended results. Shango's death is the end of a
chain of reactions (unlike the immediate death promised by Yahweh to
anyone who "touches the Mount"), an entire narrative that theorizes
the relationships among the human, the divine, and natural phenomena.

Similarly, while the sign remains unchanged throughout the Old Testament account, in the Shango myth, there is a transformation of the
lightning itself from agent of destruction to a sign of moral retribution.

Yet it is the human interaction with the natural phenomenon as sign that causes the change in its meaning. Shango becomes the lightning. Human hubris leads to death and destruction, which leads to self-destruction, which leads to the "human" self's resurrection or transformation into a natural force. Shango's metamorphosis changes (corrects, if you will) the "self" from human to natural and, most important, imbues nature with the character of the human who is capable of learning—indeed, has learned—right from wrong, or at least responsibility from recklessness. Nature can thus be imbued with morality and can serve humanity by transforming society for the better. Nature has lost its arbitrariness with the losing of Shango's human life.

Just as Shango dies (kills himself) only to be reborn *as* lightning, Jackson "dies" metaphorically to be reborn in her narrative: "I felt as though my soul had come into the chamber letting the lightning into the house." Sasson is correct in equating the "house" in this case with Jackson's soul. Later in her writings, Jackson writes of an out-of-body experience in these terms: "Now when my spirit left my body I was sensible of it as I would be now to go out of this house and come in again. . . . I found my body was no more than a chain to me, or any other piece of thing" (112). But in an occurrence that goes beyond a New Testament, Christian sense of accepting Christ into one's soul, lightning, once an external, terrifying force, actually takes possession of Jackson. In fact, she actually *becomes* lightning as she takes on its characteristics in her movements, her supernatural abilities, and the role of moral monitor in her community.

Jackson's behavior after the conversion-possession scene demonstrates many of the characteristics of the Shango possession-devotee. Almost immediately after her conversion, problems begin with her husband Samuel. In the very first scene of conflict, Jackson states, "My husband's bitterness blighted the spirit that was upon me, and I closed my eyes, went by him *like a flash*, and a double portion of the spirit came upon me" (77, my emphasis). The scene continues and the images of fire become more central to Jackson's manifestation of spiritual power:

> My husband went down to the cellar, got wood, made a fire, left the door open, put the coffee pot on top of the stove. So in my march appraising of God, I went from the cellar door to the stove and when I moved to get to the stove I would lay my hands on the stove and then turn to the cellar with my eyes shut all the while. These toe things caused my husband to believe it was more than nature. He expected every time I laid my hands on the stove to see the skin come off on the stove, and when I went to the cellar door, to see me fall down the cellar. He said it seemed as though I was

turned right around. Sometimes I went to the cellar leaping, sometimes in a swift march, and often on the very sill, and the coffee aboiling on the top while my hands were in the stove. (77)

THE RITUAL TEXT

> Many symbolic ritual acts are not arbitrary signs,
> like words or salutes; they are acts that draw their
> meaning from the nonritual significance of
> relevantly similar performances. What makes
> them symbolic is the recognition by the agents
> that these acts in ritual contexts do not work in
> the standard way. The spirit comes not because
> we have given it some money but because we
> have done something that shows respect.
> (*Kwame Anthony Appiah,* In My Father's House)

When I refer to Jackson's spiritual narrative as a ritual performance, I mean more than the ritual of writing one's spiritual experience. Recall the discussion in chapter 5 where I argued that the repetitious nature of Jarena Lee's *Journal* be understood as ritualized writing in which the formulaic entries were designed to emphasize not the events of the narrative but the transitions between them. By contrast, in the dream visions of Rebecca Cox Jackson's spiritual journals, to which I will turn now, Jackson actually "marks" the text as ritual space. Commentators on the visions have noted Jackson's use of directional markers throughout her dreams and visions, often trying to work out their logic in terms of regional geographical mappings of North and South, free states and slave states, and the like. Such "earthly" geographical mappings, however, fail to offer a consistent ground for interpretation.

Some of Jackson's dream visions, like "The Vision of Eliza Smith's Death," are echoed in other African American writing: "Her bed lay east and west, the head in the east. It laid on the north side of the room. She looked pale" (80). This scene resonates for readers of Hurston with Hurston's memory of her mother's death, with the bed facing east, in her autobiography *Dust Tracks on a Road*, a scene she fictionalized in her first novel, *Jonah's Gourd Vine*. These passages reflect an African American folk belief that the soul, upon death, would go east back to Africa, and thus the importance of having the deathbed face east.[22]

Other visions are more complicated. In fact, almost every account of a dream or vision in Jackson's writings begins with meticulously detailed pointing to several, and often all four, compass directions. At the risk of minimizing the pervasiveness of this textual feature, I will cite but three examples (in each case, the emphasis is mine):

In "A Dream of Slaughter" (1831):

> In a night or two after I had this dream, I also dreamed I was in a house, *entered in at the south door*. I heard a footstep quick behind me and looked at the *east window* and saw a man coming. I run upstairs, told the child's nurse a robber was in the house. She fled. I went to *the east window, then to the west*, to jump out. I found in so doing I should kill myself, so I sat down on a chair *by the west window with my face to the north*. (94)

> On the 15th of February, 1843, I had this vision. I thought I went into a house that *stood in the east*. I went in *at the west door* and I saw a table set in an *east room of the house*. The people ate and rose up, and were all standing around the table in a solemn position, all alooking down to the floor. *The table stood north and south*. (176)

And in "Vision of the Three Books Explained" (June 4, 1864):

> I was told that I should be instructed in them when they were revealed. The book that lay on the table at the *north side of the room*, I was told I should be instructed in it from Genesis to Revelations. My guide then led me to the book that lay on the table at the *west side*, and said, "Yea, thou shalt be instructed from the beginning to the end of time." He then led me to the book that lay on the table on the *east side* of the room. (289)

I have deliberately picked visions from different times in Jackson's life to show that this ritual marking persisted throughout her life.

Robert Farris Thompson in *Flash of the Spirit* has written extensively on the Kongo cosmogram as a representation of "four moments of the sun," depicting cycles of the human life span—birth, prime, death, and afterlife—and simultaneously dividing the worlds of spirit and matter, the living and the dead. I direct the interested reader to his work. What is significant for our purposes is that the cosmograms as associated with African American conjure practices were used as a way of marking ritual space for encounters with the spirit world. The figures were often marked—almost always with white chalk—on the bottoms of kettles or pots (spirits are often associated with water, and so vessels or containers were important in ritual).

Kenneth Brown, a historical archaeologist, reports on an excavation of a slave site in Mississippi in which archaeologists unearthed, among other things, a "high-ranking cabin" of the local conjurer from the nineteenth century.[23] A significant feature of the site was the placement at the four compass points of important objects that "appear to have functioned within a single context—that of a large cosmogram, and the resulting *definition of ritual space*" (111). Brown suggests further that "the curer had sanctified the floor space of the cabin for its use within the ritual performance of curing and/or conjuring. As Thompson notes, such rituals take place within *space marked out with a cross oriented to the compass directions*" (114). Obviously I cannot prove that Jackson had cosmograms in mind while she was writing her dreams and visions, but I do maintain that the compulsion with which she marks these visions in this way, usually at the very beginning of the vision, performs a ritual mapping of textual space as a space for the presence of spirit. Maria Franklin has written convincingly of "protective symbolism," which she defines as "the means by which people actively sought to protect themselves, their belongings, family, etc. by sending culturally-defined signals to others of their intention to safeguard."[24] Truly through the performance of this ritual textuality Jackson has managed simultaneously to reveal and to safeguard her private encounters with the spirit.

Performing Community: Culture, Community, and African American Subjectivity before Emancipation

RACE, CULTURE, AND COMMUNITY

The African American community has never been
monolithic. Gender, national identity, color,
leadership, and the relationships between free
blacks and slaves or with various immigrant
groups have all been issues of disagreement. Here
also is a people who, despite their differences,
were bound by a shared oppression and the
power of a collective history. At crucial times, at
points of crisis, this diverse people united to
support common goals. It was not necessary
that they walk in lockstep in order to form a
community of common direction. There were
many black experiences, yet one overwhelmingly
common black history.
(*James Oliver Horton*, Free People of Color)

James Oliver Horton's statement of the dialogical relationship between
experience and history—"many black experiences . . . one overwhelmingly common black history"—answers a question as crucial to the study
of African American identity and culture as it is unspoken. The traditional assumption has been that African American culture simply reflects
or is produced by a community formed through the historical crisis process outlined by Horton. Yet African American cultural production simply cannot be linked exclusively to crisis-producing events, though such
events often have had an impact on the forms of such cultural practices.

In discussing the linkages among history, African American culture,
and community, scholars proceed from assumptions about the interrelationship of race, culture, and community that have gone unexamined.
That is, the presence of black culture is seen as evidence of and as an
index to the presence of a collective known as "black" people. I suggest

that in the case of decendants of Africans enslaved in the United States, the relationship between culture and what I will call "peoplehood" or community rather than "race" is more complex. While this chapter is not meant to be definitive, I do want to present challenges to and open up discussion around some of the most fundamental assumptions underlying considerations of African American cultural production, with specific implications for the study of African American culture and literature of the pre-Emancipation period. Then, I will focus on one particular cultural form that has become practically synonymous with early black culture—African American spirituals.

My argument is this: the forms and practices we designate African American culture are active and constitutive of African American community rather than passive indicators of race/group identity. Seen in this light, Judith Butler's conceptualization of gender as "performance" is particularly helpful. Yet while pre-Emancipation African Americans cannot be said to be performing "race" (read: "blackness") for reasons that will become clear below, we can say that they are *performing community*, engaging in and (re)producing cultural forms and practices whose central function is community building and the production of the terms by which African Americans come to identify themselves as "a people."[1]

Indeed, it is reflection on the function of early African cultural forms and practices that leads me to the above conclusion. The classic debate between Melville Herskovits and E. Franklin Frazier over African cultural "survivals" has already been reframed by scholars such as Veve A. Clark and Mechal Sobel in terms of cultural "transformation" and "syncretism."[2] Yet even these approaches deal with the fact of cultural forms, their givenness, rather than their function. By function, I mean something akin to the dialectic between intention and effect, a dialectic that is itself dialogically related to its own historical reproduction over generations of repetitions and performances. As anthropologist Sherry Ortner writes in *Making Gender*, "intention plays a complex role in the process [of culture "making"] for while intention is central to what the actor seeks to accomplish . . . its relationship to the outcome is often quite oblique" (2). In other words, given the unique historical pressures and the metacrisis of Middle Passage and displacement that I have sketched out in this book, what was "African American culture" for? What was its function? What was it designed to do, and for whom? Thus to speak of African American culture in terms of its functionality is to recast the question of survivals, transformations, and syncretism to ask: How is it that people from a multiplicity of African tribal, national, religious, linguistic, "racial," and, indeed, cultural collective affiliations came to be viewed—and more important for my purposes, *came to view themselves—*

as a community in the late eighteenth and early nineteenth centuries in America?

In framing the question this way I have, of course, already partially suggested an answer. For to introduce a oneness-out-of-manyness theme is to make claims about origin and destination, cause and effect.[3] Yet even these terms must shift for me as they are made historically and geographically accountable. It is, therefore, a series of actual as well as theoretical departures and arrivals that work to destabilize the epistemological ground of many/one, origin/destination. Indeed, not only is such a ground destablized, it more accurately remains in suspension within a lexical and semantic field described by Hortense Spillers as "oceanic."[4]

Victor Anderson uses the term "ontological" to describe "the blackness that whiteness created," whiteness itself created by what he calls "the cult of European genius"(13). The black response, however, has been to form "*the cult of black heroic genius,*" which refers to "the exceptional, sometimes essentialized cultural qualities that positively represent the racial group in the action of at least one of the group's members" (13). The antidote for ontological blackness, for Anderson, ia "postmodern blackness," a term he takes from bell hooks: "postmodern blackness recognizes the permanency of race as an effective category in identity formation. However, it also recognizes that *black identities are continually being reconstituted*" (11, my emphasis). Central to Anderson's counterproject is the connection between ontological blackness and religion. "Racial identity is not total," he writes, "although it is always present. From a religious point of view, when race is made total, then ontological blackness is idolatrous, approaching racial henotheism" (15). Anderson's warning against both worshiping the idol of race and staging displays of "black heroic genius" is well taken. What I find particularly helpful, however, is his acute observation that "racial identity is not total."

Similarly, Kenneth Kusmer in his framework for describing black urban life draws distinctions among three forces: *external,* including "white attitudes toward blacks and how these attitudes were expressed"; *internal,* "black individual and institutional responses to the restrictions, threats, or violence imposed by external forces"; and *structural,* "factors associated with the geographical location of the black community and the wider society in which it is located" (qtd. in Horton 14). Using this grid, I suggest that African Americans, externally designated a distinct and inferior race by a narrow and self-interested White Gaze during the period under discussion, produced an African American culture constituted by a set of internal black responses to white oppression. What remains to be accounted for is the means by which the boundary between external and internal was produced and maintained by African Americans themselves. I would argue that such a boundary was precisely *structural*, as African Americans created a "geographical location" *in language* that mediated the bar splitting the binaries of insider/outsider, self/other. As Charles Long reminds us,

> the black community in America is a landless people. Unlike the American Indian, the land was not taken from him, and unlike the black Africans in South Africa, or Rhodesia, his land is not occupied by groups whom he considers aliens. His image of the land points to the religious meaning of land even in the absence of these forms of authentication. It thus emerges as an image which is always invested with historical and religious possibilities.[5]

This use of language and cultural production as the site for the creation of communal space goes beyond Benedict Anderson's "imagined community."[6] For African Americans resisted not only social and legal spatial restrictions but what they astutely perceived to be a *restrictive subjectivity*. That is, the process of racialization, upon New World arrival, monologized disparate and complex pre-Departure collective identities, blackened and, in theory, unified African peoples by encouraging them to see themselves in terms that they would never have chosen for themselves. Thus "black," "slave," "Negro," indeed, even "African," are markers of externally delineated collective signs.[7] Phillis Wheatley was one of the first early African American thinkers and creative artists to perceive and expose to view this racialization process:

> Some view our sable race with scornful eye
> "Their colour is a diabolic die."[8]

If twentieth-century, especially post–Civil Rights movement, scholars have applauded the use of these signifiers by early African American writers as proof of "race consciousness" in the positive sense, it is because the notion of race as the only means by which black or African American community can be organized has gone unexamined. My argument here is that race was only one among several principles by which early African American communities identified themselves as "a people," but that an analysis based solely on race is inadequate as a basis for understanding the crucial role of African American culture in *producing* African American community. While white society, especially in the slaveholding South, was busy with legal definitions of who was "black," "white," or "mulatto" (including "octoroon," "quadroon," etc.) in terms of biology, color, parentage, and so forth, black people had other criteria not based solely on biological/racial characteristics. Meeting the criteria of "blackness" from the white/legal point of view did not necessarily qualify one for membership in the community. If racialization as a sign of restrictive collective subjectivity depended on formulas for testing an individual's "blackness," community building was much more interactive.

It was and is, in fact, an act of collective self-definition not only *not* legally binding but legally *unbinding*. Community building strategizes a way outside the Law, a set of terms alternative to what African Americans perceived as specifically dehumanizing, externally defined collective designations. The ritual misnaming of Ashante, Igbo, Fulani, Yoruba (among others) as "blacks," "negroes," "niggers" took away the kin/collective designations by which one's pre-Departure humanity was assigned and given meaning. This lexical/cultural displacement paralleled the real-world geographical displacement as the separation from one's land and people (kin, clan, tribe, nation).[9]

Anthropologists Sidney W. Mintz and Richard Price speak to this point when they write:

> Without diminishing the probable importance of some core of common values, and the occurrence of situations where a number of slaves of common origin might indeed have been aggregated, the fact is that these were not *communities* of people at first, and they could only become communities by processes of cultural change. What the slaves undeniably shared at the outset was their enslavement; all—or nearly all—else had to be *created by them*. In order for slave communities to take shape, normative patterns of behavior had to be established, and these patterns could be created only on the basis of particular forms of social interaction. (18)

Thus African American creativity expressed itself most emphatically in the pressing need for building and maintaining institutions (19). Moreover, it is important to realize that the purpose of African American culture in the pre-Emancipation period was not to accommodate Africans to slavery but to help them to be more than slavery demanded. Thus the common view of subculture versus "wider society" must be rethought as well. As Bernice Johnson Reagon remarks: "To function simply as slaves is much too narrow to ensure that a people will prosper. There was a need to establish a structure, and a system with its own content that would allow an improved situation for survival beyond the confines of carrying out the required function as slaves."[10] From the point of view of African Americans, such sites as the slave quarters and the northern free black communities were "the wider society," because they were the social systems that offered African Americans the widest possible subject positions. "It was within the confines of the slave huts and barracks," write Mintz and Price, "that so much of the most intimate aspects of that life—sexuality, reproduction, birth, socialization, death, love, and hate—was lived out" (76). This structure of intimacy, I would argue, as a counterculture to the dehumanization of the chattel system, was a structure of community resistance as well.

In talking about community as resistance, I do not mean to say that participants in community performance necessarily consciously intend such resistance. As philosopher Howard McGary writes, an action need not be intentional to count as resistance. Significantly, McGary's analysis follows from an understanding of "behavior patterns . . . passed down from generation to generation":

> Perhaps those slaves who originated the practice had the intention of reducing oppression by engaging in the acts that established it. For strategic reasons, they may have chosen to teach these practices to their children as routine behaviors. This would have the effect of keeping the practice clandestine since even if slaves who acted in these ways were interrogated by the slaveholders, they could not reveal any intentions about reducing oppression because they did not have them.[11]

In other words, as an internal "response" to external circumstances of restraint and oppression, African American culture/community is a response that does not figure itself as a response. It is, therefore, not necessarily the practices themselves that are clandestine—they may in fact be quite open—but the "original" intentionality, which masks itself even from the participants involved.[12] In producing a resistant yet interrogation-proof resisting practice, such actions become encoded as "routine behaviors," the "regulated social practices" Wendy Hollway identifies as constitutive of subjectivity.[13] As such, these practices become (re)producers of a culturally specific collective subjectivity, and to the extent that this subjectivity-producing culture is community-based, as I shall argue below, it is a community-building culture as well.

McGary's theory is important to an understanding of the feature of black culture described as "masking." Yet while masking is described as having an intention that is hidden from the "dominant" society yet visible to those of the oppressed group or to the mask-wearer as an individual, McGary's theory of resistant action takes into account that the intention of the mask may not be available to the wearer himself (indeed, its "maskness" may not be consciously perceived). This goes beyond designating an in-group/out-group cultural sign to an understanding of the sociopsychical processes, generationally and collectively inscribed, that condition membership in a specific community. Gayle Johnson writes:

> The masked meanings of African American performance are still very much hidden in their own structures. Africanisms in African American performance are as often hidden as they are evident, and this seems somewhat by

design. The conceptual framework, the stage on which dual but non-oppositional systems of symbols or meanings are encoded, by virtue of their masked nature, was built to survive a period underground.[14]

HEARERS OF THE WORD: THEORIZING SPIRITUALS

> [D]isplaced from a logocentric world . . . the
> people of the black diaspora have, in opposition
> to all of that, found the deep form, the deep
> structure of their cultural life in music.
> (*Stuart Hall, "What Is 'Black' in*
> *Black Popular Culture?"*)

> Many people bare their ears in the belief that part
> of the virtue will be transferred from their hearing
> to their sense of sight.
> (*Zora Neale Hurston,* The Sanctified Church)

As with any folkloric "narrative," Hurston's description of an African American folk belief, whereby the cure for poor eyesight was thought to reside in improving one's hearing, "theorizes" via condensation and displacement.[15] The bared ears said to constitute the "cure" signify metonymically the aural/oral roots of an African American culture almost universally praised for its musicality. If, as Stuart Hall suggests, this orality is "overdetermined" by "black cultural repertoires constituted from two directions at once" (28), Hurston's narrative of folk cure poses orality as an antidote to a subjectivity othered by a racializing specularity. Indeed, Hall's titular interrogative depends upon a racialized designation through which "black" culture becomes powerless to account for itself, for its "blackness." Asking "What Is 'Black' in Black Popular Culture?" stages an interrogative that cannot, on a metalevel, be self-interrogating, cannot answer itself any more than laying bare one's ears can cure myopia. In the remainder of this chapter I will examine late-nineteenth- and early-twentieth-century transcriptions of spirituals along with "eyewitness" accounts from the pre-Emancipation period in order to capture something of the "performing context" of these important cultural forms. Obviously, much remains unrecoverable, and it is precisely through these silences which I have called a "spirituals matrix" that there emerges an alternative theorizing of the relationship between African American culture and community, utterance and subjectivity.

When I say "performing context," I mean to enact a shift not only from "performance" to "performing" similar to Barbara Christian's shift from "theory" to "theorizing," and away from spectatorship to auditorship or listenership, but from a static conceptualization of "audience" to the dynamic notion of "participant." Hall's three characteristics of "black popular culture" in the twentieth century—*style*, *music*, and *body*—are helpful here, as they correspond, loosely, to contemporaneous accounts of black cultural performance in the pre-Emancipation period. Music historian Eileen Southern notes that "the single most important element of the slave music was its performance as, indeed, is true of black folk music in the twentieth century. It was the performance that shaped the song into an entity, that finally determined its melody, texture, tempo, rhythmical patterns, text, and *effect upon listeners*" (200, my emphasis).

This creative potential corresponds to a feature of early African American culture pointed out by nearly all observers, contemporary and subsequent: spontaneity.[16] Writing on nineteenth-century reports of slave singing, historian Lawrence Levine notes that "*a sense of almost instantaneous community*" was "a central element in every account of slave singing" (26). This construction of "almost instantaneous community" produced its share of ethnographic angst among white recorders who as "outsiders" to the performance, Levine notes, "had difficulty resisting the centripetal pull of black religious services and songs" (29). Rather than view this as reflective of what Levine calls a "compelling communal ethos" (27), I suggest we see this "centripetal pull" as precisely that aspect of spirituals in performance which establishes the bar between outsider and insider, draws the boundaries between participants within the communal performance and those outside the performing collective. Viewed from "the other side," what to white observers appeared as a threatening collapsing of boundaries between observer and participant functioned to make African Americans—including new arrivals, newly bought and transported slaves, Northern fugitives and migrants—feel instantly "at home."

It is important to remember that the creation of cultural space and community was not limited to southern slave culture. Horton notes a similar function in nineteenth-century free black religious culture of the North:

> For recent [migrant] arrivals, the church provided both a means for entering black society and a continuity with their previous experience. . . . The style of preaching was familiar to blacks no matter where they lived. The preacher built an emotional crescendo, and the entire congregation responded both verbally and physically, finding at least temporary relief from the common pressures of black life. Religious music was an important part of any black church experience. The songs were the same and the singing style varied little from one urban church to another. The black churches of

Boston seemed entirely familiar to migrants and made a strange city seem less foreign. (34)

These "means of constituting and sustaining camraderie and community" (qtd. in Hall 28) worked brilliantly to ensure that those seeking community and kinship after suffering separation from loved ones owing to material conditions of slavery/escape, economic hardship, and the like, would be able to join virtually instantaneously in such a collective.

Moreover, as Paul Gilroy reminds us in *The Black Atlantic*, "a distinctive kinesis . . . a distinctive relationship to the body" attends black musical performance (75). As theologian Vincent Harding put it, "We are a people of the spoken word, we are a people of the danced word, we are a people of the sung word, we are a people of the musical word" (qtd. in Gravely 315 n. 38). As "people of the . . . word," African Americans perceive the meaning of "words" to involve various body and motor performances that go beyond any assumed one-to-one correspondence between speech and writing. Harding's remarks also provide an important conceptual transition, as he is referring to African American religious culture, the cultural forms that dominated eighteenth- and nineteenth-century understandings of black culture.

It was the performing context of early African American oral cultural practices that drew almost universal comment from early white spectators/recorders. Contemporary observers emphasized precisely those elements of the music that could not be captured in writing or Western musical notation:

Frederika Bremer in 1853: "I wish I could give you an idea of [it], so fresh was the melody, and so peculiar the key."[17]

Lucy McKim Garrison in 1862: "It is difficult to express the entire character of these negro ballads by mere musical notes and signs. The odd turns made in the throat, and the curious rhythmic effect produced by single voices chiming in at different irregular intervals, seem *almost as impossible to place on the score as the singing of birds or the tones of an Aeolian Harp*."[18]

An observer in 1863: "The most striking of their barbaric airs *it would be impossible to write out*."[19]

An observer in 1872: "Tones are frequently employed which *we have no musical characters to represent* . . . ranging through an entire octave on different occasions, according to the inspiration of the singer."[20]

Significantly, it is not only the music that escaped the recorders' sign systems but the words themselves as sung by slave performers. That is, linguistic vernacularity figures as that which cannot be represented in writing, or, more accurately, that for which written language can communicate only *as* representation. Written "dialect," then, is made to stand in for a sound that resists figuration within the formulas of the language's own spoken idiom. On the subject of African American vernacular rendered as "Negro dialect," James Weldon Johnson writes:

> Negro dialect is made unintelligible on the printed page by the absurd practice of devising a clumsy, outlandish, so-called phonetic spelling for words in a dialect story or poem when the regular English spelling *represents the very same sound.* . . . [T]he dialect is fundamentally English. An American from any part of the United States or an Englishman can, with not more than slight difficulty, understand it *when it is spoken.* The trouble comes in trying to get it from the printed page. (44, my emphasis)

In the absence of cassette tapes, VCRs, and CDs, observers writing down spirituals recorded what they thought they heard, and very often the texts handed down to us in writing are based on understandable mishearings.

I dwell on this point because so often in early sources, difficulties of writing down what was heard were attributed to black *voices.* Recorder William Francis Allen in 1862:

> The voices of the colored people have a peculiar quality that *nothing can imitate*; and the intonations and delicate variations of even one singer *cannot be reproduced on paper.* And I despair of conveying any notion of the effect of a number singing together, especially in a complicated shout. . . . There is no singing *in parts* as we understand it, and yet no two [singers] appear to be singing the same thing.[21]

Following the familiar lament about the tendency of black oral cultural practice to slip through the cracks of Western sign systems, Allen, in attempting to explain this phenomenon, slips into a description of the complicated structural principle often oversimplifed as "call and response."[22] What he is describing is what Eileen Southern calls "overlapping call-and-response patterns" or "heterophony":

> The lead singer always began the song. The others joined the singing on refrains, or even in the verses if they knew the words. Most often, however, the lead singer improvised new words for the verses as he sang. . . . It is important to emphasize that individuals might begin to sing the refrain before the leader concluded his solo, and that the leader might begin his next solo before the chorus had finished. (196)

That early observers were so mystified by black heterophony is no surprise, for what they failed to "hear"—indeed, what remains to be "heard" in this postmodern, postrace critical moment—is the production of black community through the structure of cultural performance. That is, African Americans are a "performing community" even as the doing of black culture *performs* community. African American culture, then, is a matter not only of, as one scholar put it, "the way we do culturally" but of the way we do "we."[23]

An example of what I mean by "performing context" can be seen in a close analysis of the familiar spiritual, "Steal Away to Jesus":

> Steal away, steal away,
> Steal away to Jesus.
> Steal away, steal away home,
> I ain't got long to stay here.
>
> My Lord He calls me,
> He calls me by the thunder,
> The trumpet sounds within-a my soul.
>
> I ain't got long to stay here,
> Steal away, steal away,
> [etc.][24]

James Weldon Johnson cites this spiritual as a classic example of African American adaptations of African call-and-response patterns, Rather than a simple lead and response, Johnson observes, the African American spiritual follows a more complex pattern of lead, response, and chorus. Thus the written text of this song fails adequately to capture the significance of its performance of/as a complex mixture of individual and communal utterance. In other words, in performance, this spiritual theorizes its own notion of "community" owing to the specific demands of African American subjectivity.

As Johnson explains, the chorus, "Steal away, steal away, [etc.]" is sung in "part harmony" while the lead, "My Lord He calls me, etc." is sung in solo. Following the lead is a part harmony and communal "response" before the chorus is repeated in part harmony, and so on (25–27). What is significant is the interaction between this performative utterance and the song text. That is, "I," sung by the community in the form of the chorus, is reinvested with communal significance; the singular "me" echoes the "I" while reinscribing it within an individual communication between soloist and "My Lord." Moreover, this individual call is figured here as communal "witness," both as response to the community's chorus, which bespeaks a longing for Jesus/home—that is, it is produced by a collective longing—and as a personal testimony that is completed only by the communal response "I ain't got long to stay here." In the latter phrasing, the "I" is reproduced as communal utterance.[25] Taken together, chorus/lead/response problematizes the boundaries between "call" and "response" by a circular, repetitious performance, since the song may begin or end with any of these elements.

African American spirituals like "Steal Away" reinvent African singing practice in accordance with the unique position of African American subjectivity in the New World. It is thus that the structure and text of spirituals is an expression of African American subjectivity. Given displacement from an African homeland via diaspora and slave trade, and family/kin separations—figured both in the "auction block" experience of enslaved African Americans and in the indenture of young children by free black families owing to material conditions of poverty—community becomes a point of mediation, a sign of a desire to return when no return is possible.[26]

This expression of community as space of desire is not "compensatory," as some scholars have argued.[27] Rather, it represents a redirection of collective psychic energies toward something or someplace else. This type of cultural adaptation goes beyond the rubrics of African "survivals" or "syncretisms," as it expresses both a deferred desire and its creative response; that is, it creates the very object of desire by its own figurative and structural displacements.

Most of the scholarship on African American spirituals focuses on debates about origins (Euramerican or African), otherworldliness versus temporal direction, style of composition, and social, historical, theological, and literary readings of the songs.[28] John Wesley Work provides one of the few discussions of the structure of spirituals. Work writes: "The movement in this music . . . demands short notes and short syllables. To gain this effect, the creators of these songs have resorted ingeniously to the use of a nameless little something represented by the letter 'A,' thereby adding a subtle force to the way in which it is employed" (38–39). The effect of the "-a" can be seen in the line from "Steal Away": "within-a my soul."[29] I would like to nominate "-a" as a figure for the excess and surplus, antistructural units of African American cultural expression.[30] Work writes that the "certain subtle effect . . . consists in certain turns, twists, and intonations, not represented by musical terms. To be appreciated it must be heard" (40). As the figure for performing community, "-a" subverts the structure of discretely identifiable notes and simultaneously provides structure; that is, it mediates between two notes somehow incomplete without it. Like the *a* of Derrida's *différance*, which stands simultaneously for presence and absence, the "-a" of spirituals becomes the figure for both the plentitude and lack in language.[31] As performance, then, "-a" represents the listener/reader's absence from the performing context even as it seeks to restore such context by its promise of plentitude. Yet crucially, the *a* of Derrida's *différance* signifies to the extent that it is *unheard*:

> The graphic difference (*a* instead of *e*), this marked difference between two apparently vocal notations, between two vowels, remains purely graphic: it reads, or it is written, but it cannot be heard. It cannot be apprehended in speech. . . . It is offered by a mute marker, by a tacit monument, I would even say by a pyramid. . . . The *a* of *différance*, then, is not heard; it remains silent, secret, and discreet as a tomb. (3–4)

In contrast, the "-a" (pronounced "uh") of spirituals is distinctly *heard*. For Derrida, "*différance*" operates as "the economy of death," which, as material "monument" and "tomb," "is not far from announcing the death of the tyrant" (4). We might say that African American spirituals theorize "a way out of no way," a way out of psychical/social/ discursive death, as they enact the ancient ritual of death and resurrection: the death of African desire and the rebirth of African American desire(s).

The Sacred Subject

SITUATED now on "the other side," as it were, of this project, I have a similar sensation to the one I experienced at "The Point of No Return" in Cape Coast Castle, Ghana, that I wrote about in the introduction. For to make any attempt at a "conclusion" is to attempt a return that is simultaneously mandated and impossible, as the idea of an originary project or set of original expectations must give way to "what is" and "what has been." In the words of Pontius Pilate, "what I have written, I have written."

Yet several issues and concepts emerge for me from this study that point not so much backward as forward (again, the terms of departure and arrival have shifted) to other possible directions that future study of African American literature, especially the study of African American women writers and writers of the pre-Emancipation period, might take. All of these issues can be summed up in the term "sacred subjects," "sacred" connoting the sense of the untouchable and unapproachable even as it lures us with a promise of fulfilled desire. Thus I have identified several desires/needs that my sojourn with these writings has produced.

First is the need for literary scholars of this period to attend more closely to the importance of religion in these texts.[1] We have traditionally treated religious claims or biblical allusions in literature as the stuff of footnotes, tangential to the main work of the text's system of signification. Yet to continue to insist on such a perspective, given texts so riddled with religious symbology and theological claims, is to opt for a blindness that is bound to hamper our scholarly insights. This is especially true of these early writers for whom Christianity and Christian discourse of salvation, conversion, and redemption are often being troped onto issues of political freedom and social liberation in complex and dazzling ways.

Second, and related, is the need to attend to the centrality of issues of spirituality in black women's literature in general in order more fully to explore the range of ways in which African American women—indeed, African women throughout the diaspora—have represented themselves as religious subjects within a variety of sacred traditions: Christianity, Islam, African and neo-African Traditional Religions, among others. While there is, admittedly, some risk in equating black women with spirituality, especially given essentialist claims that tend to conflate African

American women with "the Black Church," a deeper understanding of the ways in which sacred and secular, spiritual and political, often coexist for many women of this writing community would help to develop political and social readings of these texts in more nuanced ways.

Third, the need for greater dialogue and inclusivity of African American religious studies scholars within humanities projects of revision and reclamation, especially as issues of race, gender, culture, and community converge at the site of African American texts. While we as literary scholars have much to gain from their expertise in theology, history of religions, biblical studies, and the like, they, in turn, would benefit greatly from our ability to read the nuances and subtlety of texts with theoretical sophistication.

Fourth, the need for greater biblical literacy.

Fifth, the need for greater sophistication in the theorizing of connections between literature and religion in general, given that it is becoming increasingly difficult to "bracket" religion and religious experience as somehow extraliterary or not germane to issues of textuality.

The most pressing rationale for taking up "the sacred subject" as an integral part of the work we do as literary scholars and theorists, for me, is the undeniable fact that such large numbers of African American people have always maintained cherished religious affiliations that are fundamental to their sense of community and subjectivity—and continue to do so. Certainly the writers in this book represent this, as do writers like Alice Walker, Toni Morrison, Gloria Naylor, Lorraine Hansberry, James Baldwin, and others. Indeed, the complexity and variety of African American spiritual interrogations has only just begun.

Notes

Introduction

1. In Marilyn Richardson 45. James Melvin Washington includes Stewart in his excellent treatment of the genre of African American prayer in *Conversations with God: Two Centuries of Prayers by African Americans* (New York: Harper Collins, 1994).

2. See José Rabasa, "Dialogue as Conquest: Mapping Spaces for Counter-Discourse," in JanMohamed and Lloyd 187–215, and Fogel.

3. Anderson.

4. See Barbara Christian's reading of *Beloved* in the context of Middle Passage and African ancestral worship in "Fixing Methodologies." Hortense Spillers interrogates the meaning of "the vital sign of Africanity" for the study of American literature in "Who Cuts the Border?" Peter Paris's important contribution to religious studies reads ethics across the African diaspora in *The Spirituality of African Peoples*. Kwame Anthony Appiah complicates the meanings assigned to "Africa" in intellectual discourse in *In My Father's House*; see especially chapter 6, "Old Gods, New Worlds," 107–36. Paul Gilroy argues for the refiguring of the Atlantic as "one single, complex unit of analysis" in *The Black Atlantic*.

5. Perhaps no one has been clearer on this point than Ivan Van Sertima when he writes: "You cannot study America and you cannot study Africa the way you study Europe. Europe has, in spite of its many wars, what I would like to call 'an archival continuity.' Africa does not. America does not. . . . That is why it has become necessary to adopt what some people like to call an 'ahistorical' method. It is, in fact, the only possible historical method for dealing with such shattered worlds." Ivan Van Sertima, ed., *The African Presence in Early America* (New Brunswick, NJ: Transaction Publishers, 1992), 32.

6. Gates, *The Signifying Monkey* and *Figures in Black*; Henderson; Bakhtin, *Speech Genres*.

7. Cannon; Grant; Weems; Delores Williams; and Kirk-Duggan.

8. Theophus Smith; Anderson; Paris; Spencer, *Protest and Praise*; and Hopkins.

Chapter One
The Daughters' Arrival

1. William H. Robinson identifies this notice as the one announcing the arrival of the cargo that included Phillis Wheatley. See *Phillis Wheatley and Her Writings* 15. Karla F. C. Holloway argues that "race has a cultural presence" in literature by black women, in *Moorings and Metaphors* 11.

2. Consider, for example, the northern locations of writers such as Wheatley (Boston), Ann Plato (Hartford, Connecticut), Maria W. Stewart (Hartford and

Boston), Jarena Lee (Cape May, New Jersey, and Philadelphia), Zilpha Elaw (Pennsylvania), Nancy Prince (Massachusetts), and Rebecca Cox Jackson (Philadelphia and Watervliet, New York). Thus I follow the "northward turn" of scholars such as Frances Smith Foster in *Written by Herself* and Carla Peterson in *Doers of the Word*.

3. Greene's early study remains definitive on the subject of colonial New England. See also William D. Piersen's *Black Yankees*. On the topic of New England's heavy involvement in the transatlantic slave trade, see Ronald Bailey, "The Slave(ry) Trade and the Development of Capitalism in the United States: The Textile Industry in New England," in Inikori and Engerman, 205–46.

4. Historical Treatments of U.S. slavery include Genovese, Levine, Blassingame, and Stuckey. Deborah Gray White's study of black women under slavery also concentrates on the U.S. South. Two helpful overviews of the historical literature on American slavery are Berlin, "Time, Space, and the Evolution of Afro-American Society," and Hines.

5. Blassingame discusses the "Sambo" figure as predominant among plantation house servants (304–5). Histories of slavery in the northern United States predominantly remain local. Two important general studies are McManus and Litwack, *North of Slavery*. For regional treatments of slavery in New England, see Greene and Piersen. On U.S. free black communities, see Berlin, *Slaves without Masters*; Curry; and Horton, *Free People of Color*.

6. Quoted in Herbert A. Aptheker, ed., *A Documentary History of the Negro People in the United States*, vol. 1, *From the Colonial Times through the Civil War* (New York: Citadel Press, 1951), 6. For historical treatments of black women before Emancipation, see Lerner, Loewenberg and Bogin, and Sterling.

7. This was especially true after the passage of the 1850 Fugitive Slave Act, which made it a federal crime for anyone in a nonslaveholding state to harbor a fugitive from a slaveholding state. One of the casualties of this law was Solomon Northup, born free in New York and captured, sold southward, and enslaved in Louisiana. See Northup's account in his autobiography, *Twelve Years a Slave* (1853; Baton Rouge: Louisiana State University Press, 1968).

8. See Piersen; Horton, *Free People of Color*; and Litwack, *Been in the Storm So Long*.

9. See Porter, "Organized Educational Activities" and *Early Negro Writing*; Joyce; Dann; Howard Holman Bell, ed., *Minutes of the Proceedings of the National Negro Conventions, 1830–1864* (New York: Arno, 1969); and Carter G. Woodson, *Negro Orators and Their Orations* (New York: Russell and Russell, 1969).

10. Ongoing developments in the field of historical archaeology are continuing to add to our knowledge of African American material culture from the period. One famous example is the discovery in 1990 of the African Burial Grounds in Lower Manhattan, which dates back to 1712. This discovery alone unearthed over 1.5 million artifacts and 390 sets of skeletal remains, which are still being cataloged, labeled, tested, and analyzed. *African Burial Ground*, Five Points Archaelogical Project Liason Office, April 1993. See also *New York Times*, December 26, 1991, and August 9, 1992; *Washington Post*, August 3, 1992; *Amsterdam News*, February 20, 1993; *USA Today*, September 15, 1992.

11. Henry Louis Gates, Jr., "On the Rhetoric of Racism in the Profession," in *Literature, Language, and Politics*, ed. Betty Jean Craige (Athens: University of Georgia Press, 1988), 26.

12. In this sense, William L. Andrews's *To Tell a Free Story* can also be considered a part of the vernacular/tropological school.

13. Spillers, "Cross-Currents."

14. James C. Scott defines the "hidden transcript" as a "*writing between the lines*" and an "*infrapolitics*" best conceived of as "*a condition of practical resistance rather than as a substitute for* [resistance]." See *Domination and the Arts of Resistance* 183, 191.

15. The corollary to this argument, of course, is that Henderson's theory allows no space for the testimonial relations of discourses between black women and white men in any form.

16. See also Deborah E. McDowell's critique of essentialism in "Boundaries," in *Afro-American Literary Study in the 1990's*, ed. Houston A. Baker and Patricia Redmond, and the responses by Hortense Spillers and Michael Awkward that follow McDowell's essay. The debates within this important volume—which reprints papers from a conference where leading African Americanists convened to discuss scholarly directions for the field in the midst of the flurry of intellectual and publishing activity of the 1980s—presents engagements with many of the issues of tradition, subjectivity, and critical theory I have been addressing.

17. Refiguring "race" as a "cultural presence" is distinct from the deconstruction of race that Henry Louis Gates argues for in the introduction to his edited volume *"Race," Writing, and Difference*. What Gates deconstructs is the opposition between race as "an objective term of classification" and "race" as "a dangerous trope" (5). As I read Karla Holloway, the move to resituate race vis-à-vis culture does not seek to deconstruct a dualism between biology and language but aims at embracing race within a larger framework that allows for multiplicity, heterogeneity, and complexity, all of which are signified in her work by "community."

18. bell hooks uses the term "talkin' back" to signify "speaking as an equal to an authority figure."

19. Hortense Spillers calls for an "archaeological" critical project that "questions matters of lexis, syntax, and semantics and tries to decide what common fund of rhetorical legacies (and betrayals?) writers across time and in the same time were drawing," in "Cross-Currents" 258.

20. For a detailed treatment of the theological significance of black women's understanding of "conversion," see Kimberly Rae Connor's *Conversions and Visions in the Writings of African-American Women*.

21. Here I am building on Frances Smith Foster's recent *Written by Herself*, which lays out the broad historical and literary parameters of this body of work.

22. For an elaboration on African American women's "matriarchal" lineage, see Henry Louis Gates's series introduction to the Schomburg Library of Nineteenth-Century Black Women Writers (New York: Oxford University Press). Marilyn Richardson dubs Maria Stewart the first black woman political writer, in her edited volume of selected Stewart writings.

23. In Shields 186–87.

24. See discussion on the broadside "Dreadful Riot on Negro Hill" above.

Chapter Two
Diaspora Subjectivity and Transatlantic Crossings

1. For the most accurate biographical information on Wheatley and a comprehensive bibliography of commentary, reviews, and criticism on *Poems* from 1773 to 1981, see Robinson, *Phillis Wheatley: A Bio-Bibliography*. See also Jean Fagan Yellin and Cynthia D. Bond for a more recent but selective listing in *This Pen Is Ours: A Listing of Writings by and about African-American Women before 1910 with Secondary Bibliography to the Present* (New York: Oxford University Press, 1991). For a detailed treatment of Wheatley's reputation and reception in the eighteenth and nineteenth centuries, see Henry Louis Gates, Jr., "Phillis Wheatley and the 'Nature of the Negro,'" in *Figures in Black* 61–79. The most complete volume of Wheatley's poetry to date appeared as a part of the Schomburg Library of Nineteenth-Century Black Women Writers: *The Collected Works of Phillis Wheatley*, ed. John C. Shields (New York: Oxford University Press, 1988). In addition to a facsimile reprint of the 1773 *Poems on Various Subjects Religious and Moral*, this excellent volume reprints variants and miscellaneous prose. All citations of Wheatley's work will be taken from this edition.

2. Baker, *The Journey Back*; Gates, *Figures in Black*; Alice Walker; June Jordan; O'Neale; Russell J. Reising, "Trafficking in White: Phillis Wheatley's Semiotics of Racial Representation," *Genre* 22 (Fall 1989): 231–61; Phillip Richards, "Phillis Wheatley and Literary Americanization," *American Quarterly* 44, no. 2 (June 1992): 163–91; Foster.

3. See Reising, "Trafficking in White," and Richards, "Phillis Wheatley and Literary Americanization."

4. Mbiti. For a similar ritualistic critical intervention, see Barbara Christian's "fixing ceremony" in which she reads Toni Morrison's *Beloved* in the context of the Middle Passage, in "Fixing Methodologies."

5. This identification is made by William H. Robinson in his *Phillis Wheatley: A Bio-Bibliography*.

6. Julian D. Mason states what is still a popular assessment: "On the basis of the poems which have survived her short career, she [Wheatley] must be labeled as primarily an occasional poet, one interested in the clever crafting of verse." Introduction to *The Poems of Phillis Wheatley* (Chapel Hill: University of North Carolina Press, 1966).

7. See Gates, *Figures in Black*, and Baker, *The Journey Back*. See also June Jordan and Alice Walker.

8. Margarita Matilda Odell, *Memoir and Poems of Phillis Wheatley. A Native of Africa and a Slave. Dedicated to the Friends of the African* (Boston: George W. Light, 1834). Wheatley died in abject poverty and near-obscurity in 1784 at the approximate age of thirty-one.

9. For a comprehensive treatment of the use of Phillis Wheatley's image and poems in debates over black inferiority, see Gates, *Figures in Black*.

10. A related "deficiency," according to Odell, was Wheatley's habit of "forgetting" her own poems, a problem said "to have affected her own thoughts only, and not the impressions made upon her mind by the thoughts of others, communicated by books or conversation" (*Memoir* 19).

11. Patricia Hill Collins argues that "Black women have a self-defined standpoint on their own oppression" (32).

12. Mazrui writes, "So much of the history of the slave experience in the Western hemisphere amounted to the following command addressed to the captives, 'Forget you are African, remember you are Black!'" (110).

13. Toni Morrison refers to displaced Africans as "the not-Americans" (48).

14. Wheatley's references to herself as "Afric" and "Ethiop" can be found in the following poems: "To Maecenas" (line 40), "To the University of Cambridge" (line 28), "On Recollection" (line 62), "An Hymn to Humanity" (line 31), and "To His Honour the Lieutenant-Governor on the Death of His Lady" (line 28). Houston Baker discusses these references as "sign-vehicles" (after Eco) and reads "the complex mappings" of the terms as moving "in the direction of an extended African consciousness" (*The Journey Back* 12).

15. In using the term "survivor" I mean to connect Wheatley and other first-generation Africans in the Americas to such celebrated communities as Jewish survivors of the Nazi Holocaust as well as to the various discourses of survivorship of individual "holocausts" like rape and incest that have historically characterized black women's lives.

16. On African "survivals," the classic debate has been between anthropologist Melville J. Herskovits (*The Myth of the Negro Past* [1924]) and sociologist E. Franklin Frazier (*The Negro Church in America* [1964]). See also Karla F. C. Holloway, ed., *Africanisms in American Culture* (Bloomington: Indiana University Press, 1990); Sobel; Mintz and Price; and Thompson. Americanist literary scholars are also beginning to apply the concept of "cultural syncretism" with respect to American and African American literature and culture. See Shelly Fisher Fishkin, *Was Huck Black?: Mark Twain and African American Voices* (New York: Oxford University Press, 1993); and Eric Sundquist, *To Wake the Nations: Race in the Making of American Literature* (Cambridge: Harvard University Press, 1993).

17. Mukhtar Ali Isani, "'An Elegy on Leaving ———': A New Poem by Phillis Wheatley," *American Literature* 58, no. 4 (December 1986): 609–13. See also Shields.

18. In addition to Curtin, see Edward Reynolds, *Stand the Storm: A History of the Atlantic Slave Trade* (Chicago: Ivan R. Dee, 1985), which provides an analysis in terms of African, European, and American life and culture. See also the essays in Inikori and Engerman.

19. In *African Religions and Philosophy*, John S. Mbiti writes of the interconnectedness of African ontology as comprising God, Spirits, Man, Animals, and Plants, and "[p]henomena and objects without biological life" (15–16). Moreover, he writes that Africans are particularly tied to the land, as they conceive of subjectivity within the matrix of space: "The land provides them with the roots of existence, as well as binding them mystically to their departed. . . . To remove

Africans by force from their land is an act of such great injustice that no foreigner can fathom it" (26). On African Sacred Cosmos, see also Sobel and Hopkins.

20. I discuss the correspondence between Obour Tanner and Wheatley more fully in chapter 1.

21. Phillip Richards argues that Wheatley "assimilates" Anglo-American discourse in her poetry, in "Phillis Wheatley and Literary Americanization."

22. The first four lines of "On Being Brought" form a versified "conversion narrative," prefiguring black women's appropriation of a genre that will come to be dominated by Jarena Lee, Zilpha Elaw, Rebecca Cox Jackson, Julia A. J. Foote, Amanda Berry Smith, and others, in the nineteenth century. The conversion narratives of Lee, Elaw, and Foote are collected in Andrews, *Sisters of the Spirit*. Jackson's writings appear in Humez, *Gifts of Power*. Amanda Berry Smith's *Autobiography* appears in its entirety as part of the Schomburg Library of Nineteenth-Century Black Women Writers (New York: Oxford University Press, 1988). See also Houchins.

23. Mae Henderson, "Response to Baker," in Baker and Redmond 160.

24. The advertised proposal ran in the *Boston Censor* on February 29, March 14, and April 18, 1772. There were no local (American) publishers willing to publish a book of poems by an African slave, which necessitated their being published in England (August 6, 1773). Wheatley, who had sailed to London in May of 1773, was on hand to oversee the publication and printing of the volume. "Cambridge" and "On Being Brought" were repositioned to third and fifth, respectively, in the final volume.

25. The subtitle "Wrote in 1767" appeared in the 1772 proposal.

26. John Shields points out that most of the "editorial tampering" with Wheatley's verse was done in poems published after her death in 1784. The evidence confirms that during her lifetime, Wheatley displayed an astonishing amount of editorial control over her poetry.

27. Wheatley published her first poem, "On Messrs. Hussey and Coffin," on December 21, 1767, in the *Newport Mercury* also at the age of fourteen.

28. Here I also disagree with Russell Reising, who views Wheatley's poetics within a dialectic of "accommodation" and "resistance." If Wheatley's popularity depended on the "opacity" of her antislavery message to New England readers, then revisions should show an increase in the veiling of her language from earlier drafts to those published in *Poems*. Instead, Wheatley actually revised poems in order to make the antislavery message more clear. This is, to me, evidence that with the passing years, Wheatley became not more "domesticated" but more overtly abolitionist. See Reising, "Trafficking in White."

29. The final version of these lines reads: "While an intrinsic ardor prompts to write, / The muses promise to assist my pen."

30. The conceptualization of slavery as "sin" would have been available to Wheatley's eighteenth-century audience. Diaries of slave traders making this connection abound. See also Samuel Sewall's *The Selling of Joseph: A Memorial* (1703), ed. Sidney Kaplan (Amherst: University of Massachusetts Press, 1969), perhaps the earliest text specifically equating European slavery with biblical wrongdoing.

31. On African Americans' use of the biblical account in Exodus, see Theophus Smith's recent cultural history, *Conjuring Culture* 55–80. See also Hopkins 23–24.

32. See Olaudah Equiano, *The Interesting Narrative of Olaudah Equiano or Gustavus Vassa, the African*, in Gates, *Classic Slave Narratives*. See Reynolds, *Stand the Storm*.

33. Ronald Bailey, "The Slave(ry) Trade and the Development of Captialism in the United States: The Textile Industry in New England," in Inikori and Engerman 205–6.

34. Thomas W. Wilson and Clarence E. Grim, "The Possible Relationship between the Transatlantic Slave Trade and Hypertension in Blacks Today," in Inikori and Engerman 339–60. Several medical historical studies have been conducted in recent years to explore the possibility that black Americans' propensity to hypertension may be linked not only to diet and heredity but also possibly to the harsh physical conditions of the Middle Passage. While I find this interesting, I do not believe the Middle Passage constituted an "evolutionary gateway" that would have altered African physiology to as great a degree as some researchers think. See also Kenneth F. Kiple and Brian T. Higgins, "Mortality Caused by Dehydration during the Middle Passage," in Inikori and Engerman 321–38.

35. Foucault, *Power/Knowledge*. See also Henriques et al.

36. Russell Reising offers an extensive reading of the word "refin'd" (line 8) in its biological, theological, and cultural senses. See "Trafficking in White" 243–45.

37. Hortense Spillers writes that "[t]he historic triangular trade interlarded a third of the known world in a fabric of commercial intimacy so tightly interwoven that the politics of the New World cannot always be so easily disentangled as locally discrete moments." See "Who Cuts the Border?" 9.

38. A similar aesthetic effect is created in the following lines from "To Maecenas": "When gentler strains demand thy graceful song, / The length'ning line moves languishing along" (Shields 10, lines 15–16).

39. I use "speech genres" after Bakhtin as a way of grouping together the sociodynamics of everyday speech communication as they encode relations between "speaker" and "other." See "The Problem of Speech Genres," in *Speech Genres*.

40. While all public accounts of Susannah and Wheatley report that the relationship was close—Wheatley herself remarked that she "was treated by her more like her child than her servant" (letter to Obour Tanner, Boston, March 21, 1774; Shields 177)—both the letter lamenting Susannah's death and the poem "Ode to Neptune" encode ambivalence owing, no doubt, to the mistress-servant relationship that Susannah had a tendency to exploit. Anecdotally, Susannah is said to have been responsible for denying Wheatley associations with other black people. In any event, Wheatley would have made the acquaintance of many slaveholding "ladies," and her near-caricaturing of them in these two poems is instructive.

41. On the nuances of environmental discourse, especially its use in both pro- and antislavery arguments, see Winthrop Jordan.

42. On nineteenth-century black women's negotiations of the Cult of True Womanhood, see Carby.

43. William D. Piersen notes that the slave markets in New England often purchased slaves first "seasoned" in the West Indies, although they were often advertised (untruthfully) as "direct from Africa." During the eighteenth century, about half of the slaves purchased in the New England market came from the islands (though they were usually born in Africa). Moreover, New England was a "market of last resort," the final stop on a long route that brought slaves from the West Indies up along the North American coast from as far south as Charleston, whereby the "undesirable 'refuse' slaves [were sold] northward." Among those "refuse" slaves were those deemed "refractory" or resistant to training (including runaways and slaves accused of murder) and the very ill. (See Piersen 4.) This fact has led some scholars to speculate that Wheatley may have been sent to the West Indies before arriving in Boston, as her frail condition may have marked her for "refuse."

44. Houston Baker reads "economic deportation" and "chattel principle" as foundational to African American experience of slavery, in *Blues*. I would argue that these principles developed later in African American consciousness. Loss of kin and community would have been the most immediate and fundamental experience of the process of dehumanization.

45. For information on British antislavery lobbies and legislation, see James Walvin, *The Black Presence: A Documentary History of the Negro in England, 1555–1860* (New York: Schocken Books, 1971). See Olaudah Equiano's description of a similar case in *Interesting Narrative*, in Gates, *Classic Slave Narratives* 134–35.

46. See *Narrative of the Most Remarkable Particulars in the Life of James Albert Ukasaw Gronnoisaw an African Prince*, ed. W. Shirley (1770). Both Olaudah Equiano's *Interesting Narrative* (1789) and Mary Prince's *History of Mary Prince* (1816) are reprinted as part of Gates's *Classic Slave Narratives*. A study of the relationship between Wheatley and slave narrators, especially her eighteenth-century contemporaries, is long overdue.

Chapter Three
"The Too Advent'rous Strain"

1. Gates's reading of Wheatley's "oral examination" is based on his keen observation that discourses of black inferiority from the eighteenth century forward were grounded in the presumed lack of black intellectual ability. However, Winthrop Jordan writes of "the absence of clearcut distinctions and interlacing of mental capacity with spiritual grace" that characterized the discourse of colonial America. Because of these interlocking discourses, "the issue of the Negro's mental ability first arose historically out of doubts concerning his ability to participate in the experience of conversion." Thus in the eighteenth century, "the concept of intelligence had not yet become disassociated from the ideal of religious experience." See Winthrop Jordan 189–90.

2. See Robinson, *Phillis Wheatley: A Bio-Bibliography.*

3. There have been only two article-length treatments of Wheatley's funeral

elegies to date: Gregory Rigsby, "Form and Content in Phillis Wheatley's Elegies," *College Language Association Journal* 19, no. 2 (1975): 248–57; and Mukhtar Ali Isani, "Phillis Wheatley and the Elegiac Mode," in Robinson, *Critical Essays*, 208–14. Other attempts to treat the poems sympathetically include Robinson, *Phillis Wheatley and Her Writings* 97–99 and David Grimstead's historical monograph, "Anglo-American Racism and Phillis Wheatley's 'Sable Veil,' 'Length'ned Chain,' and 'Knitted Heart,'" in Hoffman and Albert 338–444, esp. 352–58. See also John Shields's treatment in "Phillis Wheatley's Struggle for Freedom in Her Poetry and Prose," included in *Collected Works* 229–70, esp. 245–52.

4. Wendy Hollway, "Gender Difference and the Production of Subjectivity," in Henriques et al. 227–63.

5. Cotton Mather's pamphlet *The Negro Christianized* appears in Ruchames 59–70.

6. See Russell Reising, "Trafficking in White: Phillis Wheatley's Semiotics of Racial Representation," *Genre* 22 (Fall 1989): 231–61. While Reising offers brilliant and original readings of Wheatley's odes, he follows the general tendency of Wheatley criticism in seeing in the elegies only "predictable images of consolation and heavenly solace" (238).

7. Bakhtin refers to this as "answerability" or "responsibility," which positions "art" and "life" in dialogical relation to one another, united by the consciousness of the writing subject: "Art and life are not one, but they must become united in myself—in the unity of my answerability" (*Art and Answerability* 2).

8. I use the term "elegiac pact" in the sense in which Phillipe Lejeune uses the phrase "autobiographical pact," as a way of discerning literary genre within the matrix of the expectations readers bring to the genre and writers' adherence to and/or thwarting of that contract. See Lejeune.

9. Rigsby ("Form and Content"), for example, groups the elegies according to subject matter. To date, no study of *Poems on Various Subjects Religious and Moral* has considered the narrativity of the volume. While there is some evidence that Wheatley's poems were subjected to minor editorial changes, most of this editing occurred in editions and reprints issued after the 1773 edition. The extensiveness of Wheatley's own revising process, however, as demonstrated by the ongoing recovery of her manuscripts, makes it probable that the ordering of the original 1773 edition is her own. The 1772 "Proposal for Printing by Subscription" lists the poems in "the Order in which they were penned, together with the Occasion" (Shields 188). Wheatley, of course, revised many of these poems before publishing them, and it is logical to assume that she would have had a hand in revising their order as well. I am not, of course, arguing that Wheatley was fully conscious of the implications of her arrangements. It is also interesting to note that while the elegies are scattered throughout *Poems*, the 1779 "Proposal" for a second volume of her writings lists nine new elegies grouped together by genre.

10. In this sense, Wheatley inverts William L. Andrews's paradigm of the dictated slave narrative as "literary ventriloquism," in *To Tell a Free Story* (35). For Andrews, throughout much of the first century of black autobiography, the

black story/text was controlled by white amanuenses and "editors." Wheatley's telling of the "Other's" story in the funeral elegies, then, is an early example of black "control" of white stories/texts.

Chapter Four
"Social Piety" in Ann Plato's *Essays*

1. Not only is Wheatley's gender completely unacknowledged, but ownership is assigned to John Wheatley, even though it was his wife, Susannah Wheatley, who, reportedly, "picked Phillis out" on the auction block (and who "claimed" her as a personal servant) and Mary Wheatley who tutored her. Moreover, it was John Wheatley who wrote the short biographical sketch that prefaces the 1773 *Poems*. Further, seventeen prominent male citizens signed the letter of authentication that accompanied *Poems* even though Wheatley was well established in a community of powerful women—Susannah and the Countess of Huntingdon, who was her literary patron. When we consider Wheatley's correspondence with Susannah Wheatley and Obour Tanner, the appellation "Negro Servant" with its sole concern for racial affiliation can be read as a complete erasure of the significance of gender. (To which might be added the fact that Wheatley was only the second American woman, after Puritan poet Anne Bradstreet, to publish a book of poems.)

2. Toni Morrison, "Unspeakable Things Unspoken: The Afro-American Presence in American Literature," *Michigan Quarterly Review* 28, no. 1 (Winter 1989): 1–34. Henry Louis Gates writes of the difference between Wheatley's "Attestation," with its white male signers, and Pennington's "Preface" to Plato's writings, in *The Signifying Monkey*: "Not a lot changed . . . between Wheatley's 1773 publication . . . and Ann Plato's except that by 1841 Plato's attestation was supplied by a black person" (130). Obviously I do not agree. Moreover, while noticing the difference in the race of the authenticators, Gates misses the implications for gender.

3. On the placement of black Puritans in "Negro Pews," see Alice Morse Earle, *The Sabbath in Puritan New England* (New York: Scribner's, 1892), esp. chapter 5, "Seating the Meeting," 45–65. See Pennington. Though Pennington began his short tenure at the Talcott Street Church in 1840, he did not disclose his fugitive status until 1845. For biographical information on Pennington, see David O. White, "The Fugitive Blacksmith of Hartford: James W. C. Pennington," *Connecticut Historical Society Bulletin* 29, no. 1 (Winter 1984): 5–29.

4. Barbara Smith writes of the "simultaneity of oppressions" that characterize black women's lives, in *Home Girls: A Black Feminist Anthology* (New York: Kitchen Table Press, 1983). Mae Henderson extends this concept as a function of black women's subjectivity and discourse in "Speaking in Tongues."

5. Henderson refers here to the courtroom scene from Zora Neale Hurston's *Their Eyes Were Watching God* during which Janie Starks must plead her case to a heterogeneous audience of spectators. Hurston's imaginative and Henderson's critical and tropological refigurings of black women's subjectivity and discourse "on trial," however, engage dialogically with the historical trials and examinations out of which emerge the authorship of both Wheatley and Plato.

6. I wish to thank Professor James Miller of Trinity College (Hartford) for sending me what little information is in print on Ann Plato. The 1830 Census is helpfully available in Woodson, *Free Negro Heads of Families*. I examined Hartford city directories between 1828, the year of the the first directory to record free blacks, and 1860–61. Other information about blacks in Hartford is available through the Connecticut Historical Society, Hartford, Connecticut.

7. The relevant lines are:

> Now eighteen years their destin'd course have run,
> In fast succession round the central sun.
> How did the follies of that period pass
> Unnotic'd, but behold them writ in brass!
> In Recollection see them fresh return,
> And sure 'tis mine to be asham'd, and mourn.
>
> (Wheatley, "On Recollection," lines 31–36)

> Now fifteen years their destined course have run,
> In fast succession round the central sun;
> How did the follies of that period pass,
> I ask myself—are they inscribed in brass!
> Oh! Recollection, speed their fresh return,
> And sure 'tis mine to be ashamed and mourn.
>
> (Plato, "Lines," lines 14–19)

8. I refer, of course, to Henry Louis Gates's groundbreaking observation that black writers, from the beginnings of Afro-American literary tradition, read and revised each other's work. Gatesian "signifyin(g)," however, does not take up the issue of what motivates such rereading and rewriting. I would argue, by extension, that black writers' investment in the writings of other black writers is a function of African American intersubjectivity and community interaction.

9. Michael Awkward argues for the use of sociohistorical context as a part of intertextual analysis, in *Inspiriting Influences*.

10. See Porter, "Organized Educational Activities" and *Early Negro Writing*; Joyce; Dann; Howard Holman Bell, ed., *Minutes of the Proceedings of the National Negro Conventions, 1830–1864* (New York: Arno, 1969); and Carter G. Woodson, *Negro Orators and Their Orations* (New York: Russell and Russell, 1969).

11. The text Hamilton "holds in [his] hand" is Peter Williams's *Oration on the Abolition of the Slave Trade: Delivered in the African Church in the City of New York, January 1, 1808. With an Introductory Essay by Henry Sipkins*. This text is reprinted in Porter, *Early Negro Writing* 343–54.

12. This outpouring of oratorical genres was, of course, not unique to African Americans; the era between the American Revolutionary War and the Civil War was often self-styled "the golden age of American oratory." As Lawrence Buell writes, "the prestige of oratory overshadowed that of poetry, not to mention fiction and drama, and resulted in the persistence, well into the Romantic period, of the Neoclassical tendency to define belles lettres as a branch of rhetoric." See Buell 137.

13. *Freedom's Journal*, the first black periodical newspaper, was published weekly in New York and ran from March 16, 1827, to March 28, 1829. The *Colored American*, also published in New York, ran from March 1837 to December 1841.

14. See Peterson.

15. Some historians, like Rosalyn Terborg-Penn in "Black Male Perspectives on the Nineteenth-Century Woman," argue that "on the whole during the antebellum period, black male leaders were more sympathetic to woman's rights than white male leaders" (28). Terborg-Penn states that black men's political disenfranchisement put them in a position to better empathize with women because "the legal and political discrimination that black men suffered was shared by all women as well" (29). Yet this perspective depends on an interracial framework that presents "all women" as a monolithic category distinct from racial difference.

16. Harriet E. Wilson appeals "to my colored brethren universally for patronage, hoping they will not condemn this attempt of their sister to be erudite, but rally around me a faithful band of supporters and defenders." See the preface to *Our Nig; or Sketches from the Life of a Free Black* (1859).

17. "Addressivity" is Bakhtin's term for the "dialogic turn" that confers upon the utterance "the quality of turning to someone" (*Speech Genres* 95–99). The utterance is determined, then, by an addressee *"for whose sake . . . it is actually created"* (94).

18. Here Bakhtin presages Houston Baker, who reads black modernism as evidence of the "mastery of form" of late-nineteenth-century minstrelsy. See Baker's *Modernism and the Harlem Renaissance* (Chicago: University of Chicago Press, 1987).

19. A necessary component of the addressivity of all utterances, according to Bakhtin, is "the superaddressee," one who will "coincide *personally*" with the subjectivity of the speaker (*Speech Genres* 95).

20. Because of the racism experienced by the few black children allowed to attend the white schools in Hartford, in 1830 the black community of Hartford petitioned for separate schools for their children (David O. White, "Hartford's African Free Schools, 1830–1868," *Connecticut Historical Society Bulletin* 39, no. 2 [April 1974]: 47–53). We know that Ann Plato was teaching in the Second District by 1844 because of the notes of Reverend Thomas Robbins, a white clergyman assigned to report to the Hartford School Society on the progress in the black schools. Yet her reference to having passed her "examination" in "Lines," a poem "To My Infant Class," and the remark by Robbins in 1845 that "she has taught some time" make it possible that Plato was already teaching in 1841 or about to begin her coeducational classes of black children. I mention this only because the style of *Essays* makes it entirely possible that her primary audience was her pupils. In this light, *Essays* should be read as of the same genre as Pennington's *Textbook of the Origin and History . . . of the Colored People* (1841), which was, according to Vernon Loggins, "intended for Negro children" (197). Such a reading would account for what several scholars have perceived as a "didactic" style in *Essays*, which I will refigure as her pedagogical mission. For Plato is ultimately concerned with preparing a rising generation of

black youth for the realities and possibilities of life as free black persons in nineteenth-century America.

21. Though free blacks are often discussed as if they are a privileged "class" (as compared to African Americans still enslaved), their "status" was notoriously precarious. Not only were free blacks constantly vulnerable to capture and enslavement by overzealous slave catchers on the lookout for fugitives (see Solomon Northup's *Twelve Years a Slave*), but they inhabited the lowest social stratum in every northern city. A visitor to Philadelphia in the 1840s, for example, observed that free blacks were often "crammed into lofts, garrets and cellars, in blind alleys and narrow courts" (qtd. in Curry 49). Curry's quantitative analysis documents the hardship faced by the vast majority of free blacks before 1850. See also Woodson's early monographic introduction to *Free Negro Heads of Families*.

22. "Finalization" is Bakhtin's term for "boundedness" or "outsidedness" and is often translated as "consummation." It is through "finalization" that one experiences one's own "outsidedness" or "otherness," a process that allows for a relationship to one's "self" as "other." See *Art and Answerability*, esp. 101–2.

23. For the relationship of these changes to gender, see Richard D. Shiels, "The Feminization of American Congregationalism, 1730–1835," *American Quarterly* 33, no. 1 (Spring 1981): 46–62.

24. A supreme example of the belief in God as an agent moving in history is in Absalom Jones's rhetorically brilliant *Thanksgiving Sermon, Preached January 1, 1808, in St. Thomas's or the African Episcopal Church, Philadelphia: On Account of the Abolition of the African Slave Trade*: "Our God . . . came down into the United States, when they declared, in the constitution which they framed in 1788, that the trade in our African fellowmen should cease in the year 1808 . . . ." (in Porter, *Early Negro Writing* 338).

25. Deathbed scenes are frequent in American women's literature of the period, part of the convention of sentimentality that forges identification with the reader through the use of highly emotion-charged scenes. See Jane Tompkins, *Sensational Designs: The Cultural Work of American Fiction, 1790–1860* (New York: Oxford University Press, 1985). These scenes show up most often, in African American women's writings, in the genre of spiritual autobiography and as part of the authenticating strategy of sanctioning the black woman preacher's call to public ministry. The best example is Zilpha Elaw's *Memoirs*, in which she actually represents her dying sister, newly converted after a long illness, voicing the call from God amid other utterances such as singing, speaking in tongues, etc. See *Memoir of the Life, Religious Experience, Ministerial Travels, and Labours of Mrs. Zilpha Elaw*, in Andrews, *Sisters of the Spirit*, esp. 71–76.

26. On the epitaph as a figure for autobiography, see Paul de Man, "Autobiography as Defacement," *Modern Language Notes* 94 (1979): 919–30.

Chapter Five
"I Took a Text"

1. For the formation, duties, and responsibilities of the A.M.E. Book Concern see the *Articles of Association of the African Methodist, Episcopal Church, of*

the City of Philadelphia, in the Commonwealth of Pennsylvania (Philadelphia: John Ormond, 1799). An important early history of the denomination is Payne, *History of the African Methodist Episcopal Church.* See also George, Harry V. Richardson, and Sernett, *Black Religion.*

2. *The Life and Religious Experience of Jarena Lee, a Coloured Lady, Giving an Account of Her Call to Preach the Gospel,* in Andrews, *Sisters of the Spirit,* 25–48. *Religious Experience and Journal of Mrs. Jarena Lee, Giving an Account of Her Call to Preach the Gospel,* in Houchins. Hereafter I will refer to the 1836 edition as *Life* and the 1849 text as *Journal.* All further citations will be taken from these two editions.

3. Clifford Geertz, "Blurred Genres: The Refiguration of Social Thought," in *Critical Theory since 1965,* ed. Hazard Adams and Leroy Searle (Tallahassee: Florida State University Press, 1986), 514–23.

4. See Andrews's introduction to *Sisters of the Spirit.* To date, the most extended treatment of Lee's work is Frances Smith Foster's cultural history *Written by Herself.* Joanne Braxton includes a thematic discussion of Jarena Lee's narratives in *Black Women Writing Autobiography.* Susan Houchins's discussion in the introduction to the Schomburg volume *Spiritual Narratives* is also helpful to the situating of Lee's writings in the context of women's religious history. See also Jean Humez's historical treatment of Lee along with the lives and writings of four other nineteenth-century preaching women, " 'My Spirit Eye.' "

5. See Kagle.

6. Kagle explains that the Methodist emphasis on "good works" meant that diaries kept by Methodists "place greater stress on physical acts and show less anxiety about an internal struggle for grace" than similar diaries/journals by other religious group members, for example, Quakers and Puritans. This would account for the emphasis on frenetic activity that characterizes Lee's *Journal.*

7. This is based on the pagination of the *Journal* in which the portion that appeared in 1836 covers the first twenty pages of the text.

8. Hayden White, "The Value of Narrativity," in *On Narrative,* ed. W.J.T. Mitchell (Chicago: University of Chicago Press, 1981), 1–24.

9. Will B. Gravely writes that African American churches "became the institutional core of free black community life, serving as an educational venture, housing literary societies and libraries, and hosting schools and benevolent associations. Their buildings were the meeting-houses of black freedom." Will B. Gravely, "The Rise of African Churches in America, 1786–1822," in Fulop and Raboteau 135–51.

10. See, for example, Rabateau.

11. On African preaching, see Raboteau; Henry Mitchell, *Black Preaching: The Recovery of a Powerful Art* (Nashville: Abingdon Press, 1990); and Davis. For a treatment of the sermon in black literature, see Hubbard. Much work has been done on spirituals by scholars in history, ethnomusicology, religion, sociology, and other disciplines. See Cone, Work, Johnson and Johnson, Lovell, Southern, Stuckey, Levine, Fisher, Spencer, *Protest and Praise,* and Kirk-Duggan.

12. Christian "The Race for Theory."

13. Spencer (*Protest and Praise*) refers to all of these forms as black "sacred music." I maintain that all of these "sacred genres" should be regarded as "song."

14. See Lovell 227; Southern.

15. Subsequent editions were compiled in 1803, 1818, and 1837. See Spencer, *Black Hymnody*, and Southern.

16. Southern implies that spirituals developed out of "wandering refrains" attached to orthodox hymns, working from the assumption that Euramerican hymnody came first and was merely varied by black songsters and singers in performance. A more likely scenario is that spirituals coexisted alongside traditional hymnody, and Allen's inclusion of "wandering verses" was a way of making otherwise standard Watts and Wesley hymns palatable to his African American congregation, a congregation already familiar with spirituals derived from African singing practices. Allen obviously had the musical taste of his congregation in mind when he wrote in the preface to the 1818 edition, *African Methodist Pocket Hymn Book*: "Having become a distinct and separate body of people, there is no collection of hymns, we could, with propriety adopt. However, we have for some time, been collecting materials for the present work; and we trust, the result of our labour will receive the sanction of the congregation under our charge" (qtd. in Spencer, *Black Hymnody* 7).

17. See Southern 165, 77–86.

18. Lee mentions in *Religious Experience and Journal* that she took her handwritten manuscript to an unnamed editor for "corrections."

19. A similar search for religious community appears in *The Interesting Narrative of Olaudah Equiano or Gustavas Vassa, the African* (1789) when Equiano recounts his experimentation with Quakerism, Roman Catholicism, and other denominations and faiths before his "arriving" at true conversion through Methodism. Equiano, however, does not mention the cultural dimensions of Methodism because he did not have access to the specific Afro-Christian practices via African Methodism that were open to Lee. Thus Lee's cultural specificity is a new development in this type of narrative line.

20. Lee uses the term "missionary" here rather than "minister" or "preacher." This designation probably means that this is a special service held for servants or slaves.

21. Lee uses "psalm" here in the generic sense of a song or hymn rather than to designate the biblical poems themselves. Lee says that the psalm was "read," yet it is versified in the manner of psalms used for singing as early as the time of the Puritans. It could be—especially if, as I suspect, this was a special service being given for servants—that the psalm was indeed sung and "lined-out" (minister reading one line at a time and congregation singing in response), as were psalms in the early American church. Because of illiteracy and lack of hymn books, "lining-out" (a method of singing blacks dubbed "Dr. Watts") continued in the black churches long after it ceased being the unsual practice in white churches, and it continues to this day. It, of course, fits right into black call-response worship style and cultural practice, hence its practice even in black congregations where parishioners are highly educated. See Southern; Melva W.

Costen, "Singing Praise to God in African-American Worship Contexts," in Wilmore, *African-American Religious Studies* 392–404; Spencer, *Black Hymnody*.

22. Joseph Pilmore (1739–1825). In 1769, he volunteered as the first Methodist from England to preach in Philadelphia at St. Paul's Episcopal Church; he frequently led services at both the Free African Society—founded by Richard Allen, Absalom Jones, and others, who broke away from St. George's Methodist Episcopal Church because of racial discrimination—and at the newly formed Bethel A.M.E. Though St. Paul's was known as "the most evangelical of the three Anglican churches in the city," and Pilmore attracted a large audience of black worshipers before the formation of black religious institutions, Lee still fails to find in his "ministrations" and worship style the community she is seeking. For information on Pilmore and early black churches in Philadelphia, see Nash.

23. See n. 1 above.

24. See Marcellus Blount, "The Preacherly Text: African American Poetry and Vernacular Performance," *PMLA* 107, no. 3 (May 1992): 582–93. Blount refigures performance as "verbal performance viewed as cultural event" (583).

25. Matrix in the sense developed by Houston Baker in *Blues* of "blues matrix." My figure of African American cultural expressivity as "performing community" posits, for the nineteenth century, a distinct but related "spirituals matrix."

26. See also Spillers, "Moving On down the Line," a poststructuralist treatment, and her earlier "Martin Luther King and the Style of the Black Sermon," in Lincoln, *Black Experience in Religion* 76–98. See also Jon Michael Spencer's brilliant *Protest and Praise*. Spencer's understanding of the relationship between preaching and singing in African American religious contexts helped shape my own understanding of these connections. Spillers, also, in "Martin Luther King" refers to the black church as a "singing church." I will use the term "preaching," then, to refer to the "sermon" in performing context, rather than as a static "text," as is the usual practice in literary analysis.

27. Folklorist Alan Dundes writes that "folk categories have an internal analytic capability" (qtd. in Davis 37).

28. The first sermon recorded is Lemuel Haynes, "A Black Puritan's Farewell" (in *Afro-American Religious History: A Documentary Witness*, ed. Milton C. Sernett [Durham: Duke University Press, 1985], 51–59). Other early examples of African American sermons are collected in Porter, *Early Negro Writing*.

29. Spencer, *Protest and Praise*. "Order of service" is the isochronic structure for the event of religious worship for which singing, intonation, testifying, shouting, clapping, etc., serve as "antistructure."

30. Qtd. in Porter, *Early Negro Writing* 344–45.

31. "Merciful[ly] striving" resonates strongly with W.E.B. Du Bois's notion of African American culture as "Our Spiritual Strivings," in *The Souls of Black Folk* (New York: Penguin, 1989), 3. See Alice Walker.

32. In "Gender and Genre: Black Women's Autobiographies and the Ideology of Literacy," *African American Review* 26, no. 1 (Spring 1992): 119–29, I note that in the case of both Lee and Zilpha Elaw's narratives, the first sin is a misuse of language. For Lee it is lying; for Elaw, cursing.

33. For Bakhtin, "finalization" refers to "the inner side of the change of speech subjects. This change can only take place because the speaker has said (or written) *everything* he wishes to say at a particular moment or under particular circumstances" (*Speech Genres* 77).

34. Michael Holquist (in "Answering as Authoring: Mikhail Bakhtin's Trans-Linguistics" in *Bakhtin: Essays and Dialogues on His Work,* ed. Gary Saul Morson [Chicago: University of Chicago Press, 1986], 59–71) notes, correctly, that "agency" is checked by the participation of all speakers in socially determined "speech genres," which allows for the reentry of the social dimension of human subjectivity.

35. Critics who maintain that Bakhtin is first and foremost a theorist of ideology and power relations (for example, Ken Hirschkop and David Shepherd) tend to draw on the works of contested authorship, such as *Marxism and the Philosophy of Language* and *The Formal Method in Literary Scholarship.* Even when these works are taken into account, in my view, power relations remain secondary rather than primary considerations. On the debate over the "disputed texts," see Morson and Emerson, esp. chapter 3.

36. Two excellent critiques of Bakhtinian dialogics are Fogel and José Rabasa's "Dialogue as Conquest: Mapping Spaces for Counter-Discourse," in JanMohamed and Lloyd.

Chapter Six
Rituals of Desire

1. Jarena Lee was born on February 11, 1873, in Cape May, New Jersey. Rebecca Cox Jackson was born on February 15, 1795, in Horntown, Pennsylvania, about nine miles outside of Philadelphia. Both were born free.

2. Humez, *Gifts of Power* 262. Rebecca Cox Jackson's journals, which were written between 1830 and 1864, were preserved in manuscript form in various Shaker archives until they were gathered, edited, and published in one volume in 1981 by Humez as *Gifts of Power.* All citations of Jackson's writings will be taken from this edition.

3. I cannot emphasize enough the representative nature of both Lee's and Jackson's writings. While both are autobiographical, the writers clearly structure and order the events of their texts and employ strategies of dialogue and tropes in ways that highlight their own sense of religious doctrines and ideologies. Note, for example, Jackson's representation of Lee's speech with the Quaker/Shaker "thee," which is not found in Lee's representations of her own speech in either the *Life and Religious Experience* or the *Religious Experience and Journal.*

4. See, for example, Jean Humez's introduction to her edited volume, *Gifts of Power*, and "'My Spirit Eye.'" See also William Andrews's introduction to *Sisters of the Spirit*, Braxton, Evans, and Alice Walker 71–82.

5. In recounting her first meeting with the Shakers, Jackson claims to have read "no books but the Bible" (141). Given that Jackson was completely surrounded by A.M.E. Church activities during her early years in Philadelphia (her brother Joseph Cox, with whom Jackson lived even after her marriage, was an

A.M.E. minister and held several important offices at Bethel), I find it hard to believe that Jackson could have escaped either reading or hearing read or recounted Jarena Lee's *Life and Religious Experience*. Humez points out that this remark is strategic, used by Jackson to defend herself against the charge that her theological stance and practice of celibacy came only after she had read the Shaker writings, rather than being derived independently and communicated directly by the Spirit. I regard this statement in the same light as similar statements made by Lee. At the end of her *Life*, Lee claims that she "never had more than three months schooling" (*Gifts of Power* 48). This claim could be accurate in terms of formal education, but Lee's *Life* and *Religious Experience and Journal* (1849) show a remarkably developed prose style. I see the statement as a strategy by which Lee answers both the increasing literacy requirements of the A.M.E. clergy, which threatened to exclude women and lower-class blacks who had less access to education, and as a claim that her own religious insights were of God and not obtained through formal education. On the literacy requirements of the A.M.E. Church, see Payne, *History of the African Methodist Episcopal Church*. Moreover, throughout Lee's narrative, temporal sequences almost always occur in threes: "three months," "three weeks," etc. Again, this is less an attempt to be historically accurate than a device that signals the fullness of God's time. For more on such strategies of temporal representation, see my "Gender and Genre: Black Women's Autobiographies and the Ideology of Literacy," *African American Review* 26, no. 1 (Spring 1992): 119–29. The tendency to see black women's spiritual narratives as, simply, transparent recordings of experiential "facts" is a problem in the criticism of these narratives. Their very sophisticated rhetorical, strategic, and representational qualities have largely gone unappreciated. A noteworthy exception is James H. Evans's treatment of Jackson's fictional strategies in *Spiritual Empowerment* 53–94.

6. I borrow the term "investment" from Wendy Hollway's "Gender Difference and the Production of Subjectivity," in Henriques et al. 227–63. Hollway uses the term to describe the process by which people take up particular subject positions in certain discourses rather than others. "Investment" replaces, for her, terms like "motivation," with its biological overtones, or "drive," which recalls a mechanistic psychoanalysis: "By claiming that people have investments . . . in taking uncertain positions in discourses, and consequently in relation to each other, I mean that there will be some satisfaction or pay-off or reward . . . for that person. The satisfaction may well be in contraction with other resultant feelings. It is not necessarily conscious or rational" (238).

7. The increasingly rigid literacy standards, standardization of hymnals, and attempts to clamp down on "female praying bands," and the like, are discussed in Payne, *History of the African Methodist Episcopal Church*. See also Southern. Lee had a run-in with just such institutionalization when the A.M.E. Book Concern refused to publish her 1849 *Religious Experience and Journal* on the grounds that "it is impossible to decipher much of the meaning contained in it."

8. My trope "troublin' the waters" is, of course, taken from the New Testament and the African American spiritual "Wade in the Water" commonly sung at Afro-Protestant baptisms. In both versions, healing is said to occur only through a prior "troubling" of the waters "in a certain season" (John 5:4).

9. Holy Mother Wisdom is the Shaker term for the female attribute of the Deity. Many fine studies of Shaker social life and theology have been published since the mid-1970s, most notably, Desroche, Whitson, and Brewer. On Rebecca Jackson's establishment of the mostly black Philadelphia Shakers, see Richard E. Williams.

10. Though Jackson claims this vision occurred before her meeting with the Shakers in 1843, Humez's argument that it was written *after* that first meeting is convincing. It appears as an insertion, beginning with the words "I should have mentioned this, in between the Savior on the cross and my heavenly lead" (*Gifts of Power* 136). Humez points out that both this vision and the subsequent retelling of her first meeting with the Shakers are deliberately placed out of the chronological order of their writing, as evidenced by their inclusion of events that occurred several months earlier (see 136 n. 18, 138 n. 21). Once again, Jackson demonstrates a self-conscious manipulation of details for full religious and ideological effect.

11. The distinction between natural and spiritual, generational and regenerational, extends to Shaker reading practices as well. Natural readings were based on literal interpretations of texts, which the Shakers eschewed. In this sense, they were not fundamentalists. Spiritual readings were based on the interaction between text and communications from the spirit world directly through the reader's experience. I would argue, then, that Jackson's revision of Lee's text is based on a "spiritual," rather than "natural," reading of Lee's work. See Desroche 79–81 and 148–62 for an excellent discussion of Shaker methods of biblical interpretation and exegesis.

12. See Margarita Bowen, *Empiricism and Geographical Thought: From Francis Bacon to Alexander Humboldt* (Cambridge: Cambridge University Press, 1981), 100; Mazrui, "The Map and the Master," in *The Africans*. The compass as an artifact and signifier of Western culture calls to mind the watch that engaged Olaudah Equiano aboard the slave ship that transported him (*Interesting Narrative*, in Gates, *Classic Slave Narratives* 39).

13. See also Murphy.

14. I discuss this more fully in chapter 7.

15. John S. Mbiti writes of time and space as key to the understanding of African religions, in *African Religions and Philosophy*.

16. This line appears in the African American spiritual "Steal Away to Jesus."

17. While I have taken this passage from Humez's edition, Diane Sasson, in *Shaker Spiritual Narratives*, uses the Berkshire Athenaeum manuscript, which she arranged into lines for metrical effect. Thus the paragraph reads:

"Sen In the yeare of 1830 July
I Was Wakened by thunder and Lightning At the brak of day
and beed Wich Had bin my resting plac
in time of thunder for five Years Was now Taking away
A bout five years Ago I Was Afected by Thunder
and alwayes after in time of Thunder and Lightening
I woud hav to go to beed Becos it mad me So sick
now my only plac of reast is taking A Way

and I roes up and Wolket the floore beak and fouth
Ringing my hnades and criing under great fearre
I heared It sayed to me
this day thy souls is requiered Of thee
and all my Sines from my Childhood
rushed In my mind like A over Swelling tiid
and I expected every clap of Thunder
to launch my Soul at the Bare of God
Withall my Sines that I had ever dun
I hav now langigs to Describe my feeling. (Qtd. in Sasson 160)

Clearly Sasson's rendering raises important questions about voice in early African American narrative, especially as so many of the early narratives were taken down by amanuenses and subjected to other editing. See, for example, *The History of Mary Prince* in Gates, *Classic Slave Narratives*.

18. Sasson cites Jarena Lee and "Steal Away."

19. "It was because I had disobeyed the Spirit, that brought me out of Egypt and was then bringing me through the Wilderness down to the Jordan, where I was to be given to Joshua, whom I did not know" (84). "March 30, 1844 Saturday, P.M. The Lord spoke to me through his preacher whome he called me out out of Egypt that is thunder and lightning" (200).

20. See Theophus Smith and Hopkins.

21. See Humez, *Gifts of Power* 15 n. 16: "Jackson recorded instances of the windstorm functioning as a medium for divine communication with her."

22. See Thompson, Raboteau. The persistence of these folk beliefs has been corroborated by the findings of the African Burial Ground project in New York, which is systematically studying the graves of 390 African Americans found in Lower Manhattan during a construction project. The earliest known mention of the African cemetery dates from 1712, and the burial ground was apparently in use well into the nineteenth century. Among the discoveries, excavators have found that "all the bodies were buried with their heads to the west, allowing them to sit up and face the rising sun on Judgment Day" (David W. Dunlap, "Unfree, Unknown: Buried Slaves Near City Hall," *New York Times*, December 26, 1991). Other researchers report, "Many were buried with coins in their hands and on their eyes. A shell found with one skeleton suggests a traditional slave saying: 'By the sea we came, buy the sea we shall go'" (Bruce Frankel, "Black Cemetery in NYC New Key to Colonial Times," *USA Today*, September 15, 1992). The continued gathering, cataloging, and interpretation of data from this and other archaeological sites will enrich the study of early African American history and culture in the future.

23. Kenneth Brown, "Material Culture and Community Structure: The Slave and Tenant Community at Levi Jordan's Plantation, 1848–1892," in *Working toward Freedom: Slave Society and Domestic Economy in the American South*, ed. L. E. Hudson (Rochester: Rochester University Press, 1994), 95–118.

24. Maria Franklin reads cosmograms and other artifacts as part of the protective ritual of enslaved Africans and their communities, in her fine Ph.D. dis-

sertation, "Out of Site, Out of Mind: The Archaeology of an Enslaved Virginian Household, ca. 1740–1778" (University of California–Berkeley, 1997).

Chapter Seven
Performing Community

1. Judith Butler, *Gender Trouble: Feminism and the Subversion of Identity* (New York: Routledge, 1991).

2. Herskovits, Frazier. Veve A. Clark, "Developing Diaspora Literacy and *Morasa* Consciousness," in Spillers, *Comparative American Identities* 40–61; Sobel.

3. Mintz, in Mintz and Price, emphasizes the "many" to "one" syntax. Most scholars have tried to get around the heterogeneity of African peoples transported to the New World by arguing that the majority of enslaved Africans came from particular regions of Western Africa. I realize that such arguments were necessary to counter racist assumptions about black inability to conceive of themselves collectively. On the heterogeneity of Africa, see Appiah.

4. Spillers, "Mama's Baby, Papa's Maybe."

5. Charles H. Long, "Perspectives for a Study of African-American Religion in the United States," in Fulop and Raboteau 26.

6. Benedict Anderson theorizes "imagined community" as the temporal-spatial mode of cognition underwriting notions of community and nationhood: "The idea of a sociological organism moving calendrically through homogeneous, empty time is a precise analog of the idea of nation, which also is conceived as a solid community moving steadily down (or up) history." See Benedict Anderson, "The Cultural Roots of Nationalism," in Donald and Hall 98.

7. Mazrui discusses European "invention" of Africa and racialization as "the dis-Africanisation of the diaspora." The primacy of sight in the construction of African "otherness" during initial contacts of Europeans with African people is discussed in Winthrop Jordan's comprehensive *White over Black*, esp. 3–43.

8. "On Being Brought From Africa to America," lines 5–6.

9. On the trauma associated with the severing of Africans from their land, see Mbiti.

10. Bernice Johnson Reagon, "African Diaspora Women: The Making of Cultural Workers," in *Women in Africa and the African Diaspora*, ed. Rosalyn Terborg-Penn, Sharon Harley, and Andrea Benton Rushing (Washington, DC: Howard University Press, 1989), 170.

11. McGary and Lawson.

12. Here I must draw a distinction between James Scott's notion of the "hidden transcript" and the traditional notion of "masking," which conceives of a mask worn by a member of the in-group not visible to the out-group.

13. Wendy Hollway, "Gender Difference and the Production of Subjectivity," in Henriques et al. Note the individual rather than collective focus.

14. Gayle Johnson, "The Way We Do," *Black American Literature Forum* 25, no. 1 (Spring 1991): 16.

15. Christian, "The Race for Theory."

16. See, for example, Levine, Herskovits, Southern, Lovell, Work.

17. *The Homes of the New World* 1:371, qtd. in Southern 190.

18. Allen et al., *Slave Songs of the U.S.* vi, qtd. in Southern 191.

19. Henry G. Spaulding, "Under the Palmetto," *Continental Monthly*, August 1863; rpt. Katz, *The Social Implications of Early Negro Music in the United States* 5; qtd. in Southern 192.

20. M. F. Armstrong and Helen W. Ludlow, *Hampton and Its Students* 172; qtd. in Southern 192.

21. Allen, *Slave Songs*, qtd. in Southern iv–vi.

22. Most scholars treat call-and-response as a strict utterance-answer phenomenon, similar to Western classical notions of "dialogue," rather than as an oral practice that often involves *simultaneous* and *overlapping* utterance. See, for example, Robert Stepto's use of call-and-response as a linear model for African American literary history, in *From Behind the Veil*.

23. Johnson, "The Way We Do" (cited above, n. 14).

24. This particular written arrangement of the lines is taken from Johnson and Johnson 26–27.

25. This movement from a singular "I" to a collective "I"/"we" recalls Wheatley's poem "On Being Brought From Africa to America," in which the "I" becomes communal in line 5 with "our sable race."

26. Spillers, "Moving On down the Line."

27. See Mays and Fisher.

28. See chapter 5, n. 11.

29. Another well-known example is "Lord I want to be a Christian in-a my heart."

30. On "surplus" and "antistructure" see Spencer, *Protest and Praise*.

31. See Jacques Derrida, "Différance," in *Margins of Philosophy*, trans. Alan Bass (Chicago: University of Chicago Press, 1982), 1–27.

Afterword

1. Some of this work has been pioneered by scholars like bell hooks and Cornel West in *Breaking Bread*; Hortense J. Spillers in her article on the African American sermon, "Moving On down the Line"; Mae G. Henderson in "Speaking in Tongues"; and Barbara Christian, "Fixing Methodologies."

Selected Bibliography

Anderson, Victor. *Beyond Ontological Blackness: An Essay on African American Religious and Cultural Criticism*. New York: Continuum, 1995.

Andrews, William L. *To Tell A Free Story: The First Century of Afro-American Autobiography, 1760–1865*. Urbana: University of Illinois Press, 1986.

——, ed. *Sisters of the Spirit: Three Black Women's Autobiographies of the Nineteenth Century*. Bloomington: Indiana University Press, 1986.

Appiah, Kwame Anthony. *In My Father's House: Africa in the Philosophy of Culture*. New York: Oxford University Press, 1992.

Awkward, Michael. *Inspiriting Influences: Tradition, Revision, and Afro-American Women's Novels*. New York: Columbia University Press, 1989.

Baker, Houston A. *Blues, Ideology, and Afro-American Literature: A Vernacular Theory*. Chicago: University of Chicago Press, 1984.

——. *The Journey Back: Issues in Black Literature and Criticism*. Chicago: University of Chicago Press, 1980.

——. *Workings of the Spirit: The Poetics of Afro-American Women's Writing*. Chicago: University of Chicago Press, 1991.

Baker, Houston A., and Patricia Redmond, eds. *Afro-American Literary Study in the 1990's*. Chicago: University of Chicago Press, 1989.

Bakhtin, Mikhail Mikhailovich. *Art and Answerability: Early Philosophical Essays*. Edited by Michael Holquist and Vadim Liapunov. Translated by Viam Liapunov. Austin: University of Texas Press, 1990.

——. *The Dialogic Imagination: Four Essays*. Translated by Caryl Emerson and Michael Holquist. Austin: University of Texas Press, 1981.

——. *Speech Genres and Other Late Essays*. Edited by Caryl Emerson and Michael Holquist. Translated by Vern W. McGee. Austin: University of Texas Press, 1986.

Benstock, Shari, ed. *The Private Self: Theory and Practice of Women's Autobiographical Writings*. Chapel Hill: University of North Carolina Press, 1988.

Berlin, Ira. *Slaves without Masters: The Free Negro in the Antebellum South*. New York: Pantheon Books, 1974.

——. "Time, Space, and the Evolution of Afro-American Society on British Mainland North America." *Journal of Negro History* 85, no. 1 (February 1980): 44–78.

Blassingame, John W. *The Slave Community: Plantation Life in the Antebellum South*. New York: Oxford University Press, 1979.

Boime, Albert. *The Art of Exclusion: Representing Blacks in the Nineteenth Century*. Washington, DC: Smithsonian Institution Press, 1990.

Brawley, Benjamin. *Early Negro American Writers: Selections with Biographical and Critical Introductions*. New York: Dover Publications, 1970.

——. *The Negro in Literature and Art in the United States*. New York: Duffield and Company, 1930.

Braxton, Joanne. *Black Women Writing Autobiography: A Tradition within a Tradition*. Philadelphia: Temple University Press, 1989.

Braxton, Joanne, and Andree Nicola McLaughlin, eds. *Wild Women in the Whirlwind: Afra-American Culture and the Contemporary Literary Renaissance.* New Brunswick, NJ: Rutgers University Press, 1990.

Brewer, Priscilla J. *Shaker Communities, Shaker Lives.* Hanover, NH: University Press of New England, 1986.

Brown, Elsa Barkley. "African-American Women's Quilting: A Framework for Conceptualizing and Teaching African-American Women's History." In *Black Women in America: Social Science Perspectives,* edited by Micheline R. Malson, Elisabeth Mudimbe-Boyi, Jean F. O'Barr, and Mary Myer, 9–10. Chicago: University of Chicago Press, 1990.

Buell, Lawrence. *New England Literary Culture: From Revolution through Renaissance.* Cambridge: Cambridge University Press, 1986.

Cannon, Katie. *Black Womanist Ethics.* Atlanta: Scholar's Press, 1988.

Carby, Hazel V. *Reconstructing Womanhood: The Emergence of the Afro-American Woman Novelist.* New York: Oxford University Press, 1987.

Christian, Barbara. *Black Feminist Criticism: Perspectives on Black Women Writers.* New York: Pergamon Press, 1985.

———. *Black Women Novelists: The Development of a Tradition, 1892–1976.* Westport, CT: Greenwood Press, 1980.

———. "Fixing Methodologies: Reading *Beloved.*" In *Female Subjects in Black and White: Race, Psychoanalysis, Feminism,* edited by Elizabeth Abel, Barbara Christian, and Helene Moglen, 363–70. Berkeley and Los Angeles: University of California Press, 1997.

———. "The Race for Theory." In *The Nature and Context of Minority Discourse,* edited by Abdul R. JanMohamed and David Lloyd, 37–49. Oxford: Oxford University Press, 1990.

Collins, Patricia Hill. *Black Feminist Thought: Knowledge, Consciousness, and the Politics of Empowerment.* New York: Routledge, 1991.

Cone, James H. *The Spirituals and the Blues.* Maryknoll, NY: Orbis Books, 1991.

Connor, Kimberly Rae. *Conversions and Visions in the Writings of African-American Women.* Knoxville: University of Tennessee Press, 1994.

Cott, Nancy F. *The Bonds of Womanhood: "Woman's Sphere" in New England, 1780–1835.* New Haven: Yale University Press, 1977.

Curry, Leonard P. *The Free Black in Urban America, 1800–1850: The Shadow of the Dream.* Chicago: University of Chicago Press, 1981.

Curtin, Philip D. *The Atlantic Slave Trade: A Census.* Madison: University of Wisconsin Press, 1969.

Dann, Martin E., ed. *The Black Press 1827–1890: The Quest for National Identity.* New York: Putnam's, 1971.

Davidson, Cathy N. *Revolution and the Word: The Rise of the Novel in America.* New York: Oxford University Press, 1986.

———, ed. *Reading in America: Literature and Social History.* Baltimore: Johns Hopkins University Press, 1989.

Davis, Gerald L. *I Got the Word in Me and I Can Sing It, You Know: A Study of the Performed African-American Sermon.* Philadelphia: University of Pennsylvania Press, 1985.

Desroche, Henri. *The American Shakers: From Neo-Christianity to Presocialism.* Translated by John K. Savacool. Amherst: University of Massachusetts Press, 1971.

Donald, James, and Stuart Hall, eds. *Politics and Ideology.* Philadelphia: Open University Press, 1986.

Draper, John W. *The Funeral Elegy and the Rise of English Romanticism.* New York: New York University Press, 1929.

Eakin, Paul John. *Fictions in Autobiography: Studies in the Art of Self-Invention.* Princeton: Princeton University Press, 1985.

Epstein, Barbara Leslie. *The Politics of Domesticity: Women, Evangelism, and Temperance in Nineteenth-Century America.* Middletown, CT: Wesleyan University Press, 1981.

Evans, James H., Jr. *Spiritual Empowerment in Afro-American Literature: Frederick Douglass, Rebecca Jackson, Booker T. Washington, Richard Wright, Toni Morrison.* Lewiston, NY: Edwin Mellen Press, 1987.

Fisher, Miles Mark. *Negro Slave Songs in the United States.* New York: Citadel Press, 1981.

Fogel, Aaron. "Coerced Speech and the Oedipus Dialogue Complex." In *Rethinking Bakhtin: Extensions and Challenges,* edited by Gary Saul Morson and Caryl Emerson, 173–96. Evanston, IL: Northwestern University Press, 1989.

Foster, Frances Smith. *Written by Herself: Literary Production by African American Women, 1746–1892.* Bloomington: Indiana University Press, 1993.

Foucault, Michel. *Power/Knowledge: Selected Interviews and Other Writings, 1972–1977.* Translated by Colin Gordon, Leo Marshall, John Mepham, and Kate Soper. New York: Pantheon Books, 1980.

———. "What Is an Author?" In *Critical Theory since 1965,* edited by Hazard Adams and Leroy Searle, 138–47. Tallahassee: Florida State University Press, 1986.

Frazier, E. Franklin. *The Negro Church in America.* New York: Schocken Books, 1974.

Frederickson, George M. *The Black Image in the White Mind: The Debate on Afro-American Character and Destiny, 1817–1914.* Middletown, CT: Wesleyan University Press, 1971.

Friedman, Lawrence J. *Gregarious Saints: Self and Community in American Abolitionism, 1830–1870.* Cambridge: Cambridge University Press, 1982.

Fulop, Timothy E., and Albert J. Raboteau, eds., *African-American Religion: Interpretive Essays in History and Culture.* New York: Routledge, 1997.

Gates, Henry Louis, Jr. *Figures in Black: Words, Signs, and the "Racial" Self.* New York: Oxford University Press, 1987.

———. "From Wheatley to Douglass: The Politics of Displacement." In *Frederick Douglass: New Literary and Historical Essays,* edited by Eric J. Sundquist, 47–65. Cambridge: Cambridge University Press, 1990.

———. *"Race," Writing, and Difference.* Chicago: University of Chicago Press, 1986.

———. *The Signifying Monkey: A Theory of Afro-American Literary Criticism.* New York: Oxford University Press, 1988.

Gates, Henry Louis, Jr., ed. *Black Literature and Literary Theory*. New York: Methuen Books, 1984.

———, ed. *The Classic Slave Narratives*. New York: New American Library, 1987.

———, ed. *Reading Black, Reading Feminist: A Critical Anthology*. New York: Meridian, 1990.

Genovese, Eugene D. *Roll, Jordan, Roll: The World the Slaves Made*. New York: Vintage Books, 1976.

George, Carol V. R. *Segregated Sabbaths: Richard Allen and the Emergence of Independent Black Churches, 1760–1840*. New York: Oxford University Press, 1973.

Gibson, Donald B. "Response to Gates." In *Afro-American Literary Study in the 1990's*, edited by Houston A. Baker, Jr., and Patricia Redmond, 44–50. Chicago: University of Chicago Press, 1989.

Gilroy, Paul. *The Black Atlantic: Modernity and Double Consciousness*. Cambridge: Harvard University Press, 1993.

Grant, Jacqueline. *White Women's Christ and Black Women's Jesus: Feminist Christology and Womanist Response*. Atlanta: Scholar's Press, 1989.

Gravely, Will B. "The Rise of African Churches in America (1786–1822): Reexamining the Contexts." In *African-American Religion: Interpretive Essays in History and Culture*, edited by Timothy E. Fulop and Albert Raboteau, 133–51. New York: Routledge, 1997.

Greene, Lorenzo Johnston. *The Negro in Colonial New England, 1620–1776*. New York: Columbia University Press, 1942.

Gutman, Herbert G. *The Black Family in Slavery and Freedom*. New York: Vintage Books, 1978.

Hall, Stuart. "What Is 'Black' in Black Popular Culture?" In *Black Popular Culture: A Project by Michelle Wallace*, edited by Michelle Wallace and Gina Dent. Seattle: Bay Press, 1992.

Harley, Sharon, and Rosalyn Terborg-Penn, eds. *The Afro-American Woman: Struggles and Images*. Port Washington, NY: Kennikat Press, 1978.

Harris, Barbara, and JoAnn McNamara, eds. *Women and the Structure of Society: Selected Research from the Fifth Berkshire Conference on the History of Women*. Durham: Duke University Press, 1984.

Henderson, Mae Gwendolyn. "Speaking in Tongues: Dialogics, Dialectics, and the Black Woman Writer's Literary Tradition." In *Changing Your Own Words: Essays on Criticism, Theory, and Writing by Black Women*, edited by Cheryl A. Wall, 16–37. New Brunswick, NJ: Rutgers University Press, 1989.

Henriques, Julian, Wendy Hollway, Cathy Urwin, Couze Venn, and Valerie Walkerdine. *Changing the Subject: Psychology, Social Regulation, and Subjectivity*. London: Methuen, 1984.

Henson, Robert. "Form and Content of the Puritan Funeral Elegy." *American Literature* 32, no. 1 (March 1960): 11–27.

Herskovits, Melville J. *The Myth of the Negro Past*. Boston: Beacon Press, 1990.

Higginbotham, A. Leon, Jr. *In the Matter of Color: Race and the American Legal Process, The Colonial Period*. New York: Oxford University Press, 1978.

Hines, Darlene Clark, ed. *The State of Afro-American History Past, Present, and Future*. Baton Rouge: Louisiana State University Press, 1986.

Hirschkop, Ken, and David Shepherd, eds. *Bakhtin and Cultural Theory*. Manchester: Manchester University Press, 1989.

Hoffman, Ronald, and Peter J. Albert, eds. *Women in the Age of the American Revolution*. Charlottesville: Unversity of Virginia Press, 1989.

Holloway, Karla F. C. *Moorings and Metaphors: Figures of Culture and Gender in Black Women's Literature*. New Brunswick, NJ: Rutgers University Press, 1992.

Holquist, Michael. *Dialogism: Bakhtin and His World*. London: Routledge University Press, 1990.

Hood, Robert E. *Begrimed and Black: Christian Traditions on Blacks and Blackness*. Minneapolis: Fortress Press, 1994.

hooks, bell. *Talking Back: Thinking Feminist, Thinking Black*. Boston: South End Press, 1989.

hooks, bell, and Cornel West. *Breaking Bread: Insurgent Black Intellectual Life*. Boston: South End Press, 1991.

Hopkins, Dwight N. *Shoes That Fit Our Feet: Sources for a Constructive Black Theology*. Maryknoll, NY: Orbis Books, 1993.

Horton, James Oliver. *Free People of Color: Inside the African American Community*. Washington, DC: Smithsonian Institution Press, 1993.

Horton, James Oliver, with Lois E. Horton. *Black Bostonians: Family Life and Community Struggle in the Antebellum North*. New York: Holmes and Meier, 1979.

Houchins, Susan, ed. *Spiritual Narratives*. The Schomburg Library of Nineteenth-Century Black Women Writers. New York: Oxford Unversity Press, 1988.

Hubbard, Dolan. *The Sermon and the African American Literary Imagination*. Columbia: University of Missouri Press, 1994.

Humez, Jean McMahon, ed. *Gifts of Power: The Writings of Rebecca Cox Jackson, Black Visionary, Shaker Eldress*. Amherst: University of Massachusetts Press, 1981.

———. " 'My Spirit Eye': Some Functions of Spiritual and Visionary Experience in the Lives of Five Black Women Preachers, 1810–1880." In *Women and the Structure of Society: Selected Research from the Fifth Berkshire Conference on the History of Women*, edited by Barbara Harris and JoAnn McNamara, 129–43. Durham: Duke University Press, 1984.

Hurston, Zora Neale. *Mules and Men*. 1935. Bloomington: Indiana University Press, 1978.

Inikori, Joseph E., and Stanley L. Engerman, eds. *The Atlantic Slave Trade: Effects on Economies, Societies, and Peoples in Africa, the Americas, and Europe*. Durham: Duke University Press, 1992.

Jackson, Blyden. *A History of Afro-American Literature*. Vol. 1, *The Long Beginning, 1746–1895*. Baton Rouge: Louisiana State University Press, 1989.

JanMohamed, Abdul R., and David Lloyd, eds. *The Nature and Context of Minority Discourse*. New York: Oxford University Press, 1990.

Johnson, James Weldon, and J. Rosamond Johnson. *The Book of American Negro Spirituals*. New York: Harper and Row, 1926.

Johnson, Paul E., ed. *African American Christianity: Essays in History*. Berkeley and Los Angeles: University of California Press, 1994.

Jordan, June. "The Difficult Miracle of Black Poetry in America; or, Something Like a Sonnet for Phillis Wheatley." In *Wildwomen in the Whirlwind: Afra-American Culture and the Contemporary Literary Renaissance*, edited by Joanne M. Braxton and Andree Nicola McLaughlin, 22–34. New Brunswick, NJ: Rutgers University Press, 1990.

Jordan, Winthrop D. *White over Black: American Attitudes toward the Negro, 1550–1812*. New York: W. W. Norton, 1977.

Joyce, Donald Franklin. *Gatekeepers of Black Culture: Black-Owned Book Publishing in the United States, 1817–1891*. Westport, CT: Greenwood Press, 1983.

Joyner, Charles. "'Believer I Know': The Emergence of African-American Christianity." In *African-American Christianity: Essays in History*, edited by Paul E. Johnson. Berkeley and Los Angeles: University of California Press, 1994.

Kagle, Steven E. *American Diary Literature, 1620–1799*. Boston: Twayne Publishers, 1979.

Kaplin, Sidney, and Emma Nogrady Kaplan. *The Black Presence in the Era of the American Revolution*. Amherst: University of Massachusetts Press, 1989.

Katzman, David M. *Seven Days a Week: Women and Domestic Service in Industrializing America*. Urbana: University of Illinois Press, 1978.

Kirk-Duggan, Cheryl A. *Exorcising Evil: A Womanist Perspective on the Spirituals*. Maryknoll, NY: Orbis Books, 1997.

Kristeva, Julia. "My Memory's Hyperbole." in *The Female Autograph*, edited by Domna C. Stanton, 219–35. Chicago: University of Chicago Press, 1987.

Lejeune, Phillipe. *On Autobiography*. Translated by Katherine Leary. Minneapolis: University of Minnesota Press, 1989.

Lerner, Gerda. *Black Women in White America: A Documentary History*. New York: Vintage Books, 1973.

Levine, Lawrence W. *Black Culture and Black Consciousness: Afro-American Folk Thought from Slavery to Freedom*. New York: Oxford University Press, 1977.

Lincoln, C. Eric. *The Black Church since Frazier*. New York: Schocken Books, 1974.

———, ed. *The Black Experience in Religion*. New York: Anchor Books, 1974.

Lincoln, C. Eric, and Lawrence H. Mamiya. *The Black Church in the African American Experience*. Durham: Duke University Press, 1990.

Litwack, Leon F. *Been in the Storm So Long: The Aftermath of Slavery*. New York: Vintage Books, 1979.

———. *North of Slavery: The Negro in the Free States, 1790–1860*. Chicago: University of Chicago Press, 1961.

Loewenberg, Bert James, and Ruth Bogin, eds. *Black Women in Nineteenth-Century American Life: Their Words, Their Thoughts, Their Feelings*. University Park: Penn State University Press, 1976.

Loggins, Vernon. *The Negro Author: His Development in America to 1900.* Port Washington, NY: Kennikat Press, 1964.

Long, Charles H. *Significations: Signs, Symbols, and Images in the Interpretation of Religion.* Philadelphia: Fortress Press, 1986.

Lovell, John. *Black Song: The Forge and the Flame; the Story of How the Afro-American Spiritual Was Hammered Out.* New York: Macmillan, 1972.

Lubiano, Wahneemah. "But Compared to What?: Reading Realism, Representation, and Essentialism in *School Daze, Do the Right Thing,* and the Spike Lee Discourse." *Black American Literature Forum* 25, no. 2 (Summer 1991): 253–82.

———. "Constructing and Reconstructing Afro-American Texts: The Critic as Ambassador and Referee." *American Literary History* 1, no. 2 (Summer 1989): 432–47.

Mason, Julian D. *The Poems of Phillis Wheatley.* Chapel Hill: University of North Carolina Press, 1966.

Mays, Benjamin E. *The Negro's God as Reflected in His Literature.* New York: Negro Universities Press, 1969.

Mazrui, Ali. *The Africans: A Triple Heritage.* Boston: Little Brown, 1986.

Mbiti, John S. *African Religions and Philosophy.* Oxford: Heinemann, 1990.

McDowell, Deborah E. "Boundaries: Or, Distant Relations and Close Kin." In *Afro-American Literary Study in the 1990's,* edited by Houston A. Baker and Patricia Redmond, 51–70. Chicago: University of Chicago Press, 1989.

McGary, Howard, and Bill E. Lawson. *Between Slavery and Freedom: Philosophy and American Slavery.* Bloomington: Indiana University Press, 1992.

McManus, Edgar J. *Black Bondage in the North.* Syracuse, NY: Syracuse University Press, 1973.

Mintz, Sidney W., and Richard Price, eds. *The Birth of African-American Culture: An Anthropological Perspective.* Boston: Beacon Press, 1992.

Moore, R. Laurence. "Religion, Secularization, and the Shaping of the Culture Industry in Antebellum America." *American Quarterly* 41, no. 2 (March 1988): 83–109

Morgan, Edmund S. *Visible Saints: The History of a Puritan Idea.* New York: New York University Press, 1963.

Morrison, Toni. *Playing in the Dark: Whiteness and the Literary Imagination.* Cambridge: Harvard University Press, 1992.

Morson, Gary Saul, ed. *Bakhtin: Essays and Dialogues on His Work.* Chicago: University of Chicago Press, 1985.

Morson, Gary Saul, and Caryl Emerson. *Mikhail Bahktin: Creation of a Prosaics.* Stanford: Stanford Unversity Press, 1990.

———, eds. *Rethinking Bahktin: Extensions and Challenges.* Evanston, IL: Northwestern University Press, 1989.

Murphy, Joseph M. *Working the Spirit: Ceremonies of the African Diaspora.* Boston: Beacon Press, 1994.

Nash, Gary B. *Forging Freedom: The Formation of Philadelphia's Black Community, 1720–1840.* Cambridge: Harvard University Press, 1988.

Ngugi Wa Thiong'o. *Moving the Centre: The Struggle for Cultural Freedom.* London: James Currey, 1993.

Olney, James, ed. *Autobiography: Essays Theoretical and Critical.* Princeton: Princeton University Press, 1980.

———, ed. *Studies in Autobiography.* New York: Oxford University Press, 1988.

O'Neale, Sondra. "A Slave's Subtle Civil War: Phillis Wheatley's Use of Biblical Myth and Symbol." *Early American Literature* 21 (1986): 144–65.

Ortner, Sherry B. *Making Gender: The Politics and Erotics of Culture.* Boston: Beacon Press, 1996.

Ortner, Sherry B., Nicholas B. Dirks, and Geoff Eley, eds. *Culture/Power/History: A Reader in Contemporary Social Theory.* Princeton: Princeton Unversity Press.

Ostriker, Alicia Suskin. *Stealing the Language: The Emergence of Women's Poetry in America.* Boston: Beacon Press, 1986.

Paris, Peter J. *The Spirituality of African Peoples: The Search for a Common Moral Discourse.* Minneapolis: Fortress Press, 1995.

Payne, Daniel A. *History of the African Methodist Episcopal Church.* Nashville: Publishing House of the A.M.E. Sunday School Union, 1891.

———. *Recollection of Seventy Years.* New York: Arno Press, 1968.

Pennington, James W. C. *The Fugitive Blacksmith; or, Events in the History of James W. C. Pennington, Pastor of a Presbyterian Church, New York, Formerly a Slave in the State of Maryland.* In *The Great Slave Narratives,* edited by Arna Bontemps, 193–267. Boston: Beacon Press, 1969.

Peterson, Carla. *Doers of the Word: African American Women Speakers and Writers in the North, 1830–1880.* New York: Oxford University Press, 1995.

Piersen, William D. *Black Yankees: The Development of an Afro-American Subculture in Eighteenth-Century New England.* Amherst: University of Massachusetts Press, 1988.

Plato, Ann. *Essays; Including Biographies and Miscellaneous Pieces in Prose and Poetry.* Edited by Kenny J. Williams. New York: Oxford University Press, 1988.

Porter, Dorothy B. *Early Negro Writing, 1760–1837.* Boston: Beacon Press, 1971.

———. "The Organized Educational Activities of Negro Literary Societies, 1828–1846." *Journal of Negro Education* 5, no. 4 (October 1936): 555–76.

Pryse, Marjorie, and Hortense J. Spillers, eds. *Conjuring: Black Women, Fiction, and Literary Tradition.* Bloomington: Indiana University Press, 1985.

Quarles, Benjamin. *Black Abolitionists.* New York: Oxford University Press, 1969.

———. *Black Mosaic: Essays in Afro-American History and Historiography.* Amherst: Universisty of Massachusetts Press, 1988.

———. *The Negro in the Making of America.* New York: Macmillan Press, 1987.

Raboteau, Albert J. *Slave Religion: The "Invisible Institution" in the Antebellum South.* New York: Oxford University Press, 1978.

Redding, J. Saunders. *To Make a Poet Black.* Ithaca: Cornell University Press, 1988.

Reynolds, Edward. *Stand the Storm: A History of the Atlantic Slave Trade.* Chicago: Ivan R. Dee, 1985.

Richardson, Harry V. *Dark Salvation: The Story of Methodism as It Developed among Blacks in America*. Garden City, NY: 1976.

Richardson, Marilyn, ed. *Maria W. Stewart, America's First Black Woman Political Writer: Essays and Speeches*. Bloomington: Indiana University Press, 1987.

Richmond, M. A. *Bid the Vassal Soar: Interpretive Essays on the Life and Poetry of Phillis Wheatley and George Moses Horton*. Washington, DC: Howard University Press, 1974.

Robinson, William H. *Black New England Letters: The Uses of Writing in Black New England*. Boston: Trustees of the Public Library of the City of Boston, 1977.

———. *Critical Essays on Phillis Wheatley*. Boston: G. K. Hall, 1982.

———. *Phillis Wheatley: A Bio-Bibliography*. Boston: G. K. Hall, 1981.

———. *Phillis Wheatley and Her Writings*. New York: Garland Press, 1984.

———. *Phillis Wheatley in the Black American Beginnings*. Detroit: Broadside Press, 1975.

Ruchames, Louis, ed. *Racial Thought in America*. Vol. 1, *From the Puritans to Abraham Lincoln, a Documentary History*. Amherst: University of Massachusetts Press, 1969.

Ruether, Rosemary Radford, and Rosemary Skinner Keller, eds. *Women and Religion in America*. Vol. 1, *The Nineteenth Century*. San Francisco: Harper and Row, 1981.

Ruether, Rosemary Radford, and Eleanor McLaughlin, eds. *Women of Spirit: Female Leadership in the Jewish and Christian Traditions*. New York: Simon and Schuster, 1979.

Sadoff, Diane. "Black Matrilineage: The Case of Alice Walker and Zora Neale Hurston." In *Black Women in America: Social Science Perspectives*, edited by Micheline R. Malson, Elisabeth Mudimbe-Boyi, Jean F. O'Barr, and Mary Myer, 197–219. Chicago: University of Chicago Press, 1990.

Sasson, Diane. *The Shaker Spiritual Narrative*. Knoxville: University of Tennessee Press, 1983.

Scott, James C. *Domination and the Arts of Resistance: Hidden Transcripts*. New Haven: Yale University Press, 1990.

Sernett, Milton C. *Black Religion and American Evangelicalism: White Protestants, Plantation Missions, and the Flowering of Negro Christianity, 1787–1865*. Metuchen, NJ: Scarecrow Press, 1975.

———, ed. *Afro-American Religious History: A Documentary Witness*. Durham: Duke University Press, 1985.

Sherman, Joan R. *Invisible Poets: Afro-Americans of the Nineteenth Century*. Urbana: University of Illinois Press, 1974.

Shields, John, ed. *The Collected Works of Phillis Wheatley*. Schomburg Library of Nineteenth-Century Black Women Writers. New York: Oxford University Press, 1988.

Shockley, Ann Allen. *Afro-American Women Writers, 1746–1933: An Anthology and Critical Guide*. New York: New American Library, 1988.

Smith, Cynthia. "'To Maecenas': Phillis Wheatley's Invocation of an Idealized Reader." *Black American Literature Forum* 23, no. 3 (Fall 1989): 579–92.

Smith, Sidonie. *Where I'm Bound: Patterns of Slavery and Freedom in Black American Autobiography.* Westport, CT: Greenwood Press, 1974.

Smith, Theophus H. *Conjuring Culture: Biblical Formations of Black America.* New York: Oxford University Press, 1994.

Smith, Valerie. *Self Discovery and Authority in Afro-American Narratives.* Cambridge: Harvard University Press, 1987.

Sobel, Mechal. *Trabelin' On: The Slave Journey to an Afro-Baptist Faith.* Westport, CT: Greenwood Press, 1979.

Southern, Eileen. *The Music of Black Americans: A History.* 2d ed. New York: W. W. Norton, 1983.

Spencer, Jon Michael. *Black Hymnody: A Hymnological History of the African-American Church.* Knoxville: University of Tennessee Press, 1992.

————. *Protest and Praise: Sacred Music of Black Religion.* Minneapolis: Fortress Press, 1990.

————. *The Rhythms of Black Folk: Race, Religion, and Pan-Africanism.* Trenton, NJ: Africa World Press, 1995.

Spillers, Hortense J. "Cross-Currents, Discontinuities: Black Women's Fiction." In *Conjuring: Black Women, Fiction, and Literary Tradition,* edited by Marjorie Pryse and Hortense J. Spillers, 249–61. Bloomington: Indiana University Press, 1985.

————. "Mama's Baby, Papa's Maybe: An American Grammar Book." *Diacritics* 17, no. 1 (Summer 1987): 65–81.

————. "Moving On down the Line." *American Quarterly* 40, no. 1 (March 1988): 83–109.

————. "Who Cuts the Border?: Some Readings on 'America.'" In *Comparative American Identities: Race, Sex, and Nationality in the Modern Text,* edited by Hortense J. Spillers, 1–25. New York: Routledge: 1991.

————, ed. *Comparative American Identities: Race, Sex, and Nationality in the Modern Text.* New York: Routledge, 1991.

Stanton, Domna. *The Female Autograph.* Chicago: University of Chicago Press, 1987.

Stepto, Robert B. *From behind the Veil: A Study of Afro-American Narrative.* Urbana: University of Illinois Press, 1979.

Sterling, Dorothy, ed. *We Are Your Sisters: Black Women in the Nineteenth Century.* New York: W. W. Norton, 1984.

Stout, Harry S. *The New England Soul: Preaching and Religious Culture in Colonial New England.* New York: Oxford University Press, 1986.

Stuckey, Sterling. *Slave Culture: Nationalist Theory and the Foundations of Black America.* New York: Oxford University Press, 1987.

Tate, Claudia. *Domestic Allegories of Political Desire: The Black Heroine's Text at the Turn of the Century.* New York: Oxford University Press, 1992.

Thompson, Robert Farris. *Flash of the Spirit: African and Afro-American Art and Philosophy.* New York: Vintage, 1984.

Walker, Alice. *In Search of Our Mothers' Gardens.* San Diego: Harcourt, Brace, Jovanovich, 1983.

Walker, Wyatt Tee. *"Somebody's Calling My Name": Black Sacred Music and Social Change.* Valley Forge, PA: Judson Press, 1979.

Wall, Cheryl A. *Changing Our Own Words: Essays on Criticism, Theory, and Writing by Black Women*. New Brunswick, NJ: Rutgers University Press, 1989.

Walsh, Michael. "Reading the Real in the Seminar on the Psychosis." In *Criticism and Lacan: Essays and Dialogue on Language, Structure, and the Unconscious*, 64–83. Athens: University of Georgia Press, 1990.

Weems, Renita J. "Reading Her Way through the Struggle: African American Women and the Bible." In *Stony the Road We Trod*, edited by Cain Hope Felder, 57–77. Minneapolis: Fortress Press, 1991.

West, Cornel. *Prophesy Deliverance!: An Afro-American Revolutionary Christianity*. Philadelphia: The Westminster Press, 1982.

White, Deborah Gray. *Ar'n't I a Woman?: Female Slaves in the Plantation South*. New York: W. W. Norton, 1985.

Whitson, Robley Edward, ed. *The Shakers: Two Centuries of Spiritual Reflection*. New York: Paulist Press, 1983.

Williams, Delores. *Sisters in the Wilderness: The Challenge of Womanist God-Talk*. Maryknoll, NY: Orbis Books, 1993.

Williams, Patricia. *The Alchemy of Race and Rights: Diary of a Law Professor*. Cambridge: Harvard University Press, 1991.

Williams, Richard E. *Called and Chosen: The Story of Mother Rebecca Jackson and the Philadelphia Shakers*. Metuchen, NJ: Scarecrow Press, 1981.

Wills, David W. "The Central Themes of American Religious History: Pluralism, Puritanism, and the Encounter of Black and White." In *African-American Religion: Interpretive Essays in History and Culture*, edited by Timothy E. Fulop and Albert Raboteau, 7–20. New York: Routledge, 1997.

Wilmore, Gayrauyd S. *Black Religion and Black Radicalism: An Interpretation of the Religious History of Afro-Americans*. Maryknoll, NY: Orbis Books, 1991.

————, ed. *African-American Religious Studies: An Interdisciplinary Anthology*. Durham: Duke University Press, 1989.

Woodson, Carter G. *Free Negro Heads of Families in the United States in 1830, together with a Brief Treatment of the Free Negro*. Washington, DC: The Association for the Study of Negro Life and History, 1925.

————, ed. *The Education of the Negro Prior to 1861*. New York: Arno Press, 1968.

Work, John Wesley. *American Negro Songs and Spirituals*. New York: Crown Publishers, 1940.

Yellin, Jean Fagan. *Women and Sisters: The Antislavery Feminists in American Culture*. New Haven: Yale University Press, 1989.

Zilversmit, Arthur. *The First Emancipation: The Abolition of Slavery in the North*. Chicago: University of Chicago Press, 1967.